Pop Finance ◆

Brooke Harrington **Pop Finance** ◆

Investment Clubs and the New Investor Populism

Princeton University Press *Princeton and Oxford*

Copyright © 2008 by Princeton University Press

Published by Princeton University Press, 41 William Street,
Princeton, New Jersey 08540

In the United Kingdom: Princeton University Press, 6 Oxford Street,
Woodstock, Oxfordshire OX20 1TW

All Rights Reserved

Library of Congress Cataloging-in-Publication Data

Harrington, Brooke, 1968–
Pop finance : investment clubs and the new investor populism / Brooke Harrington.
    p.   cm.
Includes bibliographical references and index.
ISBN 978-0-691-12832-0 (hardcover : alk. paper)
1. Investment clubs—United States. 2. Investments—Social aspects—United States. I. Title.
HG4532.H37 2008
332.63′22068—dc22   2007036121

British Library Cataloging-in-Publication Data is available

This book has been composed in Minion with Helvetica Neue display

Printed on acid-free paper. ∞

press.princeton.edu

Printed in the United States of America

10   9   8   7   6   5   4   3   2   1

For Rose, Bill, and Margit, with love and gratitude

Contents

◆

Acknowledgments ◆

I have loved writing this book, and the many wonderful people it has brought my way as research participants, teachers, mentors, reviewers, and editors. Of the many events that needed to happen in order for this book to see the light of day, the catalysts were the two sets of mentors—one at Harvard and one at Stanford—who helped me build my research plan into something worth doing. Thanks are due first to my dissertation committee—Peter Marsden at Harvard University, David Frank at UC Irvine, and Lotte Bailyn at MIT's Sloan School of Management—who believed in me enough to guide me through a project that was somewhat unconventional for a doctoral student. Having now been in their position, supervising others' dissertations, I have even more appreciation for the time they put in to working with me. I also had the good fortune to work with Dick Scott, Mark Granovetter, and Jim March while I was a visiting student at Stanford; long before I ever met them, their work inspired me to choose a career as an economic and organizational sociologist. Their guidance on this project was an act of generosity for which I will always be grateful.

In addition to Harvard and Stanford, several institutions have provided me with the financing and time I needed to pursue this research. I am grateful for the grants I received from the National Science Foundation (grant #94496), the Russell Sage Foundation, the Center for Retirement Research, and Brown University. For providing me with productive work spaces, libraries, and wonderful colleagues, I am indebted to the Princeton University Department of Sociology, Stanford's Graduate School of Business, the Santa Fe Institute, and the Max Planck Institute for the Study of Societies. The material in the book has also benefited from the critiques provided when I presented my research at Mark Granovetter's economic sociology workshop, Woody Powell's lecture series at SCANCOR, the Credit Suisse First Boston Thought Leaders Forum, the Santa Fe Institute, and the departmental colloquia at Princeton, MIT, Stanford, Cornell, and Northwestern.

That I was able to gather any of the data reported in this book is due to the leaders and members of the National Association of Investors Corporation (now known as BetterInvesting), an organization that represents and provides educational materials to investment clubs throughout the United States. Bob O'Hara, the vice president of the organization, put its considerable resources at my disposal, including the list of member clubs for me to survey and the financing to conduct the study. Jonathan Strong then made it happen, arranging all the logistics for the study from NAIC's headquarters. To the thousands of anonymous investment club members who responded to my mail survey, thank you; I hope what you find here will be interesting and helpful. To the seven investment clubs in the San Francisco Bay Area who not only allowed me to observe their meetings for a year but also took me into their homes, invited me to their parties, and generally treated me like an auxiliary member, I cannot really thank-you enough. Since I promised anonymity to all the participants, I will not name them here, although I have the special permission of the San Francisco Gay Men's Investment Club to acknowledge them and two of their members—so here's a big thank-you to Charles and Ray! To the other participants, I remember you with gratitude.

As I began to write up this work, several very smart people contributed ideas that took my interpretations and analyses in new directions. These include Emilio Castilla—now of MIT's Sloan School of Management—who taught me about methodology as a peer tutor in Stanford's Sociology Department; Campbell Harvey of Duke University's Fuqua School of Business, and Andrew Roper of Stanford's Graduate School of Business, who provided some excellent leads to information on the stock market; Maggie Neale of the Stanford Graduate School of Business, Barbara Lawrence of the UCLA Andersen School of Business, and Barbara Reskin of the University of Washington, who helped me see and clarify the "value in diversity" aspect of my findings; Brian Uzzi of the Kellog School of Management at Northwestern and Michael Woolcock of the World Bank, who independently suggested the connection between the investment club phenomenon in the United States and microfinance in the developing world; Cass Sunstein of the University of Chicago Law School, who found value in my work on group decision-making and whose citations of my then-unpublished papers brought me into contact with many more interesting scholars; Viviana Zelizer of Princeton University and Victor Nee of Cornell University, who encouraged my work as an economic sociologist; Terry Odean of the Haas School of Business at Berkeley, whose work in behavioral finance has been very influential for my understanding of investment clubs; my colleagues at Brown University, who read and reviewed early drafts; Gary Fine of Northwestern University, who first helped me identify my social psychological leanings and helped me realize them in the form of three coauthored journal articles; Julia Rubin of the Bloustein School of Public Policy at Rutgers University, who saw the value of my work for public policy and has been a supportive colleague since the day we started graduate school together in 1993; and Richard Swedberg of Cornell University, who reminded me why being an intellectual was worthwhile and gave me some of the best, most timely, pep talks I have ever received.

The book has also benefited from the support of several people outside academia, including Bill Miller and Michael Mauboussin of Legg Mason Funds Management, and Steve Murphy of the New York Stock Exchange. For moral support, I thank Laura Masterson, Jim and Martha Lyons, Barbara and Bob Wilson, Marie and Jerry Caruso, Christine Rayner, Cormac McCarthy, and the entire Ottina-Cserr household. Laura's offer of a real Hermes silk scarf as a reward for completing this book was a stroke of motivational genius, even by her high standards of psychological insight. And of all the things for which I could thank my parents in connection with this project, I want to tell them how grateful I am for something they probably didn't even realize they were doing: by raising me in a house literally piled from floor to ceiling with books, and filled with lively conversation, they made me into a person whose notion of professional happiness was engaging with ideas and writing a book of my own.

In addition, there are several people who have no idea how much they've contributed to my work but who nonetheless deserve acknowledgment. Two are Gordon Thomas and Max Morgan-Witts, whose book *The Day the Bubble Burst*—an account of the stock market crash of 1929—gave me my first glimmer of enchantment with studying investor behavior; it became the basis of my first research paper ever (in seventh grade!) as well as a harbinger of my adult career. I am also very grateful to Charlie Fishbein, proprietor of the Coffee Exchange in Providence; most of this book was written there, in a table by the window that has since become my "lucky spot," under the influence of Charlie's coffee.

Finally, I want to thank my editor, Ian Malcolm, for his belief in and commitment to my work over the course of years. I would have liked to make things a bit easier on him by being more like Evelyn Waugh, who could turn out a full-length novel—revisions and all—in six weeks, or Anthony Trollope, who wrote an average of forty pages a week while holding down a full-time job in the British postal service. Unfortunately, I wrote at a pace more akin to that of Marcel Proust, whose description of the book-writing process captured everything that made the experience both joyous and miserable for me: "this writer . . . would have to prepare his book with meticulous care, perpetually regrouping his forces like a general conducting an offensive, and he would have also to endure his book like a form of fatigue, to accept it like a discipline, build it up like a church, follow it like a medical regime, vanquish it like an obstacle, win it like a friendship, cosset it like a little child, create it like a new world."[1] Ian, thank you for sticking with me throughout this process, and for the kindness, grace, humor, and integrity you have shown at every stage. With any luck, I'll have a second book for you before Zachary graduates from college.

Pop Finance ◆

A fully sociological perspective . . . asks not what social science can tell us about financial markets, but what financial markets tell us about society . . . it is economics as a mode of thought, and the economy as a mode of social action which must be explained.
—ELLEN HERTZ[1]

Investment Clubs and the "Ownership Society" ◆

SECTION ONE

Ten Years That Shook the Market

At the close of the twentieth century, an unprecedented 53 percent of American adults held investments in the stock market. Who were these people, and what was their economic and social impact? The rise of market populism was so swift that no one really knows. This book attempts to shed light on that phenomenon, which attracted enormous participation and interest in the U.S. stock market over the course of one remarkable decade.

A report by the U.S. Congress called it "an explosion in stock ownership."[2] The *New York Times* proclaimed a new era of "shareholder democracy,"[3] and *Newsweek* called it "one of the great social movements of the 1990s."[4] More recently, the Bush administration has said that the mass investment in the stock market by ordinary Americans—people who are neither wealthy nor trained in finance—ushered in the era of the "ownership society": a shift the president claims will transform the economy, culture, and politics of the United States.

However, we have very little information at hand to evaluate these assertions. The present study aims to address this gap in knowledge using the conceptual and analytical tools of economic sociology. These tools provide a means to examine macrolevel change through the microlevel behavior of agents within the market system, shifting attention "from studying the institutions in which economic activity is embedded to analyze the actual calculative practices of actors."[5] Before going into more detail about the analytical framework of economic sociology, an example may help to get the subject of the book in focus.

The "New Investor Class"

Consider Cate: "Twenty years ago, I was a twenty-six-year-old secretary living in a house with two roommates. I decided I didn't want to be a secretary any more. I wanted to be rich." She did it. Cate estimates her net worth at about $1 million, including her home and her stock portfolio. She is single, and while she still makes less than her male coworkers, she says, "I'm set for life. I'll probably be one of those old ladies who'll leave a fortune to the animal shelter."

What's interesting is *how* she did it. Cate joined an investment club made up of men and women from her workplace. The group met once a month in a conference room at work, and for about two hours the ten members discussed the portfolio they owned in common. They checked the stocks' performance and considered what to buy with the cash they put in each month—an average of $35 per person. The club, called Bulls & Bears, owned about sixteen stocks, and their portfolio was worth $45,000, owned jointly by six men and four women. The club was also racially diverse, including two African-Americans (one male, one female), a Pakistani woman, and an Asian-American male; the other members were white and born in the United States.

While Cate's personal wealth does not derive primarily from her share of the investment club, she credits the club for her financial education. She prides herself on savvy financial decisions. For example, she took out a home equity loan at 9 percent interest so that she could invest more in the stock market, figuring that she would make a lot more than 9 percent on those investments. Like Cate, the other members of Bulls & Bears participated in 401(k) plans through their employer but did not feel that they could rely on those programs to provide them with a secure income in retirement. They were all in their mid-forties, and saw themselves as individually responsible for providing their financial safety nets.

Cate and her investment club were part of the mass movement of Americans into investing during the 1990s—a stock market version of Manifest Destiny. During the market boom of that period, millions joined investment clubs and collectively poured *hundreds of billions* of dollars into the stock market. The only study that attempted to capture the national scope of the phenomenon estimated that 11 percent of the U.S. adult population belonged to an investment club.[6] That's about twenty million people.[7] Even in 2003, in the period of market decline and stagnation that followed the boom, one organization that provides investment education materials to investment clubs estimated that their membership included almost half a million individuals who collectively owned $125 billion worth of the stock market and invested $190 million each month.[8] The present study will be the first to examine the socioeconomic significance of this phenomenon.

The Performance Puzzle in Investment Clubs

This study was catalyzed by a puzzle: according to data collected by NAIC, the National Association of Investors Corporation, the stock portfolios of clubs composed of men and women together significantly outperformed those held by clubs composed of men only or women only. Analyzing all twelve years' worth of portfolio performance data available as of 1997, when I embarked on the study, I found that the performance differences between mixed groups—those composed of men and women in varying proportions—and their single-sex counterparts were statistically significant and amounted to about a 2 percent advantage for mixed groups in terms of annualized returns on investment. I dubbed this effect the "diversity premium." While a 2 percent difference may seem quite small, the compounding effect magnifies the advantage tremendously within a few years. (See section 2 for a detailed discussion of portfolio performance measures.) Curiously, there was no statistically significant difference in the portfolio performance of all-male or all-female groups.

The findings were unexpected for two reasons. First, economic theory would suggest that the personal characteristics of investors should make no difference in the performance of their stocks. Second, sociological research has repeatedly shown that compositional diversity causes decreased performance in work groups more often than not. (See chapters 3 and 4 for a review of the literature and detailed findings on investment club performance.) Yet the positive effect of gender diversity appeared robust in this data set, and I set out to uncover the origins of the "diversity premium."

Since there had been no prior research on investment clubs, I was unable to embark directly on a large-scale survey project. Instead, I took a multimethod approach, building knowledge of the groups through observation and interviews, and then moving on to survey research. The qualitative phase of the study involved conducting an ethnography of seven investment clubs in the San Francisco Bay Area over the course of a year. This portion of the project was guided by two goals: to develop theory and to generate questions for a survey to be mailed to investment clubs nationally. The survey, which gathered both club-level and individual-level information, was intended to create a broader picture of investment club performance, composition, and practices, as well as to provide a context and benchmark for the qualitative findings. In the chapters that follow, I discuss my methodology in more detail and report the findings from both the qualitative and the quantitative studies.

Why Study Amateur Investors?

In examining investment clubs and the diversity premium, a major objective of this book will be to document the real-world behavior of American investors and to offer an alternative to what might be called the "official" account of stock market dynamics presented by economics and finance. As a recent study put it, "Stock markets have long been the research domain of financial economists who gloss over social relations on the assumption that social connections are marginal sources of friction in financial markets."[9] Marginalization of social influences on investor behavior can allow some economists to preserve the elegance of their models at the expense of excluding large swaths of empirical phenomena from analysis. In particular, the behavior of amateur or "retail" investors has been described as "noise trading," as against the behavior of finance professionals, who are thought to embody the behavioral assumptions of neoclassical economic theory.[10] That is, finance professionals are presumed to make decisions that are rational in the sense of being motivated solely by the desire to maximize their self-interest and being informed by a shared set of facts, which they all interpret in the same way.[11] If one starts from these assumptions, investing becomes a process of rational analysis with the goal of maximizing gains and minimizing losses. While economists and finance scholars acknowledge that many people do not invest in this way, they argue that deviations from the model do not matter: only the behavior of rational individuals—such as finance professionals—really counts in understanding how financial markets work.[12]

There are two problems with this view. First, amateur investors are not marginal, as the case of investment clubs shows. It is difficult to minimize their $125 billion in U.S. stock holdings—and that represents only the assets of clubs that belong to NAIC. This figure is comparable to the holdings of one of the largest institutional investors in the world: the California Public Employees' Retirement System (CalPERS), which has $143 billion in assets under management and is the nation's largest pension fund.[13] The amateur investors of NAIC exert a large influence on the market compared to the number of individuals involved: while CalPERS represents over 1.2 million California public employees, NAIC clubs involve just 472,000 individuals in total. Though investment clubs do not act as a single unit, as CalPERS and other pension funds do, there is still a consistent pattern of stock ownership among the clubs. For example, NAIC clubs own $562 million worth of General Electric, $423 million worth of Intel, and $1.3 billion worth of the insurance company AFLAC—about 7 percent of shares outstanding.

A second blow to the marginalization of amateur investors is the evidence that they are not so different from professionals after all. In fact, empirical studies of Wall Street firms suggest that investing professionals deviate considerably from assumptions of rational, self-maximizing decision making; the evidence suggests that their decisions are driven as much by considerations of status and preservation of social networks as by considerations of profit. For example, an anthropological study of Wall Street pension funds portrays an environment in which fund managers feel com-pelled to make "economically counterproductive" decisions in order to preserve relationships within their professional circles.[14]

If professional investors do not fit well into the rational paradigm, one might wonder if anyone *does*. The evidence on the practices of investment professionals implies that the influence of social behavior on investing is not limited to amateurs but rather pervades the stock market. As one prominent economist put it, "apart from a few lonely Warren Buffetts, institutional investors exist in a community that is exceptionally closely knit by constant communication and mutual exposure."[15] So the behavior of amateur investors, instead of being exceptional for its permeability to social influences, turns out to be the norm, with the capacity to shed light on investor behavior at multiple levels. And if amateur investors matter in shaping the activity of the stock market, it becomes important to understand how the 53 percent of American adults who now own stocks see the market in which they are investing: what do *they* think they are doing?

Of all the ways to approach this phenomenon, investment clubs provide a particularly appealing starting point, not only because of their economic significance, but also because they offer the opportunity for detailed observation of the social processes involved in investing. They allow the complex set of practices that comprise the stock market to be studied on a manageable scale.[16] Second, investment club meetings make the decision processes of investors available for analysis. Among individual investors, decision making can be very difficult to study because so much of the process is internal; little of the process is accessible directly to researchers. In other words, while it is not difficult to find out what investors do, it is difficult to discover *why*.

In investment club meetings, members have to articulate their reasons for wanting to buy or sell stocks. They have to debate the pros and cons explicitly. Their decisions can be observed unfolding in "real time" rather than being reconstructed retrospectively, with all the potential biases that implies. Observation provides more accurate data through direct access to the process of investment decision-making in groups: a widespread but underresearched phenomenon about which we need to learn much more.

Many of the most important decisions affecting the U.S. economy are made in small groups such as the Federal Open Markets Committee, which sets interest rates and fiscal policy for the country, as well as the numerous investment committees that decide how to spend the money of America's corporations and nonprofits. Investment clubs are worthy of study in their own right, but they are also valuable to investigate as instantiations of an important socioeconomic practice that has received very little attention from social scientists.

What Is a Sociological Perspective on Investing?

This book is addressed to multiple audiences and agendas. On the one hand, its objectives are scholarly, and the findings are intended to enlarge the scope and theoretical repertoire of economic and organizational sociology. On the other hand, sociology has a long tradition of crossing boundaries and speaking to nonscholarly audiences on topics of broad public interest. A study of investment behavior among ordinary Americans lends itself to both purposes and sets of readers. With this in mind, the book will approach its subject as directly and accessibly as possible. However, a brief introduction to the perspective that has informed this research is in order.

Economic sociology seeks to understand the social underpinnings of money and markets. Its core assumption, which informs this book throughout, is that social and economic forces are inseparable. While this assertion may seem uncontroversial, it runs quite contrary to fundamental assumptions within economics and finance, which have heretofore claimed the study of financial behavior as their own. Economic sociology seeks to repair a gap between the disciplines of sociology and economics that arose just over a century ago. Prior to that, the two fields were one; indeed, until the end of the nineteenth century there was no sociology per se, only political economy or political philosophy. Adam Smith's first book was titled *A Theory of Moral Sentiments*, a subject that few modern economists would dare to broach. The change that brought about the separation of the two fields of inquiry is part and parcel of modernity itself. As one scholar put it,

> Western civilization represents itself as an economy these days . . . It is almost impossible to discuss public affairs in any terms other than economic . . . It was not always so. When the western bourgeoisie was struggling to make the modern world, politics and religion figured prominently on their agenda. They knew they had to create a whole new culture to break away from the dead hand of the military-agrarian complex. It follows from this that economics has become the religion of our secular scientific civilization.[17]

As economics sought to define itself as a science, on the model of natural sciences like physics, it developed assumptions and methodologies that distanced it from its roots and from sociology. Table I.1 summarizes important distinctions between the two fields, as they stand at present.

While economics and finance have both developed streams of "behavioral" research, which loosen many of the constraints noted above (partic-

Table I.1

Comparison of Core Assumptions in Economics and Sociology

Core Assumptions in Economics	Core Assumptions in Sociology
Individual is unit of analysis	Group is unit of analysis
Individuals are rational decision-makers	Rationality is a variable; individual decisions are grounded in socially constructed knowledge, which is not necessarily rational
Individuals are motivated by the desire to maximize their self-interest (utility)	Individuals are motivated by social concerns such as status, approval, conformity, etc.
Equilibrium—markets are fair and efficient	Power struggles—fairness is a variable
Economy and society are separate	Economy is embedded in society
Fixed preferences	Flexible preferences
Material basis for analysis	Socially constructed ideas and beliefs analyzed along with material factors
Deductive models trump data	Inductive models based on empirics
Few variables, elegant equations	Many variables, messy equations
Data are optional	Data are essential

ularly the assumptions about rationality, fixed preferences, and market efficiency), many of the basics—such as the focus on individual behavior and quantitative methods—remain intact.[18]

This book will be quite different from a work of behavioral finance or economics in the following respects. First, it will start from the supposition that all economic behavior is "embedded" in and inseparable from its social context. That is, it is nonsensical within economic sociology to discuss individual behavior without reference to the social forces—be they macro-institutional or microinteractional—that give rise to and surround it. Second, while much of behavioral economics and finance seeks to demonstrate that assumptions of classical economics—such as individual rationality and utility maximization—do not hold empirically, economic sociology *starts* with the proposition that humans are social creatures responsive to a myriad of issues, not limited instrumental or rational interests. Further, a sociological perspective regards individuals' economic behavior as influenced by factors such as social networks, status, power, socialization processes, identity, emotions, and symbols (such as language and storytelling). All this makes for much more complex models and less predictive power than is possible through the stylized assumptions of economics, but the goals of sociology lie more in the realm of explanation than prediction.

It is also worth noting that this work will be different from many other studies within economic sociology by focusing on the microlevel interaction processes that constitute stock market behavior. Much of economic sociology has been built on quantitative studies of macrophenomena, such as banks' lending decisions or corporate philanthropy.[19] In contrast, this study partakes of the tradition of "sociological miniaturism" by focusing on the behavior of small groups. These groups are partly responsible for what economists describe as "noise," and what sociologists would describe as the sound of social context; exploring this context will be the focus of the next two chapters.

Plan of the Book

To shed light on the microlevel phenomena from which macrolevel socioeconomic institutions—like the stock market—are constituted, specific issues to be addressed in the remainder of this volume will include:

- how American investors *really* think about the market, as opposed to the way the economists say they should think;
- the meaning and implications of "socially responsible investing";
- factors influencing the financial performance of investment clubs—particularly the origins of the "diversity premium";
- the implications of these findings for the corporate world, particularly with regard to diversity and performance in firms;
- the implications of this study for economic and social policy, including proposals to privatize Social Security and concerns about Americans "bowling alone";
- what this study suggests for future research on markets and other complex social systems.

Chapter 1 will locate this study within the contexts of the history of populist investor movements and the history of the investment club phenomenon; it will also provide more detail on research methodology. Chapter 2 examines how participants in the investment club movement of the 1990s understood their own behavior and developed the strategies they used to cope with the vast range of choices they faced in the stock market. Chapters 3 and 4 will examine the antecedents of investment clubs' financial performance including the sources of diversity and the group processes that affect how resources are deployed. Chapter 5 reviews the data from a follow-up study, conducted five years after the original research was concluded, to examine how participants in the observational portion of the study re-

sponded to the end of the bull market and the wave of corporate governance and financial industry scandals that rocked the economy during the
early years of the twenty-first century. Chapter 6 reviews the implications
of this study for theory and future research in sociology, as well as for
policy and practice.

The capitalistic economy of the present day is an immense
cosmos into which the individual is born, and which presents
itself to him, at least as an individual, as an unalterable order of
things in which he must live.
—MAX WEBER[1]

Stock Market Populism
Investment Clubs and Economic History ◆ 1

"Irrational Exuberance"

Much that can be said about the spirit of the 1990s in America can be encapsulated in the publication of three books in rapid succession between May and September 1999: *Dow 36,000*; *Dow 40,000*; and *Dow 100,000*. Issued by three different publishers, and written by three different sets of authors, each book vied to be the most optimistic about the upward trajectory of U.S. stocks. Though we might now wish to shelve these books in the science fiction section of the library, at the time their ideas were treated quite seriously and discussed earnestly in almost every public news forum you could name. In 1999, everyone agreed that the sky was the limit for the American stock market: the only question worth asking was, how high is the sky?

However implausible their optimism might seem in the morning-after light of the early twenty-first century, these books simply reflected the astonishing events occurring immediately before and after their publication. On March 29, 1999, the Dow Jones Industrial Average—a group of stocks issued by thirty industrial firms, which have long been used by the Dow Jones Corporation as a barometer of the U.S. stock market as a whole—closed above 10,000 for the first time in its history, having doubled its value since 1995. During the five weeks that followed this benchmark, the Dow climbed another 1,000 points—the fastest run-up in its history—and closed over 11,000 on May 3. This orgy of economic optimism culminated on January 14, 2000, when the Dow closed at what was then an all-time high of 11,722.98, followed by a descent almost as swift as its rise, with the index dropping almost 3,000 points in a few months. Despite the dramatic changes in the numbers, some aspects of the market boom of the late 1990s are still very much with us.

Among the most notable legacies of this extraordinary period is the shift in what could be called the "investor class." Once limited to a tiny elite among America's wealthiest families—the 1 percent of adults who owned stocks in 1900, which by 1952 had risen to just 4 percent—investing in stocks became a mass activity, involving over half the U.S. adult population by the end of the twentieth century.[2] Much of this growth in "market populism" occurred during the 1990s. For example, at the beginning of that decade, about 21 percent of American adults owned stocks; seven years later, the percentage had more than doubled, rising to 43 percent; by 1999, the figure was 53 percent. The last time the number of investors doubled in America, the change took twenty-five years: from 10 percent in 1965 to 21 percent in 1990.[3]

This shift in the composition of the "investor class" brought with it substantial demographic and political changes. For example, while women made up a little less than a third of American investors in 1990, they constituted fully half of the "investor class" by 1999. In addition, by 1998 the majority of the nation's registered voters were also investors, spurring declarations of a major political shift in America, with the *New York Times* announcing the birth of "shareholder democracy." The views of the nation's newspaper of record on this subject capture the expansive spirit of the era: "This may be the least appreciated economic, cultural and political development in recent years . . . we have developed a mass culture of investing, the first to exist anywhere in the world. American democratic capitalism has brought about the *democratization* of capitalism."[4]

Americans flocked to the stock market as they once flocked to lands of opportunity. And despite the market downturn, this "new investor class" appears to have continued investing, unlike the generation that followed the crash of 1929. How did this change occur, and what does it mean socially and economically?

It is significant that the initial research for this book took the form of an ethnography conducted in the Silicon Valley. Like the populist expansion of the nineteenth century, the stock market boom turned Americans' attention westward, toward the 1,500-square-mile area bounded by San Mateo to the north, Gilroy to the south, Fremont to the east, and the Pacific coast on the western edge. An area formerly known as the plum- and apricot-growing capital of California, the Silicon Valley was so entirely transformed by the mid-1990s that it surpassed Detroit as the nation's leading export region.[5] The transition was swift and dramatic. Between 1994 and 1998, thousands of people moved to the area every month to work in high-tech jobs, creating the kind of traffic jams that northern Californians had previously associated with Los Angeles. These material changes were accompanied by hyperbolic rhetoric that proclaimed, the end of the old world—economically and even socially—and rise of an entirely new regime in which none of the conventional wisdom applied and the rules would be made by smart young men and their machines.[6] Among the first casualties of this revolution were the metrics used to value companies. In the new order, anything that smacked of "bricks and mortar" was deemed useless: what counted was ideas. That meant that companies' value would no longer be assessed by whether they made a profit, or even made a product; anything with dot.com after the company name was held to be a good bet. A best-selling book of the time proclaimed, "The old rules are broken . . . Forget supply and demand . . . Old business know-how means nothing."[7]

Anyone who paid attention at that time recalls the strangely manic tenor of public dialogue about economic conditions. It resembled nothing so much as a very long infomercial, complete with hagiographic rags-to-riches stories featuring leading entrepreneurs, such as Steve Jobs and Steve Wozniak of Apple Computer. Economist Paul Krugman described the rhetoric of the "new economy" as "a rapid-fire blur of neologisms and breathless declarations that all the rules have changed, that there are limitless opportunities for those who have the courage to let go of old assumptions."[8] At the same time, skepticism about the "new economy" was so marginalized that it could scarcely bear public discussion, except under the guise of humor—the traditional method for treating many taboo subjects. For instance, in July 1997, the *Wall Street Journal* ran a front-page story quoting an investor who said that the notoriously bearish investment newsletter *Grant's Interest Rate Observer* was now worth reading only for entertainment value: "It's like [reading] the Marquis de Sade; it's interesting as long as you don't try to do it."[9]

To study investor behavior at this time and place was a bit like studying government in 1789 Paris. Investing was exciting, confusing, and tumultuous—and the only game worth playing. People who at another point in history might have joined a temperance league or a fraternal organization instead joined investment clubs, drawn by the recognition that the economy was where the action was, historically and culturally. Though some of these individuals seemingly had little economic need to invest, the president of one group spoke for many people in my study by explaining that she had joined an investment club because she was "caught up in the euphoria of the bull market." Of course, investing is driven by the profit motive, as will be discussed at greater length in subsequent chapters. But investing together during the 1990s also meant participating in a form of social organization that was both historically specific and status-relevant: in other words, fashionable.

At the height of the bull market, between late 1997 and early 1999, I studied seven Silicon Valley investment clubs, attending their monthly meetings over the course of a year and supplementing my observations of their decision-making behavior with in-depth interviews. (See this chapter's appendix for further details on sample selection and methodology.) Investment clubs, often characterized as "do-it-yourself mutual funds," are voluntary associations of ten to fifteen people who pool their money to invest in the stock market. Based on what I learned from my observations and interviews, I gathered survey data from 1,245 investment clubs and over 11,000 individuals nationally, with results I report in subsequent chapters.

Although investment clubs have existed in the United States for at least a century, they did not become extremely popular until the 1990s, when they constituted the major vehicle of the "popular finance" movement that has attracted so much attention from the media and policy makers. Through the clubs, an estimated 11 percent of the U.S. population collectively poured hundreds of millions of dollars into the stock market.[10] In addition, investment club participants during that period captured a broadly representative slice of the U.S. population, particularly groups that have previously been underrepresented in studies of investor behavior, including the very young, the elderly, and women. Approximately 60 percent of investment club members are women, and there is wide variation in age and occupational status, with members ranging from teenagers to octogenarians, and from executives to farmworkers.[11] Thus, what started as an investigation of the social underpinnings of investor behavior turned into something larger: a snapshot of historical and social transition, as millions of people were caught up in what Federal Reserve chairman Alan Greenspan called "irrational exuberance."

A Brief History of the Investment Club Phenomenon

Investment clubs make such useful research settings for studying real-life investor behavior that it is surprising that they were virtually ignored until this research was conducted in the late 1990s. The first U.S. investment club was founded in Texas in 1898, based on a European model going back several generations.[12] But the clubs were little more than an obscure hobbyist movement until the closing years of the twentieth century, when the stock market began its record-breaking upward surge and ordinary Americans rushed to participate in the boom.

Investment clubs were at the epicenter of this economic and social transformation. With each market surge, NAIC enrollments swelled—peaking in 1998 at 37,129 member clubs—as did the involvement of women. As a benchmark, NAIC's 1986 membership data show that all-women's clubs made up 38 percent of NAIC enrollments, followed by 35 percent mixed clubs and 27 percent all-men's clubs. Ten years later, mixed clubs made up 47 percent of NAIC membership, followed by 41 percent all-women's clubs; meanwhile, all-male clubs had fallen to a mere 12 percent of enrollments. Five years later, the trend had continued further in the same direction, with all-women's clubs representing 54 percent of the total NAIC enrollments, mixed clubs 38 percent, and all-men's clubs only 8 percent. Overall, the balance shifted through the massive entry of women into investing; once a minority, women comprised 62 percent of NAIC membership by 2001.

Fluctuation in investment club participation has been influenced not only by economic imperatives but also by cultural and historical conditions. For example, the 1950s witnessed a push to woo back to the stock market a generation scared away from investing by the 1929 crash. Corporations, stock exchanges, and brokerage firms urged Americans to purchase stock though a joint education/public relations campaign titled "People's Capitalism." Charles Merrill, founder of Merrill-Lynch, made his fortune by advertising extensively to individual investors and by publishing newsletters encouraging Americans to get involved in the stock market. Another pioneer of market democratization—George Funston, who become president of the New York Stock Exchange in 1951—leveraged the anticommunist sentiment of the time to claim that buying common stock was a vote for democracy and the American way.[13] The perennial appeal of the "investor as patriot" metaphor was reaffirmed fifty years later by the numerous e-mails that crisscrossed the nation following the September 11 attacks, urging Americans to buy stocks to prop up the faltering economy and signal defiant confidence in the face of the terrorism that had targeted the nation's financial center.[14]

For investment clubs, this link between investing and American identity is captured by NAIC's slogan: "Own Your Share of America." This demotic strain in the U.S. stock market is more than a marketing ploy: there seems to be a genuine sense of Manifest Destiny among American investors, characterized by belief in limitless possibilities for expansion, and the average citizen's entitlement to a piece of the economic pie. It is remarkable how readily this set of beliefs translated from the landgrabs of the 1840s to the stock market of the 1990s. As one historian put it, "the essence of speculation remains a Utopian yearning for freedom and equality which counterbalances the drab rationalistic materialism of the modern economic system."[15]

Since investment clubs have served as the primary point of entry for new investors into the stock market, it is not surprising that club enrollments have risen and fallen with waves of confidence in the market. Figure 1.1 compares NAIC's club enrollments with the Dow Jones Industrial Average since NAIC began keeping records in 1952. The trend lines match very closely, although most changes in club enrollments lag major market swings by several years. For example, investment club participation peaked first in 1962, with just over 106,000 members, following the nearly 20 percent surge in the Dow Jones Industrial Average between 1959 and 1960. The second peak in investment club participation occurred in 1970, with 169,000 members enrolled, about four years after a record high in the stock market. The decline in club enrollments began in the early 1970s as Vietnam, Watergate, and the energy crisis erased fifteen years' worth of gains in the Dow. However, the lowest enrollment levels (44,000 individual

Figure 1.1
NAIC club enrollment versus stock market growth, 1952–2005

members—fewer than the 1958 membership numbers) occurred in 1980, five years after the Dow hit its lowest point.

The Dow had regained all its lost ground by 1983, but investment club enrollments did not return to 1970 levels until 1994, when membership began soaring with the onset of the bull market; enrollment reached a peak of over 600,000 individual members between 1998 and 1999. The pattern breaks down somewhat during the period from 1999 to 2001, when there was a steep plunge in investment club participation; this may have been occasioned by the decline of the high-technology boom. Although the Dow has certainly represented a large segment of the American investment market historically, the late 1990s were dominated by the high-technology stocks listed on the NASDAQ exchange. As the high-technology boom wound down in 2001, investment club enrollments began to track the Dow more closely.

From the highs of "irrational exuberance"—marked by peaks in the early 1970s and mid-1990s—to the long period of aversion to the stock market in the intervening twenty-five years, the history of investment club enrollments echoes recent findings that individual investors do not just react to market conditions—they *overreact*, often wildly.[16]

Economic, Legal, and Technological Factors

The investment club "renaissance" of the 1990s was not due just to the upswing in the stock market during that period. More importantly, as noted in the previous chapter, new kinds of investors entered the stock market. Women and people of color, after years of being the tiniest of minorities in investing, joined the "investor class" en masse. Thus, investment clubs rose from the ashes of stagflation with a push from new kinds of investors forming new clubs, rather than building on old ones. This was part of a larger trend toward broadening the demographic composition of the investor population.

The popularization of investing and investment clubs in the United States during the 1990s was facilitated by several organizational and technological developments, most notably that of discount brokerage firms and the World Wide Web. While investment clubs have been available as an organizational form for some time, the innovations of the past decade made it possible to invest *efficiently* as a club. Specifically, changes in organizations and technology lowered the transaction costs that once made investing prohibitively expensive for all but the very wealthiest Americans.

The essence of this efficiency was the diminishing importance of brokers, who prior to the 1980s served as the sole gatekeepers of the stock market. Establishing a relationship with a brokerage firm was difficult, if not impossible, for anyone but the wealthy due to the commission system. The advent of discount brokerage firms in the 1980s created an opening in the opportunity structure of investing; commissions were lowered, and small traders found a niche. But discount brokers were able to cut commissions in part because they did not give investing advice like their full-service counterparts. Thus, the low-cost route was open only to relatively sophisticated investors. The most serious blow in favor of popularization of the stock market was finally struck by the World Wide Web. By the mid-1990s anyone with Internet access could download sophisticated investment information and execute trades.

These developments intersected nicely with NAIC's model of lowering the barriers to entry into stock market by spreading out the financial risk and the research burden of investing among the members of clubs. In addition, NAIC provides investment ideas (via a monthly magazine, *Better Investing*), training courses in investment analysis, and deeply discounted brokerage services. As of 2000, clubs were paying $40 per year for NAIC services—a relative bargain, given that the average cost of a single share of stock on the New York Stock Exchange is about $35.

To permit maximum dissemination of its populist investing message, NAIC boiled its educational strategy down to four principles:

1. Invest regularly regardless of market outlook.
2. Reinvest all earnings from investments.
3. Invest in growth firms.[17]
4. Diversify to reduce risk.

Within these constraints, NAIC recommends that investors evaluate stocks based on two basic measures: "reasonable price" and "management capability"—the ability of management to ensure a minimum 15 percent annual growth rate. The overall approach is analytical and conservative. In fact, this general strategy—originally developed by Benjamin Graham in the 1930s—is known in financial circles as the "fundamentalist" approach to the market.[18] Thus, while investing in stocks always carries risks, the NAIC method offers little in the way of the excitement associated with day traders and get-rich-quick schemes. People who are interested in high-risk, high-profit investing generally do not join investment clubs. Even in clubs that adhere loosely or not at all to NAIC principles, the group format and monthly meetings present substantial constraints to action: it is difficult to make a quick profit when decisions can only be made every four to five weeks, and must be approved by fifteen other people. This may explain part of NAIC's appeal to middle-aged women; studies of risk and financial decisions indicate that women and people in midlife are more conservative than men or people in other age groups, respectively.[19]

Even though investing was easier than ever in the 1990s—between NAIC's low-risk and easy-to-follow investment strategies and the low financial and technical barriers to entry—it still remains to be explained why investment clubs became so popular. The presence of an attractive opportunity does not in itself explain how millions of Americans came to be involved in investing. I argue that the surge of new investors—investment clubs in particular—during the 1990s was due in large part to the changing social contract between labor and management, which made investing an increasingly *necessary* source of income.

Between 1985 and 1995, three economic changes altered the conditions of American workers, pushing them toward the stock market:

- The number of workers participating in 401(k) and other defined-contribution retirement plans tripled.
- Real wages declined.[20]
- Corporate after-tax profits tripled.

Taken together, these three changes put a majority of Americans in the position of having to make up wages and benefits—particularly retirement benefits—through their own efforts. The stock market, with its historical returns of 11 percent annually, provided one of the few places to make up the shortfall.

The change in retirement benefits is particularly significant because it affected so many jobs, and because the issue of retirement planning became suddenly urgent as the baby boom generation entered middle age. NAIC's survey data indicate that retirement savings have historically been the primary objective of 80 percent of investment club members. A huge demographic shift made retirement, and the necessity for investment, an increasingly real and urgent prospect.

Until the late 1970s, most American workers could expect to receive traditional pensions—known as "defined benefit" plans—upon retirement. Under this regime, employers took full responsibility for setting aside and managing employees' retirement funds. But after the laws governing private pension plans changed in the mid-1970s, employers began shifting the risk and responsibility of retirement savings to employees. Out of this change emerged the so-called "defined contribution" plan—the most common of which is the 401(k)—in which employees must decide for themselves how much money to deduct from their salaries and how it should be invested.

The change was rather sudden for such an institutionalized aspect of the American employment system. The U.S. Census Bureau (1996) reports that between 1980 and 1992 the number of "defined benefit" (traditional pension) plans decreased by more than half, while the number of 401(k) and other "defined contribution" plans more than doubled. As of 1994, fourteen million Americans were actively participating in 401(k) plans.[21] More importantly, 52 percent of U.S. workers wound up with no corporate retirement benefits at all.[22] Even the safety net of last resort—Social Security—may be subject to the risks of the stock market if the current presidential administration has its way.[23] This has created a new imperative for individuals to become informed about investing and financial planning.

Concurrent with the growing uncertainty of retirement benefits, real wages declined as firms diverted a bigger share of revenues from wages to profits. This period was also characterized by "downsizing" of the workforce. By keeping labor costs down, profits stayed high. But for workers, this meant that employment and retirement became a great deal less secure, with risks that had once been the responsibility of employers suddenly transferred onto workers. Most importantly for those who held on to their jobs, the share of corporate profits that they used to receive as salary or wages became accessible only through the stock market. Stock options were used as currency equivalents, replacing a portion of salary while minimizing drag on profits, since corporations did not have to report stock options as obligations on the balance sheet.

On the one hand, this was simply a massive shift of cash out of the pockets of workers and into those of shareholders. This produced dramatic increases in the value of American companies' stocks, so that workers with stock options and 401(k) plans often did *better* economically in the 1990s compared with the days before such innovations. On average, American stocks returned 18 percent annually during the 1990s—far above the historical average of 11 percent annual returns the U.S. markets had enjoyed since 1926.[24] For the increasing percentage of Americans whose income and/or retirement depended on the stock market, the new financial risks they faced appeared to be well compensated by returns. But the dangers of this model became vividly apparent as the stock market declined—particularly following the collapse of Enron. Sixty percent of the 401(k) assets of Enron employees were held in company stock—shares which most Enron employees were forbidden from selling, even as the stock price plummeted and executives cashed out.[25]

The third trend pushing Americans into the stock market was the Clinton administration's 1997 revision of the tax code to favor investment income over wages and salary: the capital gains tax (which applies to profits from investments) was lowered to 20 percent, while the income of most investors was taxed in the 28 to 40 percent bracket.[26] In the year following this change in the tax code, NAIC investment club enrollment hit its all-time high of 37,129 clubs.

The economic, technological, and legal trends driving investment club formation affected women disproportionately, which is one reason that so many participants in NAIC investment clubs are female—particularly women over the age of fifty. Women have been particularly hard-hit by changes in the pension system: both private pensions and Social Security benefits are determined by salary and years of continuous employment; since women make less than men for the same jobs, tend to be employed in lower-wage industries, and often have interrupted work histories, they get fewer benefits from both public and private retirement plans.[27] Investing would appear to be a particularly attractive option for women, allowing them to compensate (at least potentially) for lower earnings and retirement security. But investing is expensive and out of reach for most women, given their income constraints and lack of exposure to investing opportunities. Thus, in addition to making investing affordable, NAIC investment clubs speak to a profound social need for investment education: Americans now bear a great deal more responsibility in managing their retirement finances, and require a great deal more investment knowledge, than previous generations.

Investment Clubs as Formal Organizations

It is important to note that the term "club" is somewhat misleading, in that investment clubs are quite different from associations that usually fall under that designation, such as book clubs or gourmet clubs. Though voluntary associations are often treated quite differently from other work groups in the scholarly literature, investment clubs are more similar to small businesses than to hobbyist groups. While some members of investment clubs may be interested primarily in the social contact offered by the groups—as are some members of corporate work groups, which appear more regularly in the research literature[28]—the ostensible purpose of investment clubs is quite businesslike and utilitarian: to make money in the stock market. And while some individuals certainly participate in investment clubs as part of a generalized "thrill-seeking" orientation to the stock market, a substantial number are driven by the intense need faced by many Americans to provide their own financial safety net—particularly for retirement.[29] Even those whose participation in investment clubs is driven more by social considerations than financial necessity must put their own money at risk and experience profits or losses that appear on their tax forms and in their bank accounts. In this sense, investment clubs are quite different from most other voluntary organizations: they can go broke, or even incur debts that members must bear.

Perhaps most importantly, no matter what an individual's motives for joining an investment club, he or she must submit to a degree of formalization, legal stricture, and hierarchy that, while common in work organizations, is not commonly associated with voluntary associations. In fact, investment clubs get the highest possible score on the "formalization index" used in surveys like the National Organizations Study to rate the degree to which command and control structures are in place to differentiate organizations from other collectivities; these include having a name for the group, as well as regular meetings governed by a stated purpose or goal, along with leaders and written rules, and a contract that members must sign.[30] Typically, investment clubs meet every month for about two hours to decide which stocks to buy or sell using the money amassed from each member's contribution, averaging $35 per person per month. The groups have hierarchical leadership structures, elect officers, make decisions jointly, and own assets (stocks) in common; new members pay an initiation fee, must sign a contract to join the club, and provide their Social Security numbers for the club's federal and state tax filings.[31] Since they are financial partnerships, many investment clubs incorporate to protect members' assets and to facilitate compliance with the accounting rules that all clubs must observe by law. Thus, investment clubs, despite their name, are actually quite formal financial partnerships and, as a subject of study, can contribute to scholarly research in much the same way as other small businesses.

Investment Clubs and the History of Speculative Manias

During the 1990s, the usually staid *Wall Street Journal* declared that investing had become "America's most exuberant entertainment business."[32] This description hints at the place of the amateur investing boom and investment clubs within the long and colorful history of speculative manias—a history that was once famously summarized by John Kenneth Galbraith as "the mass escape from sanity by people in pursuit of profit."[33]

The notion of *mass* escape is crucial, and as such is well suited to sociological analysis.

Historically, speculative activities have been characterized by the breakdown of social boundaries; American investment clubs are very much of a piece with this tradition. Indeed, a cursory review of financial history reveals that the stock market boom of the late 1990s followed the classic pattern of speculative bubbles set by the Dutch tulip bulb craze of 1620 and the British South Sea Bubble of 1720. As financial historian Edward Chancellor has ably documented, speculative crazes unfold in three phases.[34] First, an opportunity for profit arises, within an environment that encourages, or at least does not impede, speculation. Second, social and economic conventions are suspended, allowing the participation and possible enrichment of lower-status social groups. Finally, the process concludes with the bursting of the bubble and the allocation of blame and punishment. The ways in which investment clubs were viewed, by both participants and observers, followed this pattern with uncanny accuracy.

The beginnings of financial speculation have been traced to medieval Europe, where carnivals occasioned by Lent or other cultural events were among the rare social spaces in which economic activity for profit was sanctioned. Most significantly, shares in commercial ventures could be sold at such events, along with municipal bonds and lottery tickets. Later, financial bubbles were occasioned by innovations—whether driven by novelty, such as the fad in Holland for Turkish tulip bulbs, or necessity, such as the plan to nationalize the British government's debt through the issuing of shares in the South Sea Company. The populist investment boom of the 1990s could be described as a combination of novelty and necessity, driven in part by technological innovation (the World Wide Web and e-commerce, in particular) and in part by the need for many Americans to meet their financial needs privately, rather than relying on the government or their employers for a safety net.

Such events must occur within a relatively permissive atmosphere in order to precipitate a speculative mania. The Dutch and British not only possessed the great merchant empires of their time but also encouraged a freewheeling spirit of financial innovation, so it was no coincidence that they created the first two speculative crazes in history. While others developed many of the building blocks of modern capitalism—such as double-entry bookkeeping and joint-stock companies—it was Dutch and British financiers who put the pieces together to support a network of global commerce. What the economist Joseph Schumpeter wrote of the South Sea Bubble was equally true of the stock market bubble of the late 1990s in the United States: "The mania of 1719–1720 ... was, exactly as were later manias of this kind, induced by a preceding period of innovation which transformed the economic structure and upset the preexisting structure of things."[35]

Among the most important structural conditions that facilitated the stock market boom of the 1990s was the ease with which individuals who were not finance professionals could form investment associations. The notion that anyone could start an investment club was popularized by the Beardstown Ladies, a group of rural Illinois women in their fifties, sixties, and seventies who collectively wrote three investment guides (based on NAIC principles) that ended up on the *New York Times* bestseller list. If these self-proclaimed financial neophytes could do it and succeed, the thinking went, anyone could. Their success built on the "anyone can invest" message of a previous bestseller, *One Up on Wall Street,* in which phenomenally successful mutual fund manager Peter Lynch outlined his "buy what you know" philosophy. Lynch wrote: "Twenty years in this business convinces me that any normal person using the customary three percent of the brain can pick stocks just as well, if not better, than the average Wall Street expert . . . if you stay half-alert, you can pick the spectacular performers right from your place of business or out of the neighborhood shopping mall, and long before Wall Street discovers them." Lynch's evidence for this included his purchase of stock in the Limited, on the recommendation of his wife, who was impressed by the chain store during a trip to the mall.[36]

Supporting this populist message was a series of legal changes that further broke down barriers to investing, most notably the lowering of the capital gains tax and the repeal of the Glass-Steagall Act, which had separated securities brokerage from other branches of banking. The importance of a permissive legal and social atmosphere cannot be underestimated. As a counterexample, consider the case of Japan, in which the pooling of funds to buy stocks is forbidden without the purchase of a mutual fund license, which costs approximately U.S. $10 million. This legal climate effectively outlaws investment clubs, and much of what Americans would regard as populist investing behavior.[37]

In another parallel to the South Sea Bubble, the speculative mania of the 1990s was fueled by copious amounts of coffee and dubious alliances between the public and private sectors. In 1720 London, most speculation was centered around coffeehouses: Jonathan's and Garroway's, in particular, became the favored meeting places for traders. Following the collapse of South Sea share prices in the fall of 1720, recrimination centered on members of Parliament and their perceived self-interest in creating the bubble: they not only floated the original idea of paying off the national debt with public stock issues, but profited handsomely from their insider information about the South Sea Company. Fast forward to the United States in the 1990s, where we find a boom fueled by designer coffee and presided over by a secretary of the treasury who was frequently described as the "ultimate Wall Street insider": Robert Rubin, who came to government after serving as co-chairman of Goldman Sachs. While Rubin himself was never accused of misconduct in that role, the corporate financial scandals of recent years are much like those of 1720, with their revelations about collusion among financial elites and the government officials charged with regulating their activities in the public interest.

In addition to the suspension of ordinary economic rules, a signal characteristic of the carnival atmosphere surrounding financial booms is the upheaval of social norms and institutions. Just as medieval carnivals challenged the authority of the church to assign moral meaning to economic activity, speculative bubbles throughout history have brought an anarchic spirit to bear on the status order and moral conventions. As Jonathan Swift lamented during the South Sea Bubble, "We have seen a great Part of the Nation's Money get into the hands of those, who by their Birth, Education and Merit, could pretend no higher than to wear our liveries."[38] During the 1990s, a slightly more positive spin was put on this sentiment, via the oft-heard refrain "Wall Street has become Main Street." While this was sometimes portrayed as a positive development, it was also true that as soon as the stock market hit a bumpy patch—as on October 27, 1997, which saw the largest single-day point drop ever in the Dow Jones Industrial Average—financial professionals came out in droves to blame the amateur investors who had entered the market in recent years. Ironically, it turned out that amateur investors were a major source of stability in the market following the crash of October 1997; it was the professionals—specifically, pension fund managers—who were later shown to have done most of the panic selling.[39]

Class and gender roles have been shattered in every speculative mania. In 1720s Britain, stocks were one of the few forms of property that were not taxed and which even married women could own in their own name. The second subscription list for South Sea stock included the names of thirty-five women—40 percent of the eighty-eight subscribers.[40] A kind of protoinvestment club even arose when a group of women rented a shop near Garroway's and Jonathan's coffeehouses—in a part of London that came to be known as Exchange Alley—where they drank tea and traded stocks. Several women of the period became quite wealthy in their own right as a result of financial speculation. Sarah, Duchess of Marlborough (and ancestor of Winston Churchill), famously cleared £100,000 from a prescient sale of South Sea stock and as a result held the single largest share in the Bank of England.[41] Later, in the speculative boom that followed the American Civil War, the Duchess of Marlborough's role was played by women like Victoria Woodhull, the "bewitching broker," and Hetty Green, the Quaker heiress who was known as the "Witch of Wall Street." Likewise, the protoinvestment club form arose again during this new speculative mania: "Clerks formed small clubs in order to pool their limited resources . . . [and] in Saratoga, upstate New York, three young ladies set up a pool in Harlem stock and bought two thousand shares."[42]

Similarly, the 1990s witnessed the revival of group investing, particularly among women and people of modest means. The Beardstown Ladies' investment club, for example, was founded in part because the members could not get brokers to open accounts for them. As one member wrote, "brokerage houses were not particularly friendly places for women. There were few female brokers, and women, particularly older ones, were not considered desirable clients."[43] The barriers to entry were partly financial and partly cultural: brokers expected not only that women would have less money to invest, and therefore less to offer in terms of commissions, but that women would make higher demands on them in terms of investment education. Investing involves a host of terms and concepts that can be daunting to those inexperienced with finance. That is why the presence of discount brokerage firms, such as Charles Schwab, did not solve the problems faced by novice investors: there was still an education gap.

Just as there was public outrage following other speculative manias, the end of the 1990s market boom left Americans looking for someone or something to blame and punish. The backlash begins with revulsion at the object of speculative mania: for example, following the crash of the tulip bulb market in 1620s Holland—a calamity that bankrupted many—a Dutch professor of botany was said to be so incensed by the sight of the plants that he would beat them savagely with his walking stick.[44] Similar sentiments have been expressed by investors who lost money following the end of the U.S. stock market boom, although the objects of their frustrations were too elusive to be addressed via the walking stick method. Another common feature of postbubble social ritual is the punishment of elites. Like former head of the New York Stock Exchange Dick Grasso, and former Enron CEO Ken Lay following the collapse of the 1990s stock market bubble, business and government leaders who profited from speculative manias in the past were the objects of widespread public rage that sought to have them "pilloried, stripped of their wealth, and imprisoned."[45] While such efforts were not always successful, they provided material for many a broadside, song, and pamphlet. Figure 1.2 shows one example: a playing card from a deck created in London immediately following the collapse of the South Sea Bubble. The card, like all the others in the set, depicts the folly of those who hoped to get rich(er) quick through purchasing stocks. The Six of Diamonds, shown here, depicts a woman lamenting her losses in the market, with the result that she "Pawn'd her fine Brocades, / And now appears like other homely Jades."

The use of humor remains to this day the primary form of social protest in the wake of financial scandal. For example, the travails of Martha Stewart have generated endless jokes, including a parody of her flagship magazine, titled *Martha Stewart Living Behind Bars*, which features a recipe for "jailhouse chili" and tips on how to decorate a prison cell.[46] See figure 1.3, which compares this to a similar image from a popular broadside created just after the South Sea Bubble, depicting a wealthy, bewigged Englishman languishing behind bars as a result of his financial malfeasance.

Figure 1.2
Six of Diamonds card from the South Sea deck (courtesy of Bancroft Collection, Baker Library, Harvard Business School)

Figure 1.3

Humor as social protest in two financial scandals (Bubbler's Medley, courtesy of Bancroft Collection, Baker Library, Harvard Business School)

In an era of mass media, broadsides have been replaced by late-night talk shows, but the messages and motives are essentially unchanged, as the following examples suggest:

> First Enron, then Tyco and now WorldCom. How come all these companies are off billions in their accounting and nothing ever happens to them? If you bounce a $15 check at the Quickmart, the Feds are at your door! —Jay Leno

> This might be getting serious. The Securities and Exchange Commission is going to be investigating Vice President Dick Cheney. They'll begin that investigation as soon as Congress finishes investigating the Securities and Exchange Commission. —David Letterman

But by far the greatest recrimination has always been reserved for the "upstarts"—the ordinary people who breached the norms of class and gender to engage in financial speculation. The excoriation of the masses was illustrated in another card from the South Sea deck represented in figure 1.4.

Figure 1.4
Ten of Diamonds card from the South Sea deck (courtesy of Bancroft Collection, Baker Library, Harvard Business School)

While the Six of Diamonds shows a noble lady brought low by the collapse of the South Sea Bubble, the Ten of Diamonds depicts the investment losses of a cobbler and his wife, with the following subscript:

> A Wealthy Cobler which is rarely found,
> Had ventur'd in South Sea, Five Hundred Pound,
> By Aul, and End, thus prosper'd till the fall
> Of Cursed South Sea, made an End of all.

Economically empowered women have historically been favored targets for backlash. Following the collapse of the South Sea Bubble, numerous texts and works of visual art represented women investors in a degrading light, as gold diggers, harpies, and prostitutes.[47] Several centuries earlier, the growing wealth and independence of women following the Black Death plague may have catalyzed the European witch craze of the Middle Ages, in which hundreds of thousands of women were burned at the stake.[48] This precedent helps explain the extraordinary outpouring of schadenfreude that greeted the news that the Beardstown Ladies had overstated their portfolio returns.[49] The headlines trumpeted "Debacle in Beardstown"[50] and, more colorfully, "Guru Grannies Caught Cooking the Books by the Money Men: Beardstown Ladies Exposed as Bumbling Amateurs."[51] While no one accused the Beardstown Ladies of being "homely Jades," their virtue and intelligence were questioned in songs that bear a remarkable resemblance to those composed hundreds of years before. Consider, for example, the following excerpt from a song of 1720 titled "The Stock-Jobbing Ladies":

> With Jews and Gentiles, undismay'd,
> Young, tender Virgins mix;
> Of whiskers, nor of Beards afraid,
> Nor of all their cousening Tricks.
>
> Bright Jewels, polish'd once to deck
> The fair one's rising breast,
> Or sparkle round her Ivory Neck,
> Lye pawn'd in Iron Chest.
>
> The genuine Passions of the mind
> How avarice controuls!
> Even Love does now no longer find
> A place in Female Souls.

Compare this to two satirical songs published to celebrate the downfall of the Beardstown Ladies (both are set to the tune of "Camptown Ladies"):

Beardstown Ladies sing this song, bushwah, bushwah
Beardstown stock tips mostly wrong, but the books sure paid.[52]

And

Beardstown Ladies sing this song,
Doo-dah, doo-dah,
Ladies got their numbers wrong,
All the doo-dah day.
Thought they'd seen the light,
Thought they'd found the way,
Trust your money to the amateurs,
Somebody's going to pay.[53]

Artifacts such as these suggest that little about the "new economy" stock boom of the 1990s was actually new. In historical perspective, the United States during the late 1990s looks a lot like seventeenth- and eighteenth-century Europe during similar periods of speculative mania. The great bull market can be envisioned as a scaled-up version of the medieval carnivals, with the big tent located in the Silicon Valley. This particular carnival was precipitated by a number of events, including the high-tech revolution, the easing of legal regulations on investing, and the growing need to provide one's own retirement funding in an uncertain climate of 401(k) plans and an underfunded Social Security plan. The subsequent collapse of the bubble—known in the Silicon Valley as the "dot.bomb" period—not only brought about the downfall of corporate leaders but also played into the recall of California governor Gray Davis. Davis presided over the tail end of the bubble, and his historically unprecedented ouster from office can be regarded as part of the ritual cleansing that follows a mass financial debauch. His replacement by Arnold Schwarzenegger—famous for stalking through postindustrial wastelands as the Terminator—is a fitting emblem of the postapocalyptic, postboom economy.

Investment Clubs and Economic Sociology

This chapter has attempted to contextualize investment clubs not only in the social, economic, legal, and technological conditions of the 1990s, when this study was conducted, but also within the larger framework of financial history. The historical perspective suggests that investment clubs are not a fad but part of a recurrent social response to new economic opportunities and demands. Further, the increasing ability to conduct transactions in the absence of physical contact does not threaten face-to-face groups like investment clubs with obsolescence; on the contrary, "as more information flows through networked connectivity, the more important become the kinds of interactions grounded in a physical locale"—a phenomenon known as "Castells' paradox."[54] In other words, Castells suggests that face-to-face settings for transactions will be accorded increasing value by market participants as machine-mediated interaction becomes more common.

Thus, in addition to their empirical significance as part of the economic and cultural history of capitalism in the United States, investment clubs are poised to grow in both scope and influence. For scholars, they provide insight not only into the ramifications of Castells' paradox but also into other questions of great import to economic sociology, such as how value is socially constructed, who is empowered to participate in this social construction, and how microsocial factors such as these aggregate to the level of macrosocial institutions like the stock market. Chapter 2 will address these issues in greater detail.

APPENDIX ◆
Data Sources for This Study

Sample selection for this study began in May 1997 with an effort to contact as many investment clubs as possible within the San Francisco Bay Area, where I was based at the time. My objective was to gain rapid familiarity with the issues, themes, and practices common to the clubs. These contacts were made in three ways: through local NAIC officials, who invited me to their clubs; through cold-calls to a list of Bay Area clubs provided by NAIC national headquarters; and through an NAIC investment seminar at which I was allowed to make a brief presentation on my project. Of the three methods, cold-calling yielded the greatest number of successful contacts: half the clubs in the final sample were recruited in that way. Though many club officers were a bit dubious at first about allowing me to observe their meetings for a year, I was refused only two times out of dozens of calls. And once I was able to attend a club meeting, introduce myself, and explain my purpose, there was never any dissent—including instances where I was asked to leave while the members took a vote on whether to allow me to return.

In this effort I benefited enormously from NAIC's long-standing practice of encouraging outside observers to attend club meetings. Since the clubs are designed to be learning organizations, one of their official functions is to "evangelize" for the cause of stock market investing. They fulfill this role by allowing nonmembers to sit in on meetings. Often, this is a prerequisite for membership. Members are also encouraged to visit and learn from other clubs. As a result, most clubs are used to, or at least prepared for, strangers attending their meetings. The only difference in this case was my request to stay for a longer period of time than usual. The decision to observe ten meetings of each club was somewhat arbitrary, but made with an eye toward being around long enough to understand the unique dynamics of each group, and to monitor its responses to changes in the stock market. The market cooperated by racking up both record losses and record gains over the observation period.

The sample I selected was designed to provide insight into as broad a spectrum of investors as possible while remaining a manageable size for steady, long-term observation. Thus, the sample includes clubs of varying gender composition (all-male, all-female, and mixed), clubs that were brand-new as well as those that had been in business for more than forty years, composed of young people and the elderly, as well as a variety of racio-ethnic groups, occupational groups, marital statuses, and sexual orientations. Finally, I sought variation in performance, including clubs that had earned substantial profits on their investments and those that had limped along, even during a rising market. The average investment club in the United States earned an annualized rate of return of approximately 12.6 percent on their portfolios since inception; while this was somewhat above the historical average return of the U.S. stock market over the past century, it was low for the late 1990s, in which annualized rates of return for the market indexes regularly exceeded 30 percent.

The seven clubs in my observational sample—whose names, along with those of their members, have been changed to protect their privacy—included:

- Portfolio Associates, an all-men's club in continuous operation for forty-one years. It had eighteen members and was a very high performer with a 38 percent rate of return on its portfolio since inception; the club's total portfolio value had just surpassed the $1 million mark when I began attending meetings.
- Bulls & Bears, a five-year-old mixed club composed of six men and four women who were all employed by a major defense contractor. The club was a high performer, with a 23 percent rate of return on its portfolio since inception.
- Ladies with Leverage, a three-year-old club made up of fourteen women who had met through volunteer activities in a wealthy Silicon Valley suburb. The club was a low performer compared to others in the sample, with an 11.5 percent rate of return on its portfolio since inception.

- California Investors, a six-year-old club composed of fourteen men who had all been colleagues in the insurance industry and had recently retired. The club was an average performer, with a 12.6 percent rate of return since inception.
- Asset Accumulators, a five-year-old club composed of sixteen women, all former schoolteachers, who had met through membership in the American Association of University Women. The club had earned a whopping 36.5 percent rate of return on its portfolio since inception.
- Educating Singles Against Poverty, a three-year-old club composed of nine women and three men who had met through a church singles group. The club was a low performer, with a 9.4 percent rate of return on its portfolio since inception.
- Valley Gay Men's Investment Club, a newly formed club composed of men who had met through a classified ad placed in a local gay community newspaper. The group did not buy any stocks until five months into my observation period, providing too little data to calculate a meaningful rate of return. Nevertheless, observing this group allowed me to witness the process by which first-time investors orient themselves to the market.

Data gathering during this phase of the study took several forms, including taking verbatim notes of the group discussions, which were transcribed within twenty-four hours of the meetings. I tape-recorded the meetings in five of the seven clubs; as to the others, members of one of the men's groups objected to being taped, and recording devices were not permitted on the military base where one of the mixed clubs met. During the meetings, I kept track of data such as:

- Proportion of total meeting time devoted to stock selection, as opposed to social conversation or procedural issues (e.g., catching up on each others' family news and vacation plans, or interpretation and modification of bylaws). I started using a stopwatch to track this issue after I noticed that the low-performing clubs seemed to be spending very little of their meeting time on stocks.
- Stock presentations: who made them, where the presenters got their ideas, what kinds of evidence were presented, and what actions were taken.
- Voting: who made the motion to buy or sell, who seconded it, who voted for and against, who abstained.
- Artifacts: all handouts distributed at the meetings—accounting statements, agendas, and so on—plus background documents, such as the club's partnership agreement.

In addition, I gathered information about club history and members' backgrounds in two ways. First, each of the clubs in the sample pretested the survey I designed for the quantitative part of the study (they did not participate in the final survey project, however). This allowed me to gather a great deal of demographic data about members, including age, income, education, and personal investing habits. Second, I scheduled in-depth interviews with "core" club members—usually the current and past officers—to discuss the club's history in terms of formation, membership, philosophy, and investment choices. In preparation for this meeting, I reviewed each club's minutes and accounting statements (as well as any other printed material) all the way back to its inception, in order to ask more informed questions. I found that "the most reliable indicator of my impressions was saturation—the fact that after a certain amount of interviewing I began to be able to predict the tenor and directions our conversations would take."[55]

Throughout the study, I analyzed the transcripts of club meetings and interviews to detect major themes; my strategy focused on uncovering patterns in interactions, decision processes, and mental maps. I used these themes as a point of departure for an iterative process—moving back and forth between the data and an emerging conceptual structure—to describe how amateur investors understood and made decisions within the stock market. I also used my findings to develop questions for a survey that was mailed to three thousand NAIC investment clubs across the United States in January 1998.

I selected the sample for the national survey by starting from a random entry in the NAIC membership database and choosing every tenth club name until the list included three thousand names—a little less than 10 percent of the NAIC membership at the time. Each club received a packet containing two survey instruments: one designed to glean group-level information, and fifteen copies of a second survey designed to gather data from individual club members. The group-level survey was to be filled out by the club's president; the four-page instrument included thirty multiple-choice and fill-in-the-blank questions about club performance, composition, and organizational structure. The presidents were instructed to hand out the individual-level surveys at the next meeting, allowing the members time to fill out the four-page instrument (which included thirty-one multiple-choice and Likert-style questions about their demographic background and investing behavior, both inside and outside the club); the presidents were then asked to return both the club-level and individual-level surveys to NAIC in a postage-paid envelope. The individual-level surveys were all anonymous, and no identifying information about individual members was requested in the club-level survey. The only names and addresses given were those of the club presidents, which were listed in NAIC's database already as part of the club registration process.

This project netted a total of 1,279 usable responses from clubs, a response rate of 43 percent. The average club responding to this survey was 4.3 years old (s.d. = 6.4) and owned a portfolio of stocks worth $43,000 (s.d. = $7,300); on average, each club had 15 members (s.d. = 5). At the individual level, a total of 11,369 members responded to the survey, including 7,162 (63 percent) women and 4,207 (37 percent) men. The average rate of within-group individual participation in the study was 70 percent of the membership (s.d. = .18). The average member was between 45 and 50 years old (s.d. = 12.4), college educated, had an income of $58,000 (s.d. = $13,000), 11 years of investing experience (s.d. = 6.6), and had belonged to the club since its inception. While it was not possible to compare the sample frame for this study with the entire population of investment clubs, analysis of the nonresponding clubs indicated no difference in terms of composition, size, age, or portfolio value from clubs that did participate in the survey.

Please see section two of the book for details on specific measures and analytical techniques, as well as the additional data gathering and analyses I conducted to test the representativeness and validity of this survey sample.

The people recognize themselves in their commodities; they
find their soul in their automobile, hi-fi set, split-level home,
kitchen equipment.
—HERBERT MARCUSE[1]

Investment Clubs as Markets in Microcosm ◆ 2

Negative Infinity

It has been said that fads appear irrational only to those who are not caught up in them.[2] If so, it is worth asking what the stock market bubble of the 1990s looked like to the millions of individual investors who participated in it. The question is worth pursuing, not only because the perspective of nonprofessional investors has been neglected in past research, but because so much of what *has* been written has focused on the irrationality of these individuals.

This chapter will attempt to enlarge this perspective by arguing for what Daniel Kahneman, winner of the 2002 Nobel Prize in Economics, calls the "two-system view" of rationality.[3] In this view, individuals can be both rational and irrational, to varying degrees and sometimes in combination. That is, consistent with the behavioral theories of economic sociology, both rationality and irrationality are *variables*. This duality is characteristic not only of individuals but also of the economic systems in which they operate. As French cultural theorists Gilles Deleuze and Felix Guattari argued during the U.S. market boom: "Everything is rational in capitalism, except capital or capitalism itself. The stock market is certainly rational; one can understand it, study it, the capitalists know how to use it, and yet it is completely delirious, it's mad . . . the system is demented, yet works very well at the same time."[4]

Releasing the analysis of investment behavior from the constraints of static, binary thinking about rationality offers much more analytical room to explore how individuals cope with the vast array of choices presented by the stock market. Thousands of individual stocks are traded on U.S. exchanges, tens of thousands on international exchanges. These figures do not include other financial instruments, such as bonds, shares of mutual funds, derivatives, and so forth. In this sense, the stock market presents investors with what Hegel called the problem of "negative infinity": " . . . negative infinity: it is only a negation of a finite . . . In the attempt to contemplate such an infinite, our thought, we are commonly informed, must sink exhausted. It is true indeed that we must abandon the unending contemplation, not however because the occupation is too sublime, but because it is too tedious."[5] As Hegel suggests, tedium or mental exhaustion sets in when individuals are faced with an overwhelming number of choices. This clearly has implications for investment decision-making: the range of choices available in the stock market is so large as to utterly swamp and defy rational analysis. This is not to say that rationality is totally absent from investment decisions, but that our rationality is *bounded* by limits on the scope or amount of information we can process.[6] Even the most intelligent people often lack the time and other resources to investigate and prioritize all their options in a complex system like the stock market; instead, they make do with limited information and limited processing time, aided by judgment calls. In formal social scientific terms, such decision makers are said to "satisfice" rather than "optimize."[7]

On the one hand, satisficing is clearly an imperfect solution. The saga of Long Term Capital Management is a case in point: a hedge fund led by two Nobel Prize winners and one of the most successful bond traders in history lost approximately $5 billion of investors' money because of events and variables unforeseen in the principals' carefully constructed models. If three of the smartest minds in the finance world could not grasp the full complexity of the market system, it is not surprising that most investors—both professional and nonprofessional—routinely underperform the market.[8] That is, they fail to anticipate all the relevant factors bearing on any given investment decision.

At the same time, attempts to optimize often lead to the decision paralysis and withdrawal that Hegel anticipates in his discussion of negative infinity. What may be surprising is how little it takes to induce this sense of cognitive exhaustion. For example, a simple experiment in a supermarket showed that when customers were presented with two sampling booths—one offering six flavors of jam and the other offering twenty-four flavors of jam—the twenty-four-flavor booth attracted more customers but induced far less purchasing than the six-flavor booth. Apparently, customers were overwhelmed by having twenty-four choices, resulting in only 3 percent making a purchase. In contrast, the six-choice booth yielded *an order of magnitude* increase in purchases, with 30 percent of customers buying jam.[9]

If twenty-four choices of jam can produce "brain lock" in decision makers, the possibilities presented by thousands of stocks traded on U.S. and international exchanges would seem likely to elicit a similar set of responses. Indeed, preliminary evidence suggests that investors behave similarly to grocery shoppers. Research on participation in 401(k) programs indicates that individuals are overwhelmed with the increasing number of mutual funds made available by their firms;[10] as with jam, more options are not necessarily a good thing.

Markets and Mental Maps

Such findings beg the question: if the choices available in the stock market are so overwhelming, how is it that individual investors manage to buy stocks at all, as opposed to "outsourcing" their decisions to professionals, such as brokers and fund managers? Previous research has shown that when confronted with unmanageable amounts of data, individuals develop some means of narrowing the field, shrinking the range of possibilities to a manageable size relative to their information-processing capacity. However, they rarely do this narrowing in a rigorous fashion. This is true even of individuals who have professional training in the application of decision heuristics to large problem sets, such as the statisticians who—as reported by Tversky and Kahneman—made most of their decisions based on intuition and experience rather than on the formal techniques in which they had been trained.[11]

In the case of the stock market, the problem is exacerbated by lack of agreement, even among professionals, as to what constitutes a rigorous way of parsing the market into analytically manageable components. Instead, there are a number of competing taxonomies—such as the Standard Industrial Classification Codes, the STOXX system, or the Standard & Poors classification system—all of which classify the market into broad conceptual clusters according to somewhat different criteria and at varying levels of granularity. None are dominant in the realm of professional investors.[12]

In fact, finance professionals often make a name for themselves and become identified with signature methods of shrinking the universe of stocks down to a subset that constitutes their special decision pool. Thus, many fund managers are classified as "value" or "growth" investors. Even so, these labels are often contested: for example, one of the most successful mutual fund managers in history, Bill Miller of Legg Mason Funds Management, is often classified as a "value" investor even though many of his largest positions are in high-tech "growth" stocks such as amazon.com and Google. The lack of a shared cognitive model for the stock market among financial professionals makes it difficult to adjudicate whether and to what extent nonprofessionals see the market in a rational way.

Rather than attempting to resolve this debate, the present chapter will explore it by investigating the mental maps of amateur investors, and the social processes through which these maps are created. More broadly, this chapter will take an inductive approach, informed by the sociology of knowledge: the branch of the discipline concerned with how we know what we know. The goal is to build a model of the stock market from the perspective of individual investors, rather than pointing out the ways in which investors deviate from rationality as conceived deductively.

Drawing out individuals investors' mental maps means understanding how they conceptualize the market, parse it into categories meaningful to them, and make choices within those categories. Some researchers in economic sociology (most notably Viviana Zelizer of Princeton University) and in behavioral finance (particularly Richard Thaler of the University of Chicago) have approached this issue through the concept of "mental accounting"—how individuals compartmentalize and use funds according to heuristics such as "mad money" or "ill-gotten gains."[13] While this work has been very important in laying the foundation for the study of mental maps in the economy, there is still much that remains unknown about the ways in which individual investors conceptualize the stock market.

Imitative Behavior as a Response to Negative Infinity

While the "buy what you know" philosophy popularized by Peter Lynch encouraged many people to make their first leap into investing, the strategy could also be limiting, in that some individuals have interpreted it to mean that they should not go beyond their personal experiences or "comfort zones" in selecting stocks. As one investor put it in a 2001 magazine interview,

> "As an individual, there is a human limit to what I can manage. I've narrowed what I invest in to the sectors I know and understand," David says. "I want a comfort level so that when I look at an annual report, I have an understanding of the jargon, technology, and the

fundamentals of the company." David focuses on tech, biotech, computer peripherals and medical stocks. He avoids retailers, gaming, real estate and investment companies.[14]

As it turned out, the "buy what you know" strategy may not have served David very well. The technology and computing industries were among the hardest-hit in the market downturn that began in April 2000, and the industries that David was avoiding—notably retail and financial stocks—were among the most robust performers.[15] While David may have felt more comfortable buying stocks in industries that were familiar to him, he paid a price in terms of forgoing opportunities in other areas. As this anecdote suggests, what's interesting—and still poorly understood—about mental maps of the stock market is what people *think* they know, and how this helps or hurts them as investors.

For example, how do we know the value of anything, including stocks? One seventeenth-century thinker answered this question in terms that would be endorsed by twenty-first-century economic sociologists: "things have no value in themselves, it is opinion and fashion which brings them into use and gives them a value."[16] In other words, for value to be assigned, there must be a negotiation of terms among individuals. In the broadest sense, that is what investment clubs do; it is also the main business of the stock market. This is one way in which investment clubs are "markets in microcosm." Thus, the tensions and ambiguities surrounding the assignment of value are played out at both the micro- and macrolevels.

In the investment world, the value of stocks is summarized in their price. Prices change throughout the trading day, reflecting the ongoing social process of negotiation. This involves a highly specialized vocabulary and analytical tool kit. While there are numerous techniques for assessing the value of stocks, all involve making predictions about the future. Information from the past can be helpful only to a limited extent in making such predictions, and so investors are left to make judgment calls about value and risk.

Investors are compensated for assuming this risk: the greater the risk, the greater the reward. That is why relatively risk-free securities like government bonds carry low rewards (around 5 percent annually for long-term bonds), while stocks come with an "equity premium": an additional 6 percent return, reflected in the average annual gains of 11 percent in the stock market as a whole. The problem for investors is that the "equity premium" is not guaranteed: it is just an average, and some individual investors will actually lose money on stocks depending on what and when they buy and sell. In addition, the risk-return relationship is not linear.

Rather, it resembles an inverted U-shaped curve: risks pay off up to a certain point, after which they become a waste of money. As with gambling, most of the fun in investing consists of locating that fine line between risks that pay off and those that do not.

To cope with risk-reward uncertainty, investors look to each other for clues. For example, psychologist George Katona showed that there is an extremely high correlation among investors' stock purchases within neighborhoods; that is, individuals' portfolios look a lot like those of their immediate neighbors, and stock purchase ideas appear to travel by word of mouth through informal interactions, such as block parties and PTA meetings. This imitative behavior is also instrumental in drawing non-investors into the market in the first place: Katona found that the major causal factor leading non-investors to start buying stocks is not economic imperative or connection to a market "insider" but simply having acquaintances—such as neighbors or coworkers—who invest.[17]

In fact, people are constantly looking to others for clues about how to behave, particularly under conditions of uncertainty or change. Social psychologists call this phenomenon "social proof." Most of us are familiar with this process through popular sayings such as "monkey see, monkey do," or "when in Rome, do as the Romans." In this sense, investing invokes processes similar to those of any other social situation in which there are numerous unknowns—and in which individuals wish to avoid looking foolish in front of others. Investors behave much like people who find themselves at a fancy dinner party confronted by unfamiliar foods or utensils: for both groups, imitation of others is the typical strategy, regardless of whether those others are correct. Being wrong is less painful when lots of other people are wrong in the same way.

The need for social proof about value and risk is particularly appropriate in the case of stocks, because the price and volatility of a stock ultimately come down to how others evaluate it. Thus, investors are continually scanning the environment for cues from trusted information sources; these may include market "gurus" as well as friends or investment club associates. When investors ask whether a stock is worth its price, and whether it is a good risk, often they really mean: what do others think? In investment clubs, these questions are dealt with face-to-face, during meetings where members make presentations to each other about which stocks they think the club should buy or sell. These debates—in which the opinions of analysts, brokers, friends, relatives, and others are frequently invoked—are imaginative acts of storytelling, resulting in collectively constructed notions of worth and risk. The group setting is important, because social proof becomes more potent as increasing numbers of people are involved. That is, the more people you see investing in a stock, the more it seems like a good idea.[18]

Social proof is not always a positive force. Sometimes it can distort and diminish decision quality, as in the famous experiments conducted by Solomon Asch in the 1940s, in which he convinced research participants to alter their own correct perceptions on a simple and objective judgment task (estimating the lengths of several lines projected on a wall).[19] If intelligent people can be made to doubt the evidence of their own senses on a simple task, the opportunities for such distortions increase exponentially in tasks like investing, where complexity and uncertainty are givens.

Distorted perceptions and irrational behavior also increase when strong emotions are in play—such as the fear, excitement, greed, and remorse that often grip investors. The social nature of emotions has been noted by psychologists since Freud, who observed that individuals respond to the emotions of others not only by imitating but also by exaggerating them. This effect—known as "emotional contagion"—increases directly with the number of others who can be observed experiencing a given emotion.[20] Most importantly for this study, emotional contagion appears to "result in a temporary suspension of critical judgment and thinking."[21] These effects can aggregate to the macrolevel via the influence of mass media, including print, radio, television, and the World Wide Web. This is significant for the present study because very few investors keep their own counsel; most look to others—from "market experts" like Louis Rukeyser to their next-door-neighbors—to tell them how to think and feel about market news.[22] In addition, the *specific content* of emotions is contagious. Field studies show that negative emotions (such as annoyance or hostility) in instigators produce negative emotions in observers, while instigators' positive emotions (such as friendliness) produce positive emotions in others.[23] The result is a circular, self-reinforcing cycle: the emotions of some individuals stimulate others to feel the same emotions, which are then reflected back to the instigators with an escalating degree of emotional intensity.

"Buy *Who* You Are"

Imitative behavior can also be driven by self-categorization and the categorization of others as similar to or different from oneself. For example, social psychologists have found that individuals navigate ambiguous or cognitively overwhelming situations by asking two questions: first, "who am I?" and second, "how are people similar to me interpreting and responding to this situation?" In other words, "ambiguity leads to informational influence mostly from those who are categorized as being equivalent to self. *That is, self-categorization may provide the limits for informational influence.*[24] In other words, the less clarity we have about events and their meaning, the more salient our identity becomes and the more we rely on others—especially those we perceive as similar to ourselves—to help us create workable interpretations or mental maps to guide our actions. This implies that investors choose stocks in part because of their self-perceptions, meaning that "buy what you know" can translate in practice into "buy who you are."

In sociology and social psychology, identity is understood to be a social construct, built up in interaction with others.[25] Knowing who you are requires the cooperation and assent of others—family, friends, coworkers, classmates, and even strangers. In the earliest days of sociology, at the beginning of the twentieth century, Cooley called this the "looking glass self," meaning that we develop a self-concept based on the way others reflect and respond to us.[26] Several decades later, Goffman described identity as created through a call-and-response process, in which individuals make "identity claims" and rely on others to provide the consent and validation necessary for those identities to become real: "the individual must rely on others to complete the picture of him of which he himself is only allowed to paint certain parts . . . the part expressed through the individual's demeanor being no more significant than the part conveyed by others through their deferential behavior toward him."[27] Without this cooperation from others, an identity is incomplete. While the sociological view allows for the existence of an "essential" or core self, it also posits that identities are the bridges that connect us to others, linking our inner and outer realities.

In this sense, identity is the "atomic unit" of social life, the basis of the micro-macro link that "stitches (or, to use a current metaphor, 'sutures') the subject into the structure."[28] As one group of social psychologists put it, identity is "a self-conception as sharing a category membership with a set of other people."[29] However, symbolic interactionist theory holds that the self is not a single, homogenous entity but an amalgam of multiple labels and roles.[30] The self in this conception is not a unitary construct but a collage of group affiliations based on an individual's location in the social structure. Individuals can use their "portfolio" of identities as a symbolic resource to help orient themselves to new situations—including choosing which stocks to buy out of the plethora of choices offered in the market.[31]

The connection between identity and stock market activity is not new to economic sociology; but, curiously, little has been said about the impact of *individuals'* identity on their construction of mental maps of the market.

Instead, the extant research has looked at *corporations'* sense of identity and how they communicate it to relevant audiences, such as investors and analysts. For example, one study looked at why firms that had done well by listing their shares on the NASDAQ exchange often sought to "upgrade" their public images by migrating to the New York Stock Exchange. According to the authors of the study, the exchange on which a firm is listed, along with industry category and other symbolic classifications, "serve as an interpretive core from which firms derive social identity."[32] Along these lines, other studies have looked at firms' attempts to shape their public identities through the text of annual reports,[33] or—in the case of conglomerates—by shedding business units that complicate or obscure their corporate identity in the eyes of analysts and investors.[34] These studies are compelling in that they show a significant link between identity and market outcomes, such as ease of access to capital.

Extending these insights to the individual level of analysis makes sense for three reasons. First, given all the signals and symbolic communication that firms are directing toward the market, we need to understand more about how these messages are interpreted—particularly by the amateur or "retail" investors who have largely been overlooked by previous research. Second, social psychological research shows that notions of the self are the most salient aspects of our mental maps for all kinds of settings. That is, in most situations, one's self-concept dictates appropriate behavior.[35] So when individual investors follow the "buy what you know" dictum, social psychology would predict that their choices will reflect who they think they are and who they aspire to be. In some cases, buying stocks can be a way of trying on new identities—first and foremost, the identity of "investor." However, as one investment adviser wrote of the stock market, "if you don't know who you are, this is an expensive place to find out."[36]

Third, and perhaps most significantly, many cultural theorists suggest that under developed capitalist regimes, individuals literally have no choice but to live through their economic behavior—including consumption and investment. For instance, Jürgen Habermas—a cultural critic and philosopher of the Frankfurt School—argues that the "life-world" has been "colonized" by the global commercial nexus. That is, the concepts, values, and modes of thought associated with the market have intruded into daily life to such an extent that individuals can hardly think or act outside this hegemonic system.[37] The radical French political theorist Guy Debord writes that a signal characteristic of complex capitalist societies is the mediation of all human interaction by means of economic signifiers—a phenomenon he calls the "society of the spectacle." In such a society, individuals must "see the world by means of various specialized mediations (it can no longer be grasped directly)."[38] Stocks—from ticker symbols to paper certificates—may be considered one of these "specialized mediations," as implied by Debord's discussion of social relations under modern capitalism: "In societies where modern conditions of production prevail, all of life presents itself as an immense accumulation of spectacles . . . The spectacle is not a collection of images, but a social relation among people, mediated by images . . . The language of the spectacle consists of signs of the ruling production, which at the same time are the ultimate goal of this production . . . The spectacle subjugates living men to itself to the extent that the economy has totally subjugated them."[39] In other words, modern social theory regards the expression of individual identity and the mediation of interpersonal relations through signifiers like stock ownership to be an inevitable outcome of capitalist modes of production. The economic system sets the terms of every other aspect of social life. Investment clubs provide the social structure and interaction mechanisms through which individuals can perform these complex but essential symbolic functions: locating and identifying themselves within the social cartography of capitalism.

Individuals are motivated to claim identities that preserve or enhance their social status, and historically, being an investor is a high-status social activity associated with economic and social elites.[40] In particular, being a *successful* investor is associated with high status. This claim is difficult to make for the many Americans whose involvement in the market consists only of their stake in a 401(k) plan, where they have limited investment choice and thus limited bragging rights. It is far less impressive to say that your mutual fund manager made you a fortune than to explain how you made a fortune through your own financial acumen. This is particularly true in a country like the United States, in which the "self-made man" is at the top of the economic status hierarchy, and "no guts, no glory" is the rule on Wall Street.

Investment clubs offer a solution to this problem by allowing members the opportunity to claim credit for proposing profitable investment ideas, while spreading the downside risk of bad calls. Members get wide latitude to choose from among the thousands of stocks traded on American exchanges, along with over twenty-six thousand stocks available overseas.[41] While an individual member cannot claim sole credit for the performance of the group's portfolio, he or she can claim responsibility for picking the highest-performing stock or saving the group a bundle by selling a stock just before it took a fall. The sheer range of options available, and the risks involved, confer a status on the investment club member that is denied to the person who invests only with professional help. This is particularly true if the investment decision is lucrative. Because of this, status competition over the identity of "investment expert" is a constant among investment club members. Choosing a winning stock, particularly a dark horse, becomes a basis for bragging rights both within the club and outside it.

The status enhancement associated with buying and selling individual stocks may be another reason investment clubs have been so attractive to women, who have traditionally been shut out of institutions of the formal financial sector. Women have not only had trouble getting stock brokers to take them seriously as investors;[42] in addition, women have made very little headway within the world of professional finance. A recent study found that women constitute only 10.3 percent of the top management teams in American financial firms.[43] The institutional barriers that limit women's access to the formal financial sector—both as clients and employees—also limit their identity claims. Like value, identity is a social construction that requires an audience.

Investment clubs answer this need by providing a social setting in which the "call and response" process of establishing a new social identity can be completed.[44] This may be why women in NAIC investment clubs so frequently invoke terms such as "empowerment" and describe their experiences of learning to invest as "life-changing."[45] Participation in investment clubs brings with it not only an economic shift but a change of self. This also suggests why women investors have been regarded as transgressive figures since the Middle Ages; investing means upward mobility not just economically but also in status terms.

Symbols and Storytelling in the Market

Investors rely on social identity and social interaction to create mental maps of the stock market—a complex, rapidly changing environment about which even professionals cannot seem to reach a shared understanding. This insight suggests the appeal of applying a symbolic interactionist perspective to the study of investor behavior. Symbolic interactionism, one of the oldest traditions in sociology and social psychology, postulates that the central task of social life is forging connections between the self and others through symbolic means.[46] Much of social interaction in this theory is conceptualized as a series of negotiations using language and other symbols to label and categorize objects, with the ultimate goal of reaching a shared version of reality from which lines of action can be developed.

In this light, the stock market can be viewed as a collective attempt by millions of people to establish an intersubjective reality called "value," mediated through a variety of symbolic media, including the stock's ticker symbol, the exchange on which it is listed, and of course the share price.[47] For any given stock—as well as for bonds, currencies, and mutual funds—value is up for negotiation on a virtually continual basis, as long as trading is being conducted. The construction of a line of action, such as buying or selling a stock, in symbolic interaction can occur only when the symbols are placed within a meaningful, coherent structure—in other words, a story. Stories can thus be seen as cognitive "glue," allowing humans to engage in complex judgment tasks by imposing a narrative structure on fragmented symbols.[48] Indeed, some researchers have speculated that narrative is the *fundamental* organizing principle of human thought, "in which decisions grow 'naturally' from the progressive development of the narrative."[49] While it might seem surprising to seek insight into questions of economic sociology through the lens of narrative, literary critic Catherine Ingrassia points out—in an analysis of the South Sea Bubble of 1720—that "financial and emotional investment in stocks and fiction are analogous cultural practices."[50] That is, like fiction, investment in stocks requires the construction of imaginative links between signifiers (like stocks) and the signified (value). This is why narrative is so important in shaping understanding of the stock market: it is literally the lingua franca of investing.

Indeed, research in finance suggests that decision making under conditions of risk and uncertainty is heavily influenced by the stories decision makers tell. For example, people who gamble on horse races base their choices in part on which bets will yield the best stories. Betting on a sure thing does not earn one much in the way of bragging rights, but winning on a long shot does.[51] This presents a compelling analogy to the position of the individual investor: while one cannot take much credit for making money on investments managed by others (as in the case of mutual fund investments), turning a profit on the selection of individual stocks provides ample opportunity for celebration of one's financial acumen—an achievement for which the investment club provides a ready-made audience for the call-and-response process outlined by Goffman. As one observer noted, by the late 1990s stock portfolios had become essential social accessories: "Lying about how well your investments have done has replaced exaggerating the size of the fish you caught."[52] This suggests that when individuals buy a stock, they are not only buying a financial instrument that they hope will make them a profit; they are also buying a story. And in buying the story of the company, they are buying a story about themselves: the great investment decision becomes a core element in the autobiography of the modern American.

"Mommy, look! It's Abby Joseph Cohen!"

Figure 2.1

The stock anaylst as celebrity, circa 1997 (image by Hank Blonstein, reprinted by permission of *Grant's Interest Rate Observer*).

A Marketplace of Stories, or How We Learned to Stop Worrying and Love the Dot.coms

The period during which this study was conducted witnessed an efflorescence of storytelling and storytellers. For example, the formerly obscure task of stock analysis came to have the potential for fame and fortune usually associated with fronting a rock band—complete with groupies and fawning media coverage. Henry Blodgett, Mary Meeker, and Abby Joseph Cohen became the pop stars of the dot.com era (see figure 2.1). And investors—like music fans—often developed favorite market bards, to whose "songs" about the market they would return again and again. Thus there was always a core group of subscribers to publications like *Grant's Interest Rate Observer*, which maintained a consistently pessimistic outlook throughout the bull market. Troubadors of a more optimistic bent also had their die-hard fans, who stuck with the hooray-for-the-market story during the many precipitous downturns of the 1990s and beyond.

In the marketplace of stories, analysts vied with publicly traded firms to control the narratives of a stock's investment value and profit potential. Annual reports to shareholders, for instance, can be read as narratives that firms construct around their balance sheets and other financial statements, with the object of casting their performance results in the most positive light.[53] Firms pay close attention to the ways in which they are labeled, because those labels influence the firm's story. Even seemingly trivial issues, such as the categorization of firms by the federal government's industry codes, become symbolically fraught as part of the struggle to control perception, interpretation, and ultimately access to resources: "How organizations are categorized, by themselves and others, has direct consequences for their ability to acquire resources, mobilize commitment to their strategic agenda, and maintain or enhance their legitimacy in the eyes of stakeholders . . . Organizations thus have a real stake in the categories that are used to describe their activities."[54] Consequently, narrative skill has become a requirement of the executive role. As organizational researcher Joanne Martin has noted, "A story contains a blueprint that can be used to predict future organizational behavior."[55] Thus, people who tell the most compelling stories about the future earnings of a firm hold sway over the beliefs and behavior of many investors.

Throughout the 1990s, as new ideas became more important than new products, the old stories and symbols pertaining to valuation—price-earnings ratios, debt levels, and so on—fell out of favor, and storytelling became increasingly important. As one Silicon Valley venture capitalist wrote in the late 1990s: "In today's unique Internet business environment, the art of storytelling has taken on increasing importance . . . great storytellers can create self-fulfilling prophecies. Companies that grab mindshare early typically secure strong financing. Strong financing adds to the story, which in turn may make possible a killer partnership, which adds even more to the story."[56] Ultimately, investors (professionals and nonprofessionals alike) are literally being asked to "buy into" other people's versions of events.

But who gets to tell stories about the market? Traditionally, the "ownership rights"[57] to tell stories about companies and their stock value have belonged to insiders, such as CEOs, stock analysts, and fund managers. In a sense, these corporate insiders and financial professionals were like a priestly caste, empowered to interpret the mysteries of the market for the lay public. But the "new economy" brought about a kind of Reformation, both by changing the ways that stories were told and expanding the range of people empowered to tell stories. It was not only that narrative conventions broadened beyond traditional valuation measures such as price-earnings ratios. More radical still was the inclusion of financial "lay people"—that is, those outside the finance profession—in making their own stories heard. For example, the advent of the World Wide Web allowed teenagers to move markets by hyping stocks in chat rooms. If this was the Reformation, then Peter Lynch was its Martin Luther, and *One Up on Wall Street* his version of the ninety-five theses.[58]

Perhaps like Luther, Lynch was not fully aware of the revolutionary chain of events his ideas would produce. Suddenly, anyone could be a market "prophet," reaching a large audience with interpretations of 10-Ks, annual reports, and other "sacred texts" of corporate finance. But by loosening the monopoly of the "priestly caste" of financial professionals on interpreting the market, this revolution unleashed another excess of choice. As if thousands of stocks to choose from were not overwhelming enough, the proliferation of new readings of the market meant even greater information overload. This is because almost any set of facts can support multiple stories. For example, the same market conditions that yielded the "sky's the limit" story exemplified by the book *Dow 100,000* also spawned the contrarian interpretations found in *Grant's Interest Rate Observer*.

So the stock market has become like a giant game of telephone, in which companies tell stories about themselves—through annual reports or press releases—which are then interpreted by analysts and again by reporters, and often by individual investors in newsletters and on the Internet. As in a game of telephone, the stories get distorted as they are passed from one source to the next. What finance scholars call "noise trading" can be understood as investing within this environment of narrative cacophony, rather than a failure of rationality on the part of individuals. By the time a group of ten to fifteen people sits down at an investment club meeting, each member is likely to have been saturated with competing stories about the stock market. So a great deal of what goes on in these meetings becomes a process of sorting through existing stories and creating new ones. The group process involves deciding not only who is empowered to tell credible stories about the stock market (Is a friend's recommendation sufficient, or must the firm be endorsed by a professional analyst? Do some members within the club have more credibility than others?) but also what kind of information constitutes a valid narrative. How investment clubs adjudicate these questions reveals a great deal about their mental maps of the stock market.

NAIC as a Storytelling Community

One reason individuals continued to flock to NAIC investment clubs over the years was for the analytical tools. NAIC's core offering is the "Stock Selection Guide," a two-page work sheet that promises to lead from a short set of basic financial calculations to a clear recommendation to buy, sell, or hold the stock. Tools such as the SSG enjoyed decades of popularity because they offered investors respite from the "negative infinity" of stock selection, serving as kind of narrative template, permitting boundedly rational individuals to impose order on an otherwise unmanageable volume of information. The SSG also offered investors a model for creating their own stories about a stock, reducing their dependence on—and need to sort through—the cacophony of narratives offered by professional market storytellers through the mass media.

In this sense, membership in NAIC has meant membership in a special kind of storytelling community, with its own rules about what constitutes a valid narrative. Just as there are narrative conventions in the writing of mystery novels or tragedies—such as the three-part structure of rising action, climax, and resolution—the SSG provides a conceptual framework into which assorted facts can be placed to produce an intelligible story. In fact, the SSG somewhat resembles a "Mad Lib": a template in which users create a story by filling in the blanks. In lieu of the "adjective" and "noun" prompts used in "Mad Libs," the SSG asks users to plug in information on a firm's historical sales and profit growth, earnings per share, and so forth. But very much like a "Mad Lib," the result of the SSG (shown in figure 2.2) is a story. The resolution, in the case of the SSG, is a recommendation to buy, sell, or hold.

In sociological terms, the SSG aids investors in developing lines of action by taking a small number of facts about a stock, providing guidelines for interpretation, and producing a recommendation. As Ben, a member of the Valley Gay Men's Investment Club put it, the SSG can serve as a "weeding mechanism" to bring the vastness of the stock market down to a manageable size for boundedly rational decision-makers. This suggests that NAIC's ultimate product is a set of mental maps for investors.

However, the "new economy" rhetoric of the 1990s gave many NAIC members serious doubts about the adequacy of tools like the SSG to accurately guide them through the process of choosing stocks. Every club that participated in the qualitative part of my study expressed reservations about the usefulness of the SSG in a market where figures like price-earnings ratios routinely exceeded the bounds set by NAIC. "The SSG just doesn't work with the kind of numbers we're seeing these days," said Stan of California Investors. "If we followed the SSG," said Dave of Portfolio Associates, "we'd never buy anything in this market. In fact, the SSG puts everything we own in the 'sell' range." This was a startling admission of doubt from a club that had adhered to NAIC guidelines for over forty years. The skepticism and frustration were expressed even more forcefully in newer clubs, which regarded the SSG much as early modern explorers must have regarded ancient maps of the world showing a flat earth with dragons lying in wait at the edges—better than nothing, but just barely. The "new economy," like the New World, seemed to require the creation of new maps; and that is the project in which all the investment clubs in the qualitative portion of this study were actively engaged.

In creating new mental maps of the stock market, investment club members developed a variety of narrative structures as alternatives to the SSG to help them make sense of their investing options. This decision to depart from NAIC's market maps and strike out on their own was a conscious one on the part of the groups I observed. For example, I recorded the following discussion in the all-female Ladies with Leverage club in September 1997, after the treasurer announced that the club's portfolio had increased in value by only $1 during the previous three months:

> *Connie*: Maybe we should focus more on basic principles of
>   investing.
> *Karen*: As a club, we have to decide whether we want to use NAIC
>   rules for stock selection.
> *Georgia*: Sometimes it's better to buy what you know, rather than
>   trucking or something that NAIC recommends. (Other
>   members nod in assent.)

Having thus dispatched the NAIC method, the club proceeded later in the same meeting to buy shares of TriTeal Corporation—a software firm holding an initial public offering (IPO). The rationale for the purchase was "buy what you know," as mediated through interpersonal networks: specifically, a chance encounter between an LWL member and a group of men she described as "high-rolling lawyers from Louisiana" with whom she struck up a conversation while sharing a Jeep ride through Telluride, Colorado. The lawyers gave her a "hot tip" about the TriTeal IPO, and she evidently found their story persuasive, because she passed it along to her investment club, which made the purchase. Three months later, the Motley Fool website named TriTeal one of the "Nine Worst Stocks of 1997." Under the heading "How You Could Have Avoided This Loser," the Motley Fool wrote, "TriTeal had all the markings of a questionable investment— no track record, a high valuation, and too much of a connection with a 'hip' concept."[59]

While this anecdote ends poorly, it should not be taken to mean that all individual investors or investment clubs are fundamentally incompetent at developing their own market maps. Rather, as the following comparison will show, the two key points are that (1) a variety of interpretations can be made from similar sets of facts; and (2) groups vary considerably in

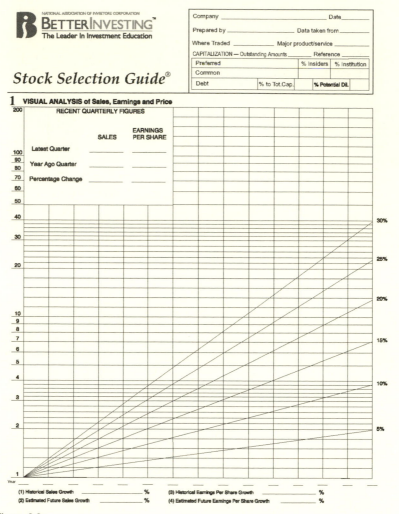

Figure 2.2a

NAIC's Stock Selection Guide (this form and the name "Stock Selection Guide® are owned by the National Association of Investors Corporation and are reproduced herein by permission).

their capacities to construct effective narratives. That is, a fundamental difference between groups is their ability to create stories that permit them both to act and to accurately interpret the facts, so that the group's actions yield the intended results. So what the Motley Fool identified as an obviously "questionable" investment—at least in hindsight—the Ladies with Leverage framed as an exciting opportunity.

These points can also be illustrated by the following comparison: during August and September of 1997 three of the seven investment clubs in

2 EVALUATING MANAGEMENT   Company _____

Year									LAST 5 YEAR AVG.	TREND UP	DOWN
A % Pre-tax Profit on Sales (Net Before Taxes ÷ Sales)											
B % Earned on Equity (E/S ÷ Book Value)											

3 PRICE-EARNINGS HISTORY as an indicator of the future

This shows how stock prices have fluctuated with earnings and dividends. It is a building block for translating earnings into future stock prices.

	PRESENT PRICE			HIGH THIS YEAR		LOW THIS YEAR		
Year	A PRICE HIGH	B LOW	C Earnings Per Share	D Price Earnings Ratio HIGH A÷C	E LOW B÷C	F Dividend Per Share	G % Payout F÷C X 100	H % High Yield F÷B X 100
1								
2								
3								
4								
5								
6 TOTAL								
7 AVERAGE								
8 AVERAGE PRICE EARNINGS RATIO				9 CURRENT PRICE EARNINGS RATIO				

4 EVALUATING RISK and REWARD over the next 5 years

Assuming one recession and one business boom every 5 years, calculations are made of how high and how low the stock might sell. The upside-downside ratio is the key to evaluating risk and reward.

A HIGH PRICE – NEXT 5 YEARS
Avg. High P/E _____ (3D7 as adj.) X Estimate High Earnings/Share _____ = Forecast High Price $ _____ (4A1)

B LOW PRICE – NEXT 5 YEARS
(a) Avg. Low P/E _____ (3E7 as adj.) X Estimated Low Earnings/Share _____ = $ _____
(b) Avg. Low Price of Last 5 Years = _____ (3B7)
(c) Recent Severe Market Low Price = _____
(d) Price Dividend Will Support = Present Divd. (H) ÷ High Yield = _____
Selected Estimate Low Price _____ = $ _____ (4B1)

C ZONING
_____ (4A1) High Forecast Price Minus _____ (4B1) Low Forecast Price Equals _____ (C) Range. 1/3 of Range = _____ (4CD)
(4C2) Lower 1/3 = (4B1) _____ to _____ (Buy)
(4C3) Middle 1/3 = _____ to _____ (Maybe)
(4C4) Upper 1/3 = _____ to _____ (4A1) (Sell)
Present Market Price of _____ is in the _____ (4C5) Range

D UP-SIDE DOWN-SIDE RATIO (Potential Gain vs. Risk of Loss)
High Price (4A1) _____ Minus Present Price / Present Price _____ Minus Low Price (4B1) = _____ = _____ (4D) To 1

E PRICE TARGET (Note: This shows the potential market price appreciation over the next five years in simple interest terms.)
High Price (4A1) / Present Market Price _____ = (_____) X 100 = (_____) - 100 = _____ (4E) % Appreciation

5 5-YEAR POTENTIAL   This combines price appreciation with dividend yield to get an estimate of total return. It provides a standard for comparing income and growth stocks.

Note: Results are expressed as a simple rate; use the table below to convert to a compound rate.

A Present Full Year's Dividend $ _____ / Present Price of Stock $ _____ = _____ X 100 = _____ (5A) Present Yield or % Returned on Purchase Price

B AVERAGE YIELD OVER NEXT 5 YEARS
Avg. Earnings Per Share Next 5 Years _____ X Avg. % Payout (3G7) _____ = _____ / Present Price $ _____ = _____ (5B) %

C ESTIMATED AVERAGE ANNUAL RETURN OVER NEXT FIVE YEARS
5 Year Appreciation Potential (4E) _____ ÷ 5 = _____ %
Average Yield (5B) _____ %
Average Total Annual Return Over the Next 5 Years (5C) _____ %

Table to Convert From Simple to Compound Rate
| Simple Rate | | | | | | | | | | | | | | | |
| Compound Rate | | | | | | | | | | | | | | | |

©2005 BetterInvesting

Figure 2.2b

my qualitative sample considered buying stock in Callaway Golf. Out of essentially identical information, each club constructed a different narrative and a correspondingly distinct line of action. For each of them, the Callaway decision revealed a great deal about the group's identity and its members' mental maps of the market.

For the all-male California Investors, discussion of Callaway Golf arose in the August meeting. Nick began the presentation with a review of the colorful history of the firm's founder, who started out selling whiskey, then opened a winery, then went into the golf club business at the age of seventy. Even before Nick got to his financial analysis of the firm, Drew anchored the discussion by saying, "I like the story of this stock." Nick said he saw "a Nike in the offing": a new megabrand being born. It was not surprising that the story resonated with this group, given that the members were retired businessmen in their sixties, and many were avid golfers. A certain identification—or sense of shared social identity—with Callaway's CEO was perhaps inevitable. While some of the financial data in the report were encouraging—gross margins were 60 percent, and the firm paid a dividend of five cents on the share each quarter—some members expressed reservations about Callaway's high P/E (price-earnings) ratio, the firm's lackluster ranking within its industry (fourteenth), and its history of volatility, as evidenced by the dramatic zigzags in the stock's price chart over the previous year. But then the tenor of discussion returned to its positive starting point as Jake noted that the firm had entered the lucrative golf ball business. Nick added that Tiger Woods was going to draw more people into golf and that all the top tour winners used Callaway clubs. Without further discussion, the club voted unanimously to buy two hundred shares.

A few days later, the mixed-gender club Educating Singles Against Poverty faced the same question—whether to buy stock in Callaway—but constructed a very different story, leading to inaction rather than to an investment. Actually, the club had been in limbo about Callaway for some eighteen months, during which the group had been able to discuss and buy other stocks. Shelley presented a handwritten SSG on Callaway, but most of it was illegible. What *could* be read did not look promising: according to NAIC guidelines, the stock was overpriced and unlikely to grow much in the next five years. Bert added that if the club had bought Callaway last month, it would have been in the "buy" range on the SSG; since then, the price had gone up.

Still, the conversation quickly turned to the merits of golf and its growing popularity. Abby noted that her seventy-seven-year-old sister had said she planned to take up golf, as did her sister's friends. Shelley said she wanted to buy Callaway stock "because its's fun, like Harley," another stock the club was considering in the leisure industry. "The Tiger Woods thing will make golf take off," Shelley added. Janet said that it sounded like the firm had big potential. Isabelle speculated that because of the baby boomers, Callaway's market would continue to grow.

Yet the discussion deadlocked once again as the group discovered that the narrative it had constructed around Callaway's public image and market potential could not be squared with the financial evidence presented to them. In other words, the group failed to produce a story line adequate to their objective—to make a decision in light of the facts presented. Thus, the group returned to sorting through the pieces that did not fit: specifically, those related to the stock price. Janet, alluding to the club's history of buying high and selling low, asked about Callaway's price stability over the past few months: "you know where I'm going with this: if we decide to buy this, we should have a committee decide *when* to buy it." Shelley said there was potential for the share price to increase but added that she thought it was near the top: the current share price was $36, with a high for the year of $38. However, she recommended that the club buy Callaway with one caveat: since they always bought just before a stock went down, they should use Janet's idea and have someone follow the stock, to see if it would come down. Bert said he was bothered by the stock's P/E of 20. He noted that the company's earnings would come out in a few days, that would likely affect the share price. Shelley volunteered to track the stock price for the club, and Janet asked Bert to get a report on Callaway from the club's broker. The final decision was neither for or against buying the stock; rather the club agreed to "appoint a committee for further study" of the matter.

The following month, in September 1997, Asset Accumulators made their assessment of Callaway Golf, as part of a broader evaluation of the leisure industry that included Brunswick bowling alleys, Carnival cruise lines, and Harley-Davidson motorcycles. Mary made the presentation on Callaway, handing out the SSG and Value Line report on the firm. The discussion touched on many of the same points reviewed by CI and ESAP. Mary noted that the stock was considered somewhat volatile, and the share price was very close to its fifty-two-week high, putting it in the "hold" range (rather than "buy") on the SSG. However, other members chimed in with positive remarks about the firm's growth potential, based on the fondness of aging baby boomers for golf and the expansion of Callaway internationally, particularly in Asia. In support of this positive construal of the evidence, Vera noted that Callaway had no debt, good financial strength, and that Value Line "likes" the stock. However, Vera's next comment changed the direction of the emergent narrative about Callaway: she pointed out that Value Line estimated that the stock would double in value within five years but added, "that's below our portfolio's current growth rate." In other words, she provided a kind of pivot point around which the group's emergent narrative turned. So even though other members continued to point out positive aspects of the stock—such as its robust performance in the face of a recent market downturn—none of the new data points altered with fundamental framing of the story, which could be summarized as: Callaway is good, but not good enough compared with what we've got. In light of this narrative, the club elected to pass on the stock. Most intriguingly, while Asset Accumulators' decision frame contained almost all the same elements as ESAP's (international growth potential, the popularity of Tiger Woods, lack of debt, volatility, and even Harley-Davidson as a comparison stock), Asset Accumulators was quite unlike ESAP in being able to develop a coherent story line and make a decision on that basis.

To summarize these comparative data: three groups evaluated the same stock during the same time period, and while they drew from the same pool of public information, they *did not* reach a common conclusion or course of action. On the contrary, the group process yielded three entirely different narrative interpretations and three equally disparate decisions about buying Callaway stock: yes, no, and maybe later. This suggests that a crucial source of variation among decision-making groups is their ability to construct adequate and credible frames or stories to fit the facts and guide action.

In support of this interpretation, members of all three groups later reflected (in interviews) on their own group's decision about Callaway stock as being characteristic of their group's identity. Brad of California Investors, for example, recalled the group's brief and rather anemic debate about Callaway as emblematic of the club ethos: "we're friends of twenty years' standing and sometimes we vote for things just to fly the flag." For ESAP, the inability to make a decision about Callaway signaled a different style: avoiding conflict by doing nothing. Craig explained that the club had dropped discussion not only of Callaway but of Harley and the whole industry because of one member's strong objections. "There are lots of stocks in the world," Craig said. "Why choose one that arouses strong feelings?" Along similar lines, Craig noted that when he made a presentation on a Canadian firm called Bombardier, one member misunderstood and thought it was a military armaments firm (in fact, Bombardier makes trains, along with recreational and commercial aircraft). Rather than correcting the misunderstanding, Craig withdrew the suggestion. "Why run roughshod over the feelings of members?" he explained. "If there's strong opposition, then we can't push." As in California Investors, social bonds sometimes took primacy over financial considerations.

The women of Asset Accumulators also saw their decision not to buy Callaway as a reflection on their identity. But it was a very different kind of identity, forged on the basis of professional ties: all the members were educators who had met through the American Association of University Women.[60] In an interview several months after the Callaway presentation, they explained their decision in terms of their shared frame of reference as teachers:

> *Berry*: It's easy to be oversold on ideas through enthusiasm.
> *Keiko*: But we're very conservative; we go by the rules.
> *Berry*: We started putting our vision statement on the [monthly meeting] agenda about three years ago . . . it keeps our sense of focus.

One way to interpret these remarks is as commentary on the construction of credible stories or maps to describe the stock market. The group's vision statement can be read as a narrative template, listing the elements necessary to make a buy or sell story persuasive:

Asset Accumulators' Vision Statement

The purpose of the club shall be to:
1. Educate club members in the fundamental principles and techniques of sound investment practices.
2. Enable members to invest funds mutually.
3. Follow growth theory of investing, allowing for diversification.
4. Invest regularly the dues collected and reinvest the proceeds therefrom.

As suggested by the illustration from Asset Accumulators, the validity of a narrative is judged not only by the credibility of the source but also by the consistency of the story with the identity of the group and its members. Indeed, a major premise of identity theories is that behavior and identity mutually affect one another, and that individuals and groups will go to great lengths to avoid behaviors that conflict with their sense of themselves. At the same time, the multifaceted nature of identity—at both the group and individual levels—provides considerable leeway in constructing lines of action.

Thus, acceptable narratives about stock purchase decisions must "make sense" at several levels simultaneously: as a way of explaining certain sets of facts about the stock (like price, revenues, and so forth) and also as a statement about the identity of the buyer(s). Other research suggests that this linkage may hold for finance professionals as much as for individual investors. For example, mutual fund managers acquire their professional identities as a result of the stocks they select for their funds; from these purchasing decisions, observers (such as analysts, journalists, and investors) infer the manager's philosophy and character. This is exemplified by books such as *The Warren Buffett Way*, which explicitly argue for the connection between what you buy and who you are.[61]

But the comparison to professional investment managers raises an important question: how do individual investors achieve congruence between their identities and their investments when purchasing individual stocks on their own, without the aid of a fund manager or adviser? In other words, how do individuals make stock purchase decisions given the simultaneous challenges of overwhelming choice and bounded rationality on the one hand, and the need for investments to be consonant with their identities on the other?

ESAP's strategy—to make no decision when the group is unable to develop a viable narrative—is not sustainable, for both financial and ontological reasons. Financially, the members' indecision wastes time and money. But perhaps more importantly, the failure to act represents a threat to their group identity. In an interview I conducted about the club's history, one of the original ESAP members noted that the group's first purchase—shares of Microsoft—was made largely to preserve their sense of themselves as a viable group. "Until we bought it," Craig said, "we were not a club." This became a recurrent theme for ESAP, with long periods of indecision and stagnation punctuated by impulsive action.

For example, after the months of indecision about Callaway, the group suddenly decided to buy stock in Amgen after a very brief discussion. It was not, the group members said later, that Amgen was a particularly compelling choice in terms of financial merits. In fact, Shelley recalled, the suggestion to buy Amgen "came out of the blue" in the January 1998 meeting. Isabelle noted that of all the stocks they had considered at that meeting, Amgen "had the lowest average return" and "didn't seem like a frontrunner." But the group was also acutely aware that, with the exception of one small purchase (fifty shares of the Applebee's restaurant chain), they had not made *any* decisions to buy or sell stock in the previous six months. Thus, Craig said, the mood in the club was "'let's buy' or 'let's act'" in order to remain a club. That the decision came down in favor of Amgen was relatively unimportant, as long as the group mustered the will to act. This also helps explain why, after a few months of inertia, the club president suggested that if the group could not agree on where to spend its money, perhaps they should just "buy pretend," by creating a fantasy portfolio without actually spending any money.

I Invest, Therefore I Am

This struggle to act in order to be—*agito ergo sum*—is reminiscent of the work of twentieth-century British philosopher John Macmurray, whose theory of "dynamic empiricism" sought to turn Descartes upside down by asserting the priority of action over thinking.[62] Similarly, Russian cultural theorist Mikhail Bakhtin argued that it is only through action that individuals construct meaningful relationships with the world at large.[63] This implies that while words and symbols can transmit information about identity, ultimately the concept of self—at both the individual and group levels—must be *enacted*. Sociological theories of identity share this view of the primacy of action.[64]

To further illustrate the point, consider another case in which two investment clubs debated over the same stock using similar information. Both Ladies with Leverage and Bulls & Bears ultimately arrived at the same decision to buy stock in Cisco Systems—a firm that produced hardware and software for computer networking. But the distinctive paths by which they reached that point suggest the tight linkage between identity and action in the minds of investors. The key contrast between the two clubs was not *whether* to purchase Cisco stock, but how. For Ladies with Leverage, the decision was relatively painless and quick, because the methods they used to reach it were consistent with their sense of themselves as a group. But for Bulls & Bears, even though every member in the group said he or she wanted to buy Cisco stock, the action steps leading to that decision emerged only after eight months of protracted, intense conflict over the implications of their decision *process* for the identity of the group. The question raised in both cases was, who do we want to be as investors, and does this course of action reinforce or undermine that identity?

As the September 1997 gathering of the Ladies with Leverage was winding down, at minute 119 of a two-hour meeting, Teresa casually mentioned that the group should consider buying Cisco. Without a discussion or analysis, the club voted unanimously to buy twenty-five shares. The whole process was completed almost in the blink of an eye. In retrospect, Tanya recalled, "everyone said 'Let's buy Cisco!' and we didn't even look at the stock before we bought it." Another member, Lydia, explained that since the decision came at the end of the meeting and two members seemed to strongly support the idea, "everyone said okay just so we could go home." Yet there was no subsequent evidence of buyer's remorse or demand for a postmortem on the decision. When interviewed several months later about the decision, Tanya explained, "when we get excited about things, it's instinct rather than looking at numbers; we just jump in." She and the other members of Ladies with Leverage seemed pleased with their Cisco purchase, despite the haphazard quality of the decision, because of its consistency with the club's implicit mission statement: as Karen phrased it, "we wanted to become part of the larger social trend of investing that everyone seemed to be interested in." In order to become part of this trend—in Goffman's terms, to claim the identity of "investor"—they had to enact it by buying stocks.

Bulls & Bears' response to the Cisco decision was also framed by its sense of identity, but led through months of tense debate that several members perceived as a struggle for the "soul" of the group. The struggle opened in August 1997, at the first Bulls & Bears meeting I attended as an observer. Jeff, the only African-American member of the group, and one of the few members who came from a marketing/sales background rather than from engineering, began his presentation by handing out an incomplete and error-riddled SSG. He had failed to show the company's earnings history and had botched several calculations badly. The analysis, however, seemed to be totally pro forma, because Jeff did not refer to it in his comments. Instead, he focused on having insider information (from friends who worked at the company) and on the enormous "buzz" the firm had generated locally. "The whole Valley is talking about Cisco," he said. In support of this, Cate, the senior woman in the club (and another member of the marketing minority) agreed that Cisco was "hot, hot, hot . . . the Microsoft of its market." A third member of the marketing staff, Dan, jumped on the "brand name" bandwagon by saying that Cisco was "the Coke of servers: overpriced, but worth it."[65] This trio was creating a popular kind of story around the core of other familiar narratives ("everybody's talking") and metaphors (Microsoft and Coke). In this respect, Jeff and his supporters performed the important task of "telling a story by being able to weave it into an on-going conversation."[66]

Unfortunately, for the majority faction in the group—the engineers who had founded Bulls & Bears—the Cisco story referenced the wrong conversation. They didn't want to hear about the Silicon Valley scuttlebutt. They wanted a narrative about Cisco that was structured around the elements of NAIC principles and what Greg called "engineers' conservatism and rigor." Greg phrased his objections by saying that he liked the firm and owned it personally, but thought the high price-earnings ratio was "tough to accept given NAIC guidelines." It wasn't clear that earnings would continue to grow at their previous pace, he said, particularly given the crisis in the Asian markets, which would dampen demand considerably. Nevertheless, he said he was willing to be convinced, *if* the presenter could only show him the analysis—in other words, if Jeff could tell the Cisco story in the analytical vernacular in which the engineers communicated. Unfortunately, the incompleteness and math errors in the form made it impossible to get meaningful answers to the growth/risk/price questions. When Jeff made a motion to buy the stock, the motion failed, with the engineers on one side and the rest of the "marketing minority" on the other.

Afterward, two of the club's founders described their frustration with Jeff's presentation. "We really wanted to buy Cisco today," Paul, the club president, said. "But I won't allow this stock to be bought until there's data." An hour-long postmeeting conversation ensued in which Greg and Paul expressed their exasperation with the members who had voted for the stock without any fundamental analysis. The bureaucrats who had joined the club could not be held accountable for anything, Paul said. Pressure to produce high-quality work wasn't the norm for them, as it was for the engineers; and the bureaucrats wouldn't tolerate confrontation. "We can't lean on anybody," Paul lamented. However, both men claimed that they were not seeking conformity of opinion; on the contrary, they said, one of the things they missed most about the "old days" in the club was the ability to have a good fight about a decision.

The struggle for the identity of Bulls & Bears—the kind of investors they would be—grew more entrenched with every subsequent meeting for the next six months. At each meeting, Jeff brought up Cisco and the opportunities that the club was missing by not buying the stock. Each time he mentioned that Cisco had been written up in the newspaper, or that the stock was up several points, the club officers would invite him to do an updated SSG analysis the next month. Finally, Jeff agreed to present an updated SSG on Cisco at the February 1998 meeting. But when the time came, Jeff claimed that there had been a misunderstanding—he "didn't think the club was in a buying mode"; then he said that he'd "forgotten his folder" with all the latest information on Cisco. But he did hold up a recent newspaper clipping in which Cisco had been written up very favorably. An uncomfortable silence ensued. Greg glared at Jeff and said sternly: "we do not buy stock without complete analysis; you can say it's a hot stock, but we're here to educate and do analysis with a consistent approach." Cate—the marketer who had previously supported Jeff's idea—jumped in to admonish him for "trying to get away with" not doing an analysis. Jeff left early, and the meeting broke up soon afterward, no one speaking or looking at each other as they left. The following month, Paul, Greg, and several other senior members of the group took matters into their own hands and presented the SSG for Cisco; Jeff seemed to see their efforts as redundant with his previous presentation, saying dismissively, "I've already done the numbers game." At the end of this meeting, however, the club voted unanimously to buy twenty shares. Jeff—voicing the *agito ergo sum* perspective on investing—pumped his fist in the air and exulted "Yes! We're spending money!" And they were: during the struggle, Cisco's stock price had risen 23 percent.[67] As if to underscore that Jeff had missed the point of the entire nine-month struggle, Greg ensured that the last word was a reiteration of the engineering identity held by the founders of the group: "if somebody comes in with a hot stock, they'd better come in with a hot analysis too."

These anecdotes suggest that individual investors are to some extent aware that they are staking an identity claim when they buy stocks. Bulls & Bears literally paid a premium of 23 percent to retain its identity as a certain type of investment club. This is not to downplay the importance of making money on these investments. Rather, in keeping with the two-system view outlined at the beginning of this chapter, the idea is that investors consider *both* the profit potential *and* the identity implications of the stocks they purchase, and that the two evaluative dimensions are closely related. This perspective sheds light on the increasing popularity of socially responsible investing.

"The Kind of People They Are"—Socially Responsible Investing

In support of the "identity investing" framework proposed in this chapter, it is worth noting one of the most intriguing aspects of the data collected in the survey portion of this study: investment club naming conventions. Investment clubs appear to put a great deal of thought into choosing their names, in ways that evoke symbolic interactionist theories. It was not surprising to find clubs choosing names that punned on the subject of money and investing, such as "The NASDORQs" or "Cents and Sensibility." Nor was it surprising to find clubs that had named themselves after their geographical locations, like the "Motown Moneymakers" or the "North County Nickel Knockers."

What *was* surprising, however, was the way in which seemingly unrelated forms of identity were woven into club naming conventions, as if the members found it necessary to identify themselves as particular *kinds* of investors. The two most salient identity categories in this regard were religious affiliation and gender. For example, clubs that found it important to identify themselves by religious belief included:

- Episcobucks
- L'Chaim Investors
- Burning Bush Investment Club
- Investors for Christ
- Mormon Bishop Investment Club

Gender-based naming conventions yielded some of the most amusing and creative club appellations in the study, including:

- The Sisters of Perpetual Profit
- Frocks for Stocks
- Dividend Divas
- Farsighted Filly Forecasters
- Dow Janes

With one exception—the "Men in Motion" club—all the gender-based names in this sample designated all-female clubs.

The asymmetrical salience of gender, along with the prominent place of religion in naming investment clubs, may be driven by the same social psychological processes that cause some people to use phrases such as "lady doctor" or "Christian broadcasting." That is, the specifications "lady" or "Christian" are markers that signal the transgression of normative expectations: the assumption that the category "doctor" by default implies a male, and that the category "broadcasting" implies secular programming. These specifications demarcate boundaries in the realm of social identity, showing how a particular individual or social group compares to the ideal type for its category. By the same token, qualifying an investment group as composed of women or people of faith tells us about normative expectations of investors: that they are male and secular in orientation.[68] Considering the longtime exclusion of women from the formal financial sector—a major reason for the rise of women's investment groups—and the history of religious tensions with the world of money and profit, the salience of these categories for club participants makes a great deal of sense.[69] These naming conventions can also be interpreted in light of the motive to avoid cognitive dissonance by "suturing" identities that appear to conflict, so as to make oneself known as a coherent whole, both to oneself and to one's reference group. The alternative is to be perceived as a compartmentalized, "split personality"—as in "devoted churchgoer" and "amoral capitalist."

Two kinds of data from my study—name choices and stock purchase decisions—suggest that members of investment clubs experienced the greatest conflicts between their burgeoning identity as investors and their self-concepts in terms of ethics and gender. Interviews and observation yielded a number of clues to the ways in which individual investors develop mental maps or "folk theories" of the market and their place within it, based on their attempts to link these disparate identities. Groups in the qualitative sample spent a great deal of energy on creating mental maps that allowed them to invest while still seeing themselves as men, women, and moral people.

A striking development that paralleled the growth of popular participation in the stock market was the proliferation of socially responsible investment funds. Such funds tailor their investment strategies to the interests and values of specific identity groups. For example, there are now funds specifically "screened" to accommodate the preferences of environmentalists, fundamentalists, Mennonites, and Muslims.[70] The secular version of the strategy usually consists of avoiding investment in firms with a poor record of "corporate citizenship" as a result of labor or human rights violations, firms that cooperate with corrupt or undemocratic political regimes, or firms that trade in products and services considered to have a negative impact on society, such as gambling, alcohol, or armaments. Portfolios screened for social responsibility—however that was defined by the fund—grew 300 percent within two years, expanding from $529 billion in 1997 to $1.5 *trillion* in capitalization by 1999.[71]

Investment funds that present themselves as "socially responsible," or as targeted to the interests of certain identity groups, help investors solve several problems simultaneously. Active management of the funds means that individuals do not have to cope with the overwhelming choices presented by the stock market. In addition, the "branding" strategies of such funds—such as commitment to avoid investing in firms with poor labor or environmental records—address individuals' need for their investments to be consistent with their self-concepts.

Socially responsible investment funds have grown in part by directly targeting social identity processes and linking them to spending on financial instruments and services. This suggests a new twist on economist Robert Shiller's observation that "investing in speculative assets is a social activity,"[72] subject to fad and fashion. With fashion moving increasingly in the direction of microcustomization (i.e., Levi's made-to-measure jeans, or Saturn's design-your-own car), it is not surprising that consumers-turned-investors would demand the same level of customization in their portfolios. And if this influence has extended into the formulation of mutual fund portfolios, the process is likely being played out all the more intensely in the portfolios of investment clubs, where individuals have much more control over individual stock selection.

At the same time, it is worth noting that socially responsible investing does not automatically imply financial sacrifices. Firms that earned high marks in terms of corporate citizenship—in terms of labor relations, environmental impact, workplace safety, and litigation history—significantly outperformed the Standard & Poor's 500 index from 2000 through 2003. While the average S&P 500 stock declined 2.3 percent over that period, the firms ranked in the top five in terms of corporate citizenship and social responsibility saw their stock rise by 23.1 percent; stocks of firms in the top fifteen rose more modestly—3.4 percent—but still handily outperformed their peers in the market index.[73] Another study, which focused on the labor relations aspect of corporate social responsibility—specifically, the hiring and promotion of women in executive positions within Fortune 500 firms— found that companies with the highest representation of women in top management outperformed their competitors by approximately 35 percent in terms of both return to shareholders (stock price) and return on equity.[74] One explanation may be that so many individual investors care about the implications of corporate citizenship that they are creating a self-reinforcing cycle, in which more and more people buy stocks of firms with good records of social responsibility, which then pushes up the share prices and provides a financial incentive to continue investing in such firms.

However, despite the demonstrated relationship between a firm's ethics and financial results, the findings collide with ingrained beliefs about the stock market as a value-neutral arena. As Philip Angelides, a board member of CalPERS—California's public employee pension fund, and the largest pension fund of any kind in the nation—described the disconnection in the minds of other finance professionals: "There is a correlation between good practices and good investment results. People in the investment industry often want to put up a wall between these two things, but they are related." The dominant view, as expressed by one investment manager, is still that "you can't be in stocks if you're going to ask moral questions."[75]

Since there is no commonly accepted map or narrative that links stock market profits with ethical behavior, individual investors have to make it up as they go along. The observational data I gathered indicate that individuals experience significant tension in their efforts to make the connection between their emergent identities as investors and their self-concepts as "good people." None of the clubs in my sample had developed a formal or explicit policy about social responsibility in investing. Yet social issues were often woven into the story these groups constructed about stocks they were considering for purchase. As Christina—president of a mixed-gender club—put it, the absence of tobacco or petroleum stocks from her club's portfolio did not arise from an explicit decision to avoid those firms, but as an apparently natural outgrowth of the members' identities. "It's just the kind of people they are," she said. "They're not interested in supporting those companies."

A similar unwritten rule was invoked when the all-female Asset Accumulators group was considering Harley-Davidson motorcycles in September 1997. Julia began her presentation of the firm's financials by mentioning that a major business magazine had picked Harley as one of its top stocks for the year. But the company was thrown out of the running almost immediately by one member's comment: Renee asked the group members if they would feel comfortable letting their kids ride Harleys. The women, brought up short, looked at each other in silence for a moment. Then Penny said no, she wouldn't want her kids riding a Harley and she wouldn't let her husband ride one either. Mary expressed some of the ambivalence that characterized all such decisions: "it's against our value system, but it's not necessarily a bad investment." Then Renee and Molly proposed a lateral move, shifting the discussion to another stock within the same industry: Callaway Golf. They'd rather stick to golf, they said, "because it's safer." In this discussion, the group was considering risk from a very different angle than most economic analysis would lead us to expect. The question was not whether golf was "safer" than motorcycles in terms of financial risk, but safer in terms of the health and well-being of loved ones.

It is important to note that this example does not support the contention made by some researchers that women have innately "stricter ethical standards."[76] The argument here is for a frame of reference informed by ethics, rather than for a biological essentialist version of investing. Indeed, the most frequent comments about social responsibility in this study came from an all-men's group: the Valley Gay Men's Investment Club. Like the other clubs in the qualitative sample, this group had no formal policy or political agenda guiding its investments other than an explicit commitment to avoid investment in Cracker Barrel or its suppliers and affiliates, because of the firm's policy of discrimination against gay people in hiring. While the issue of bias against homosexuals came up in several discussions, it was far from the group's sole focus. The club also declined to invest in Motorola, because of the firm's involvement in making the silicon chips used in land mines, and rejected a proposal to buy stock in Home Depot in part because of its record of discrimination against women employees. However, as the following dialogue shows, even these discussions were fraught with tension between moral and financial considerations. When Leonard presented on Home Depot, he began with the firm's impressive numbers. But, as with Asset Accumulators' discussion of Harley, the dialogue quickly turned to "corporate citizenship" as a second level of screening:

> *Leonard*: Some women employees have filed a sexual discrimination suit against Home Depot.
> *Sid*: Home Depot won't hire women; their ethic is to have staff who are expert in using the products themselves, and they apparently don't think women qualify.
> *Leonard*: The firm settled out of court.
> *Grant*: Women don't shop there.
> *Troy*: The women employees run the cash registers or work in the design section.

Having enumerated these breaches of corporate citizenship, the discussion reached a point of tension over the clash between identity and economic considerations. As soon as Ray, the group's treasurer, put the frame of "political correctness" on the developing story line, it veered sharply back to a narrative based purely (or at least explicitly) on economic considerations.

> *Frank*: Should we dump a stock [from consideration] because it has problems with political incorrectness?
>
> *Troy*: The firm's prices are just incredible: you can't get track lights cheaper. And Home Depot *is* breaking into the high-end design market . . . They seem to be dominating the industry.
>
> *Sid*: People often buy shares in firms with policies they don't like just so they can vote against those policies.

Ultimately, the club decided against buying Home Depot, ostensibly because of the high share price. But the discussion suggested significant role tension between making money and being "good people." Constructs like shareholder activism—buying shares as a platform for protest—can be viewed in this light as a way to mend the breach.

Such anecdotes suggest that socially responsible investing is—in keeping with the two-system view—partly an economic decision and partly a matter of social identity. On the one hand, individual investors are aware that their stock purchases constitute "voting with their dollars"; they do not want to feed the financial engines of firms whose social or environmental impact they do not support. On the other hand, by making the choice to pass up certain kinds of investments, individuals also face the very real possibility of forgoing profit opportunities—an instance of economic irrationality in the conventional sense. The behavior looks less irrational—or perhaps more socially rational—when viewed through the lens of social identity. For the gay men's group I studied, investing in firms that discriminated against gay people would have been an act of hypocrisy or self-betrayal that simply could not be squared with their identity. To behave in such a cognitively dissonant fashion is, psychologically speaking, as self-defeating as forgoing financial profits.

It is also important to note that socially responsible investing means more than simply in-group bias—or supporting the interests of other members of one's own identity group. While the lawsuit filed by gay employees deterred the gay men's club from buying stock in Home Depot, the members sent far more time talking about discrimination against women, as both employees and customers. This suggests once again that in making investment choices, individuals are often trying to square their financial decisions with a vision of themselves as "good people."

Summary and Implications

This chapter is a story about stories: the narratives that people construct about stocks and about their own identities in relation to the market. The ways in which people gather and weave bits of macroeconomic history into their own self-concepts suggests why it is so important to understand the microfoundations of economic behavior. It is not just a matter of macrolevel phenomena filtering down to the microlevel of selves and small groups: decisions made at the microlevel—the kinds of decisions documented in this chapter—can have powerful aggregate effects on the market. For example, if the narrative view of investment proposed here holds, it may help explain why investors can be reluctant to sell stocks that are performing poorly, and so ready to sell stocks that have made a profit.[77] This behavior makes little sense in terms of economic self-interest but a great deal of sense in terms of constructing a story. From a narrative point of view, making a profit is a "happy ending": the investor can sell the profitable stock and close out the narrative with a story of his or her financial acumen ("I made a killing on XYZ company"). But when a stock fails to perform, investors are faced with an unpleasant choice. They can do the "right" thing economically by selling, cutting their losses, and putting the money where it is more likely to make a profit. But the cost of this decision is an "unhappy ending": a locked-in loss, a blemish on their self-concept as investors. The evidence suggests that Americans, famous for their optimism and their love of the Hollywood ending, would prefer to hang on to their losing stocks and pay a price—potentially losing everything—rather than give up hope of snatching victory from the jaws of defeat.

In addition, my data suggest that the stocks investors own become part of the story they tell the world about themselves. That is, investors buy a stock in part because of its story and its accordance with the social identity they have or aspire to have, just the way that they "buy who they are" at the mall. Ultimately, one of the most important legacies of the populist investing boom may turn out to be the importation of the consumer-products business model into finance. Thus, the individuals I studied invested according to the identities and narratives that were most salient within their group contexts. They invested as teachers, as women, as engineers, as men, as gay people, and as ethical people—all characteristics that would seem to have little relation to the stock market, but that the participants in the study found useful as ways of making their decision process manageable.

Stories are also important as a way of understanding how and why group contexts shape the behavior of individual investors. Sociology proposes that everything we know is conditioned by a consensual, intersubjective process. That is, to understand ourselves, the stock market, or anything else, we must rely on others for input and validation. Thus, even the apparently individualist "buy what you know" philosophy requires some sort of social context—whether that means exposure to mass media, neighborhood networks, or an investment club. In other words, investors cannot develop mental maps of the stock market without social interaction.

Groups like investment clubs—or investment committees in the world of professional finance—help investors create mental maps, stories, and other ways of conceptualizing the market. They also provide a means for individuals to transcend the limits of bounded rationality; as the study about choosing among six versus twenty-four kinds of jam illustrated vividly, individuals easily become overwhelmed and unable to choose when confronted with large decision spaces.[78] Groups offer a kind of parallel-processing system, which—at its best—not only exposes individuals to different points of view but integrates the disparate perspectives into a narrative or mental map that is more complete than any individual could create. (This potential is not always realized in groups, for reasons that will be addressed in greater detail in section 2 of the book.) Looking to others for ideas or consensual validation does not necessarily imply irrationality; it may in fact be a necessity in complex, rapidly changing conditions.

My findings offer several contributions to future research in economic sociology. First, they suggest additions to behavioral economists' list of frames that shape decision making under conditions of risk and uncertainty. To established constructs such as the "wealth frame" my research adds the "identity frame" and its subtypes, such as the "good person frame." My data also extend previous research on the role of social identity in economic life, proposing that identity is an "interpretive core" not just for firms but for individual investors.[79] Second, this study helps build theory at the microinteractional level of economic sociology, showing in detail the mechanisms through which small-group behavior scales up to affect macrolevel social phenomena like the stock market. Third, these findings highlight the expressive function of investing; that is, in keeping with Kahneman's "two-system view" of rationality, my research suggests that individuals choose stocks *both* for profit-making potential *and* for identity enhancement. This may involve passing up profitable investment opportunities that clash with a group's social identity, or making unwise investments that enhance that identity. While this may be economically costly, it is far from irrational when considered from the social psychological point of view.

Money was never a big motivation for me, except as a way to keep score. The real excitement is playing the game.
—DONALD J. TRUMP[1]

Cash and Social Currency: Performance in Investment Clubs ◆

SECTION TWO

What does it mean to speak of performance in an industry where an estimated 75 percent of professional investment managers fail to outperform the benchmark Standard & Poor's 500 index? From a purely profit-oriented point of view, research in economics and finance suggests that most investors would be better off putting their money in no-load index funds rather than paying a professional to manage their money. This goes for investment clubs as well as individual investors.

Allowing for the problems of bounded rationality discussed in the previous chapter—and the very real possibility that without investment clubs, many Americans would not purchase individual stocks at all—few investment clubs outperform or even keep pace with the market index. The only study other than the present one to examine financial returns in investment clubs showed that 60 percent of a sample of 166 clubs underperformed the S&P 500.[2] My research provided much less encouraging numbers: in my sample of 1,245 NAIC investment clubs, 96 percent underperformed the S&P 500, and the average club underperformed by 20.8 percent. The comparison between these data sets is somewhat limited by a mismatch in the variables used in the two studies; my figures would probably be closer to those of the other study had my data set included brokerage fees and other transaction costs.[3]

But since this is a sociological study rather than an investing "how-to" book, the focus in this examination of investment club performance will be on the two points of sociological interest: the origins of the "diversity premium," and the ways in which retail investors understand financial performance and act to achieve it. The next two chapters will explore the key sources of variation in clubs' financial performance. Of particular interest will be exploration of performance variations related to the gender composition of investment clubs: all things being equal, groups composed of men and women together make more money in the stock market than groups composed of men or women only. This finding, based on twelve years of archival data available from NAIC, inaugurated this study, and was supported by the results of the national survey of 1,245 investment clubs I conducted subsequently.

Table II.1 shows twelve years' worth of performance data on NAIC investment clubs, sorted by gender composition. As an unexpected result of comparing these average performance rates through an analysis of variance, I found that there was no statistically significant difference between the performance of all-male clubs and all-female clubs. This suggested that neither men nor women were better investors, but rather that gender diversity itself made a distinct contribution to group performance.[4] Since I did not collect this dataset myself, and had no way to verify independently that

Table II.1
NAIC Archival Data on Investment Clubs' Rates of Return (%)

	Men's Clubs	Women's Clubs	Mixed Clubs
1986	−0.82	1.37	−0.18
1987	−3.30	−5.26	4.22
1988	−3.20	−1.80	0.08
1989	0.08	−1.20	0.79
1990	−2.45	−0.39	0.06
1991	1.91	2.67	3.27
1992	1.35	2.46	4.15
1993	−2.14	−1.67	0.70
1994	1.05	−2.02	0.03
1995	0.29	−0.12	5.23
1996	−0.29	6.33	2.52
1997	0.77	3.03	2.92
Mean	−0.56	0.28	1.98
S.D.	1.81	3.06	1.95

the results were representative of the population, I took this analysis as a starting point for further investigation rather than as proof that the gender composition of investment clubs had a significant effect on their financial performance. Ultimately, the data I collected supported the pattern illustrated in table II.1, showing through a nationally representative sample of 1,245 clubs that those composed of men and women together earned about 2 percent higher returns on their portfolios than either all-female or all-male clubs. (See chapters 3 and 4 for more detailed discussion of these performance differences.)

While the magnitude of this "diversity premium" may not seem like much, the effects can be quite large over time. All other things being equal, the process of compounding means that a 2 percent difference in the annual rate of return results in large differences over time; through compounding, investment clubs earn interest on their interest, as well as on the cash they contribute each month. While the dollar differences yielded by this process vary according to the amount of a club's contributions, the potential results can be illustrated by the following example. Imagine two investment clubs, each with fifteen members who contribute $50 per month; club A has a portfolio that earns about 10 percent annually— slightly below the historical market average rate of 11 percent per year— while club B earns slightly above-average annual returns of 12 percent. In ten years' time, the portfolio of club B will be worth almost $15,000 more than that of club A; five years after that, club B's lead will widen to $50,000. This suggests how significant the "diversity premium" can be in terms of financial outcomes.

Even more striking is the anomaly these results represent in light of current economic theory. For example, the strong form of the Efficient Markets Hypothesis[5] holds that the market factors all relevant information about a stock into its share price, and that prices change randomly. This means that no one has an edge or holds special knowledge in terms of predicting the future movements of stock prices. The theory would lead us to expect no effect whatsoever to result from the characteristics of individuals making investment decisions. And yet, as table II.1 suggested, and my survey data ultimately confirmed, some personal characteristics of investors *do* make a significant difference in their financial returns. To explore this puzzle, I created a multimethod study to examine how and under what conditions gender diversity creates performance advantages for investors.

Each of the following two chapters reports on a component of the "diversity premium" puzzle, the first of which is the diversity of the information pools from which clubs draw in making investment decisions. Men and women have very different approaches to investing, and while neither is superior, the combination in a decision-making group can produce a synergistic diversity of views that is well suited to the complexity of the stock market. However, getting individuals to articulate their differing viewpoints and engage in constructive debate does not follow automatically. Thus, the second component of the "diversity premium" is group process, which serves as the catalyst for eliciting the benefits of diversity; this includes both the decision-making process itself as well as antecedent processes, such as the recruitment and selection of new members, which create path dependencies for future interactions.

Ultimately, the puzzle of the "diversity premium" turns out to be an apt illustration of the two-system view, in that it shows why we need to consider both the financial and social aspects of market behavior. Exploring the effect of group composition and group processes on investment performance requires a distinctively sociological perspective, not only because it posits that gender and other characteristics of investors can influence the returns of their investment portfolios, but also because performance itself is subject to a surprising degree of social construction. While financial returns might seem to be a matter-of-fact issue of dollars and cents, the real meaning of investment performance seems to depend on social context for both retail investors and professionals. That is, "performance," like "value," is relative to the milieu in which one invests. To claim that performance is socially constructed or consensually defined does not imply the manipulation of numbers, as in the "creative accounting" uncovered in the corporate financial scandals of the past few years. Rather, the issues are what metrics do investors choose to define performance, and how are these metrics used and interpreted in practice?

It is important to understand that the social construction of performance is not unique to amateur investors, such as those featured in this study. On the contrary, the phenomenon appears to be pervasive throughout the market. For example, an interview study of Wall Street pension fund managers revealed that even investment professionals measure their own performance in social terms. Rather than evaluating themselves in terms of absolute gains or losses, or through comparison to a market index, these pension fund managers measured their performance *relative to one another*. As one chief executive of a $5 billion pension fund put it, "It's not necessarily realistic to expect your [fund] manager to beat the market. *You expect him to beat his peers. You want him to add value over his peers.*"[6] Similarly, a portfolio manager at a different fund said that he measured his performance not by whether his clients were up or down for the year, but by asking, "Was my W-2 bigger than so-and-so's W-2?"[7]

The epigraph for this section, in which financier and real estate developer Donald Trump talks about money as no more than a way to "keep score" in a "game," is echoed by the pension fund managers, who compare their jobs to baseball, chess, and horseshoes, totally abstracted from absolute gains or losses. These investment professionals did not indicate that losing money was of great concern for them, as long as their competitors lost *more*. Fund managers said they rarely thought about, and never met in person with, the individuals whose pensions they managed. Rather, they said their attention was focused on the "game" within their industry: "It's a competitive thing. I mean, it's like you're out there playing baseball or something; you want to win the game. And they've got a scoreboard out there and after three or five hours, or a two-week series or whatever, you look up the score and say, 'Did I win or did I lose?' "[8] One private-sector pension fund manager summed up this attitude toward investing succinctly, saying: "We love to beat these guys [our competitors]. It's fun."[9] Thus, like Trump, professional investors appear to be more interested in the status aspect of investing than in the money. This finding is consistent with economic research showing that working people in general will compete and lobby much more vigorously for status markers—like a corner office, the Employee of the Month parking space, and other nonmonetary "positional goods"[10]—than they will for a rise in salary.

So while this section of the book will examine the economic consequences of investment clubs' decisions, it will not lose sight of the social
context and construction of performance. In keeping with Kahneman's
"two-system view" of rationality, this study proposes that investors are
concerned with *both* the financial *and* the social meanings of performance.
This helps explain some findings that are otherwise difficult to compre-
hend from a purely dollars-and-cents point of view. One example is the
case of socially responsible investing outlined in the previous chapter: investors will sometimes pay a premium to buy stock in firms with which
they wish to identify themselves; conversely, such investors may also forgo
profit-making opportunities if it means investing in a company whose reputation they believe would reflect poorly on "the kind of people they are."
Similarly, a view of performance that takes both financial and social considerations into account can help us make sense of the surprisingly weak
relationship between clubs' financial performance and individuals' attachment to their groups. For example, clubs that perform well (matching or
beating the market index) do not appear to recruit new members at a
higher rate, and clubs that perform poorly do not disband at a higher rate
than others. (See appendix to chapter 4.)

In other words, while individual investors state what is very likely a
sincere desire to make a profit on their stock purchases, in practice they
behave as if unperturbed by poor results in that area. Instead, most investors—amateurs and professionals alike—appear to be keeping two sets of
mental accounts in parallel: one in which they record financial gains and
losses, and another in which they measure their investments' effect on
their social status. If the former records are tallied in dollars, the latter are
denominated in positional goods and other "social currencies." This is not
to say that financial and social currencies are mutually exclusive in practice,
but rather that they are analytically separable for the purposes of research—and that it is vital to disentangle them conceptually so as to understand the multitude of ways in which they interact. What one sociologist
said of consumption behavior in general applies well to stock purchase
decisions: "The idea that contemporary consumers have an insatiable desire to acquire objects represents a serious misunderstanding of the mechanism which impels people to want goods. Their basic motivation is the
desire to experience in reality the pleasurable dramas which they have already enjoyed in imagination, and each 'new' product is seen as offering a
possibility of realizing this ambition."[11] In this view, stock purchases provide not only an economic opportunity but also an imaginitive one—an
accessory that confers reality on a story about oneself: "I am an investor."
And it would seem that for many investors—Donald Trump, investment

club members, and professional investment fund managers alike—the status symbol is as important as the money they make or lose. Perhaps even more important, the very notion of a profit seems to be defined in terms relative to position within the social cartography. In other words, the currency of financial performance may be "pegged" to the local system of *social* currency, which provides the benchmarks (such as status) by which financial profits become meaningful.

To summarize, the following chapters will address the antecedents of performance in investment clubs. They will show why, contrary to what economic theory might lead one to expect, the composition of investment clubs matters for performance, as do the types of group processes and interpersonal ties linking members to one another. The larger objectives of these chapters will be to advance the agenda of economic sociology by showing how economic and social considerations are linked together. In addition, the focus on the interpersonal core of stock market behavior advances the general scholarly enterprise of this study, which is to put economic sociology on a more microinteractional footing. In keeping with the overall viewpoint of economic sociology, these chapters presuppose that individuals' economic behavior is neither wholly rational nor wholly irrational, but responsive to the varying structural conditions in which actors find themselves. In this perspective, microlevel behaviors such as investment decisions are driven not only by the individuals making those decisions, but also by the larger opportunity structures afforded by different types of networks, and different types of group composition.

APPENDIX ◆
Portfolio Performance Defined

Before proceeding, it will be helpful to specify how investment clubs typically measure the financial performance of their portfolios. There is an "official" NAIC method for doing this, which is automated by the NAIC accounting software and detailed in the NAIC handbook for those who use other types of accounting software or who keep their records by hand. NAIC (and this study) employ two measures of financial performance, both of which are used by investment clubs and their nearest organizational analogues, mutual funds. The ability to measure performance in these clear, externally valid terms is helpful for two reasons: first, it enables the quantification of the effect of network ties and group composition; second, it permits generalizability of the model to other kinds of teams.

The first measure is effectiveness at making a profit, calculated as the rate of return on each group's investment. The rate of return measure is calculated in two steps: the first is calculation of the internal rate of return on investment; the second is to subtract the performance of the stock market over the same period. This calculation captures portfolio performance independent of the amount of money that members contribute to the portfolio, the length of time over which the portfolio has been building, and, most importantly, independent of the vagaries of the market—all of which vary considerably in this sample.

The internal rate of return calculation compares the total amount of cash invested to the current market value of the investments. Essentially, this calculation treats the portfolio like a bank account by showing the compound interest rate that would have to be paid on the initial cash investment in order for it to result in the current market value of the portfolio. Most investment groups choose to represent investment growth on an annualized basis. This measure also adjusts for transaction costs—brokerage fees are subtracted from the market value of the portfolio—and penalizes clubs for not being fully invested; idle cash drags down overall portfolio performance. This is because of appreciation: even unsuccessful investments earn more, typically, than the minimal interest accrued by cash idling in brokerage accounts.

The second part of calculating financial returns is to compare them with returns of the stock market as a whole. This is how the performance rates of mutual funds, pension funds, and other professionally managed portfolios are measured. Though there is some variability in the choice of yardsticks for market performance, the Standard & Poor's 500 index—which includes 500 firms in a broad range of industries—is widely considered the best proxy.[12] Having calculated the overall performance for an investment club portfolio, the next step is to subtract the performance figure for the S&P 500 over the same time period. Because this measure is time-sensitive, the market benchmark is not a single number against which all portfolios are compared. Thus, performance results will vary not only based on the returns of the stocks in a portfolio but also based on the market returns over the "lifetime" of the portfolio. This levels the playing field among groups in the sample and allows their financial results to be compared fairly.

The second measure of investment club performance is efficiency at converting incoming cash into investments. Since having cash on hand drags down portfolio performance, the ability to remain fully invested—or as close to fully invested as possible—with new cash coming in at every meeting is a good indicator of these groups' ability to turn a profit. The measure overlaps somewhat with internal rate of return but also taps a distinct dimension: the ability of the investment group to perform as a decision-making body. Having cash on hand typically means that a group has been unable or unwilling to make decisions as to how to invest its contributions. This can occur for a variety of reasons, but the measure is widely used as a performance measure not only by investment clubs but by mutual funds as well. The average club in my sample had 87 percent of its cash invested, which means that for every dollar the club took in from member contributions, it left 13 cents on the table. That creates a great deal of drag on portfolio performance.

*It is hardly possible to overrate the value, in the present low state
of human improvement, of placing human beings in contact with
other persons dissimilar to themselves, and with modes of
thought and action unlike those with which they are familiar . . .
Such communication has always been, and is peculiarly in the
present age, one of the primary sources of progress.*
—JOHN STUART MILL[1]

Group Composition and
the Business Case for Diversity   ◆ 3

The significance of group composition for portfolio performance in investment clubs emerged from the outset of the study, with the evidence from
NAIC's archives showing that groups composed of men and women together earned significantly and consistently higher returns than same-sex
groups. My subsequent exploration of this phenomenon, through both
qualitative and quantitative methods, revealed that the performance difference was driven by a more complex set of compositional factors than gender alone. In fact, several different types or dimensions of diversity inter-
acted to produce the "diversity premium."

While in everyday usage, the term diversity is usually applied to readily
observable traits like gender, race, or age, recent research has been focused
on the ways in which multiple sources of diversity come together to influence group outcomes.[2] There is growing agreement within sociology and
the allied disciplines that we need to think about diversity as a constellation
of traits, of which the visible aspects are just one part. Advancing this
multidimensional understanding of diversity is one intended contribution
of the present study.

Current Research on Group Composition and Performance

Debates within the Literature

One of the most difficult things about studying the effects of diversity in
group composition is the lack of consistent findings across studies. The

current research literature is fractured across a number of fault lines, including the ways in which studies conceptualize diversity itself. For example, early research on diversity focused exclusively on readily discernible social category characteristics such as gender, age, or race.[3] Those studies found that diversity led to interpersonal conflict based on social identity processes, which lead individuals to prefer interaction with those who share their social category memberships—and to assume that dissimilar others are less trustworthy and less competent.[4] Ultimately, these conflicts detracted from work group performance. Indeed, conflict based on social category differences has been blamed more than any other factor for poor performance in demographically diverse groups.[5]

More recent research on the relationship between group composition and performance suggests that examining forms of interpersonal difference that are not as readily observable as social categories may be the key to understanding how the "diversity premium" in investment clubs occurs. Particularly promising is a stream of research on informational differences among work group members. Informational diversity is defined as differences in knowledge, skills, and education among work group members.[6] This is crucial for decision-making groups, because their performance depends on the size and content of their information pools.[7] Studies focusing on this type of diversity indicate that the more information available to a group, the better it solves problems, makes decisions, and generates creative ideas.[8] As one study concluded, "broadening a group's knowledge and perspectives can be advantageous, especially when complex problems must be solved. Many theorists have argued that knowledge diversity can improve group performance by enhancing a group's ability to be creative, discover novel solutions, and search for even more information."[9] Thus, informational diversity is particularly important in contexts where decision making and complexity are involved. This is clearly the case with investment clubs, in which diversity of information and interpretive schemas is necessary to cope with the exigencies of a complex, rapidly changing stock market.

As this brief review suggests, defining diversity in different ways—social category versus informational, for example—leads to very different conclusions about group performance. On the one hand, we have studies supporting the "diversity-as-liability hypothesis," which show that the conflicts generated by interpersonal differences outweigh the benefits.[10] As one such study concluded, "Homogenous groups do better by avoiding the process losses associated with the poor communication patterns and excessive conflict often plaguing diverse groups."[11] On the other hand, we have studies supporting the "value-in-diversity hypothesis," by showing that interpersonal differences benefit work group performance; these studies often emphasize informational diversity as well as or instead of social category diversity among their independent variables. Further complicating the debate, the studies supporting the "value-in-diversity hypothesis" have almost all been conducted in laboratories or other artificial settings, while field studies conducted in naturally occurring groups frequently report that diversity has a negative effect on performance.[12] The absence of a clear and consistent account of the relationship between group composition and performance suggests why the "diversity premium" is so remarkable: investment clubs offer a rare opportunity to investigate an occurrence of the "value-in-diversity" phenomenon in a naturally occurring context.

Informational Diversity and Decision-Making Groups

Outside laboratory settings, research showing the benefits of informational diversity have come primarily from studies of groups and teams within high-technology or new product development. For example, a study of top management teams in the semiconductor industry found that differences in knowledge and analytical styles based on variation in team members' work experiences had a positive effect on their firms' performance, as measured in sales revenues.[13] Similarly, a study of cross-functional product development teams found that they were able to produce better new product ideas than teams whose members all came from the same functional specialty.[14] The authors of the product development team study argued that the cross-functional work groups were "plugged in" to more sources of information than their more homogeneous counterparts, yielding a significant advantage in a rapidly changing market environment. The importance of information diversity in such environments was underscored by another study of cross-functional teams in a high-technology industry, which found that the teams' performance declined after about five years, because members' viewpoints had converged through working together.[15] This suggests that performance depends in part on the fit between the internal composition of the group and the demands of the task environment; as one study summed up the findings on this topic, "the amount of disagreement and variety in a group needs to match the level of variety in the task for the group to be effective."[16]

These studies suggest strong analogies with the case of investment clubs. Buying and selling stocks means making judgment calls with incomplete information, and few environments change more rapidly than the stock market.[17] Such conditions place strong demands on work groups' capacity to generate and process information. As one study of work groups in complex environments noted, "the greater the task uncertainty, the greater the amount of information that must be processed among decision makers during task execution in order to achieve a given level of performance."[18] Groups whose members are diverse in terms of the information they possess would seem to be at a significant advantage in such an environment. Thus, the conditions faced by investment clubs favor informational diversity; the question is whether and how informational diversity maps onto social category differences like gender.

Linking Social Category and Informational Diversity: Gender Differences in Investing

When it comes to money and markets, a large body of scholarly research supports the association between gender differences and informational diversity. In addition to marketing research, economic studies have repeatedly and consistently supported the notion that men and women differ significantly in both the types of financial information they possess and how they use it. For example, a 1998 study by the National Center on Women and Aging showed that women were far less likely than men to read specialty financial publications such as the *Wall Street Journal* or *Investor's Business Daily*; instead, the majority of women investors got their investing ideas from friends, relatives, or general-interest newspapers and magazines.[19] These findings were replicated in responses from the 2001 census.[20] There are also significant differences in the amount of investing experience men and women acquire over time: far more women than men rely on brokers to select and manage their investments. In contrast, men not only spend more time doing their own security analysis but also trade their securities more actively, and anticipate higher returns on their investments than women do.[21] Regardless of their investment results, however, research in economics consistently finds that women feel less confident than men in financial matters.[22]

Perhaps as a result of these variations in information sources and information processing, men and women direct their money toward different types of investments. While men favor riskier, smaller firms (often known by the shorthand "small-cap"), women put more of their investment dollars in the stocks of larger, more stable firms (known as "blue-chip" or "large-cap" companies). In general, research in finance shows that women are markedly more conservative and less willing to accept financial risk than men.[23] One study showed that women placed only 40 percent of their investment funds in stocks, compared with an average of 46 percent for men; over twenty years, all other things being equal, this 6 percent gender difference in allocation resulted in a 47 percent gap in returns—in other words, the men made almost half again as much money as their female counterparts.[24]

The data from my national survey of investment club members are consistent with the findings from previous research in economics and finance. As shown in table 3.1, the gender differences among investment club members reflect those among American investors as a whole. In comparing the average responses of 4,178 men and 7,114 women, and using F-tests to determine statistical significance, I found that the only area where there was no significant difference between men and women was in terms of investment goals: the vast majority of both genders listed retirement as their primary reason for investing. Most interesting from a scholarly point of view is the variation in the ways they go about pursuing this shared objective.

Otherwise, I found that the men in my survey sample had significantly more years of investing experience than the women, along with a greater propensity to get investing ideas from financial specialty publications and

Table 3.1
Mean Percent Differences between Men and Women as Investors

Variables	Survey Item	Men	Women	F $(df = 1,113)$
Investor Experience	Years of investment experience	13.5	10.6	145.0**
	Manage own investment portfolio	74.2	58.1	239.1**
Source of Investing Ideas	Internet	55.1	43.8	187.2**
	Broker	9.4	11.8	48.2**
	Friends	5.8	6.6	11.8**
	Media reports	24.0	19.7	116.0**
	Consumer experience	4.1	5.2	9.4*
	Financial specialty publications	62.4	57.6	17.2**
	Local newspaper	41.4	43.9	18.93**
Primary Investing Goal	Retirement	79.7	83.8	2.7
Attitude toward Risk	Hold stocks 5 years or more	41.0	57.8	188.8**
	Percent of assets in stocks	48.6	45.4	11.0*

*$p < .05$ **$p < .001$ N (total) = 11,292 N (men) = 4,178 N (women) = 7,114

the Internet, to invest in stocks as opposed to bonds, and to manage their own personal investment portfolios in addition to their work with the club. In contrast, the women in this survey relied more on friends, brokers, general-interest media, and consumer experience as their sources of investing ideas. Perhaps as a result of these differences in information, women who did manage their own portfolios outside the club invested less of their assets in stocks and managed them more conservatively, being far more likely than the men to hold stocks for five years or more instead of trading.

Gender Differences in Investing

Why might men and women have different orientations to the market? At the social structural level of analysis, labor market segration is an obvious starting point: since men and women have very different occupational experiences, gender differences in investing may in part reflect systematic differences in their ties to the economy as workers.[25] One consequence of this segregation is that significantly fewer women than men are employed in occupations and firms that provide benefits such as pensions or stock options.[26] While over 50 percent of working men have pension plans, only 45 percent of women do. Among part-time workers, who are mostly women, only 22.7 percent have pension benefits.[27] That means women are less likely than men to have been offered investing opportunities, which may contribute to the gender gap in investing experience and confidence. Even when pension plans are available, women and other low-income workers often do not participate; as a result, twice as many women as men over sixty-five years of age live below the poverty line.[28] This financial precariousness may explain why women are less willing than men to accept the risks of loss that go with investment.[29] Contributing to this hypothesis is the evidence that African-Americans—who are similarly disadvantaged in labor markets in terms of earnings and opportunities to invest through their employers—display patterns very similar to women across racial groups in their attitudes toward investing.[30]

But the gender differences may go deeper than the social structural accounts suggest. For example, several recent studies of "mental accounting" in sociology and behavioral finance indicate that men and women conceptualize and use money in very different ways. In dual-income heterosexual couples, for instance, researchers found that rather than considering all earnings as a shared resource, the partners parse incoming cash according to how it was earned and by whom. Thus, while the female partner's income is commonly classified by both partners as "hers," the male partner's income is classified as "theirs."[31] If mental maps of personal finance are shaped by gender roles, perhaps conceptualizations of the market and public finance are as well. As Marx and Engels wrote, people engage with economic issues and decisions in a very personal way: "Individuals always started, and always start, from themselves."[32]

Put more formally, gender differences in investing may be an instance of a phenomenon that behavioral finance has labeled "availability bias." This means that when individuals make decisions under conditions of risk and incomplete information—such as stock investments—they typically apply whichever ideas come most readily to mind.[33] This bias is not driven by any "objective" relevance of the ideas to a given problem but by properties of the ideas that affect their mental availability.[34] For example, one recent study showed that many individual investors buy stock in a firm simply as a result of hearing or reading about the company in the previous day's news reports.[35] Like the news headlines, some concepts and terms are more easily accessible than others; as a result, they may erroneously appear salient for a particular decision. This implies that our self-concepts— which are, after all, what we know best—may also have a role to play in our decision-making processes.

This implication is consistent with social psychological research showing that notions of the self—including constructs such as gender or professional identities—are the most salient aspects of our mental maps for all kinds of settings.[36] That is, in most situations, one's self-concept dictates appropriate behavior.[37] So when individuals choose stocks, this research implies that investors' choices will in part reflect who they think they are and who they aspire to be. This may be as sensible a strategy as any for coping with the overwhelming array of choices available to investors—in addition to the seven thousand stocks traded on U.S. exchanges, there are bonds, mutual funds, and other financial instruments from which to choose. At least when they "start from themselves," investors are working from a fairly reliable base of information, as opposed to predicting where stocks will go based on ladies' hemlines, Super Bowl winners, or similar techniques that—despite sounding fanciful—are or have been used by professional investors.[38] Since there is no single, agreed-upon way to conceptualize financial markets—even finance scholars and professional investors disagree on this issue—"availability bias" may lead many retail investors to make themselves the measure of all things financial.

"Girl Stocks" and "Boy Stocks": Evidence from the Qualitative Study

The possibility that investing decisions could be shaped by the investor's self-concept—particularly as it pertained to gender—was first suggested in the investment club study during an interview with Shelley, the president of the mixed-gender club Educating Singles Against Poverty. Reviewing the club's portfolio history, she explained that following the club's initial purchase of Microsoft, they bought shares of RPM—a firm she described as "our *boy* stock." When asked to elaborate on the term "boy stock," she said: "Well, they [RPM] made boring things like glue and ink; the men in the club really liked it." The club's third stock purchase, she continued, was "our *girl* stock": it was St. John Knits, a manufacturer of $3,000 suits and other high-end women's clothing, "something the women in the club could get excited about."

The notion that there was something intrinsically gender-linked about certain stocks arose again and again throughout the study. All the other investment clubs in the sample I observed for a year made a similar distinction among types of investments—albeit without employing Shelley's colorful terminology. In their decision making, the clubs all behaved as if men and women were experts in different sectors of the economy, and they seemed to take for granted that gender made a difference in investment behavior. This held with equal strength across female and male investors as individuals, as well as in same-sex and mixed groups. I came to think of this mapping of gender roles onto the stock market as the "logic of gender appropriateness." In other words, gender was an organizing principle of the participants' understanding of the stock market and their position within it.

This went far beyond "boy stocks" and "girl stocks" to encompass broader conceptualizations of the stock market as a gendered space. For example, throughout my observations and interviews, participants repeatedly expressed their view that the "women's sphere" of the stock market was located in the consumer products sector. Thus, the men of Bulls & Bears credited the group's female members with persuading them to buy stock in "consumer stores like Home Depot." Greg, the club president, added that "none of the men would have thought of that" sector of the economy; rather, the men in the club presented on stocks related to their own interests and training. Tim, whose professional training was in the semiconductor industry, was responsible for the club's purchase of semiconductor manufacturer AMD; Brett, who had trained as a chemical engineer, persuaded the club to purchase stock in the chemical manufacturer Crompton and Knowles. Even though all the women in Bulls & Bears worked outside their homes, and some of them worked as engineers, they differed from their male counterparts in that they did not use their professional training as a source of investing ideas. If anyone in the club noticed this asymmetry, no one mentioned it.

The association between women and consumer products stocks occured in all-female and all-male clubs as well. In the all-female Ladies with Leverage, for example, five of the club's six stock purchase decisions were in the consumer products sector of the economy; moreover, the information on which the members based their decision was primarily drawn from their experience as consumers. When they were trying to choose among three firms in the discount retail sector—PriceCostco, Barnes & Noble, and Consolidated Stores—they immediately eliminated Consolidated from the running because, as one member put it, "we'd never heard of it, it sold cheap merchandise, and we couldn't identify with it." Barnes & Noble was quickly overshadowed by the club's enthusiasm for Costco's products, of which they were all avid consumers. "Every time I go there I stand in line for twenty minutes," Lydia said. Karen added that the store does a huge back-to-school business every year. "I know," said Teresa. "I contribute to it!" Ultimately, while their financial analysis of Barnes & Noble was more promising, Karen said the group felt more comfortable and "identified with" Costco because "we all shop there and know it sells quality merchandise." Six months later Asset Accumulators, the other all-female club, held a similar discussion. The group bought Costco because, as Berry put it, the store is so popular "you can never find a parking space in their lot, and at every party you go to, they serve Costco food." She added that using her consumer experiences in this way was her main investment strategy, because "that's what Peter Lynch said to do"—a comment whose meaning will be examined in more detail later in the chapter.

Some months later, Asset Accumulators bought stock in another consumer products firm: Ethan Allen furniture. Like Ladies with Leverage, the members of Asset Accumulators used their consumer experience as their decisive source of information about the company and the investment value of its stock. Their discussion briefly reviewed the firm's financials and then moved to the quality of the firm's products and services:

Molly: My two nieces buy all their furniture there all the time.
Renee: My kids do, too.
Molly: With all the building of big houses in the Silicon Valley, furniture buying is a necessity—there are big market possibilities.
Tara: They send professional designers to your home to correct any flaws in the product and give you ideas on how to arrange the pieces.

Berry: There aren't many good midpriced furniture stores anymore. Some, like Bruener's, closed or went downmarket, leaving only really cheap or really expensive stuff. That creates a great market opportunity for Ethan Allen. It's the only firm left standing in the middle of the economic range.

Renee: My grandkids use their grandfather's Ethan Allen furniture— it's durable and high quality.

Keiko: My daughter has Ethan Allen furniture.

The club's unanimous decision to buy fifty shares was not entirely conditioned on the members' consumer experience: as the dialogue shows, they considered the firm's market share and growth prospects along with their earlier financial analysis. But the women considered their buying experiences *as women* to be a major factor in their choice of stocks. As Tara put it, "As women, we're really aware of what's going on out there, as consumers." In fact, gender was so salient to the club's perception of the stock market that the members considered transferring their investment funds to the firm owned by Muriel Siebert—the first woman to hold a seat on the New York Stock Exchange—"because she's a she."

Even more compelling evidence of this "logic of gender appropriateness" was suggested by the many instances in which women in the qualitative part of the study—members of both all-female and mixed clubs— used the consumer products model to evaluate stocks of *firms outside the consumer products sector of the economy*. For example, the first investment made by Ladies with Leverage was in a high-tech firm called Coherent, which made surgical lasers. Teresa explained that the group chose the firm because "we saw they made lasers for use in cosmetic surgery; we thought we'd all get face-lifts done by laser." In other words, the club looked at a firm that would ordinarily be classified within the technology industry and evaluated it as potential consumers. Connie added that the club "should have bought Max Factor, too—they make foundation to cover face-lift scars; that would have been perfect diversification." Frivolous as this example might appear, it resulted in a serious investment of $5,000; further, it illustrates a larger pattern that recurs throughout the data (including the discussion of socially responsible investing in the previous chapter), showing how retail investors develop a logic of valuation grounded in their own self-concepts—with particular emphasis on gender roles and norms. In this sense, I found that retail investors understood stock purchases as an extension or enactment of gender-appropriate behavior.

In another example of applying consumer thinking outside the consumer products sector, Ladies with Leverage later decided to buy shares in a financial services firm—the Charles Schwab Inc. discount brokerage—because of their experiences with the firms as customers, and despite the firm's financial outlook. Connie's presentation indicated that the stock price was very high—175 percent of the average for the industry—and the beta was double the industry average, making the stock very volatile. Volatility, plus a high price, are characteristics that make a stock like a trendy fashion item—costly and likely to lose value quickly. Based on this information, along with the historical data on the stock, Karen remarked, "it sounds like we're a year late." The SSG work sheet indicated that the stock was too expensive by NAIC standards, and Connie noted that, at the current price of $37.50, it was near its high for the year. However, the dialogue took a turn for the positive as the group members constructed a story about their consumer experiences with Schwab. Bonnie said she loved Schwab's service. Connie recalled how she had visited a Schwab branch and found the staff extremely helpful: she asked for an annual report, and though they didn't have one on hand, a staff member called headquarters to get the report sent to Connie's home.

Based on these consumer experiences, the emergent narrative in Ladies with Leverage continued to gain such momentum that even when a piece of negative information arose, it was reframed in a positive way. For example, when Tanya noted that the SSG gave Schwab particularly poor marks on management quality, other members jumped in to repair the breach in the story line:

> *Georgia*: If we were conscientious, we'd check the corporate annual report to investigate the management further. But I'm not sure it's worth being conscientious in this case.
> *Lydia*: This company is going to be hot: it's a great industry, and baby boomers will want to keep investing regardless of the economic outlook.
> *Teresa:* The number of dollars entering the market every year due to IRAs is in the billions. Schwab will make money in both good markets and bad, every time people buy and sell.

Thus, despite almost uniformly negative results from their financial analysis, the club voted unanimously to buy seventy-five shares.

Mapping Gender onto the Stock Market

What might lead women (and men) to conclude that women should focus their investment decisions on the consumer products sector of the economy? All the women in the sample were college educated, some had advanced degrees, and all had worked outside their homes at some point. It is safe to say that they all knew about many things unrelated to purchasing products. Yet in both all-female and mixed-gender settings, women seemed unwilling to use the full breadth of their knowledge as a basis for investment decisions.

One explanation may lie in the culture of capitalism itself, whose mapping of gender roles onto economic roles was noted over a century ago by economist Thorstein Veblen. While men are first and foremost tied to the economy as workers, Veblen wrote, women have historically been associated with the consumer role. In one of his earlier works, an 1898 essay titled "The Barbarian Status of Women," he argued that in traditional human societies, women are themselves commodities for male consumption; for her husband, a woman is "a trophy of his exploit," wholly owned by him and subject to trade.[39] As societies evolve from agragrian to capitalist modes of production, Veblen claimed, this commodification of women is sublimated such that women's economic function becomes the conspicuous "consumption of food, clothing, dwelling and furniture" in order to display their husbands' (or fathers') prowess as producers.[40] Even for women who work outside their homes, he wrote, "decency still requires the wife to consume some goods conspicuously for the reputability of the household and its head. So that, as the latter-day outcome of this evolution of an archaic institution, the wife, who was at the outset the drudge and chattel of the man, both in fact and in theory—the producer of goods for him to consume—has become the ceremonial consumer of goods which he produces."[41] The culture of capitalism and the socioeconomic position of women have changed a great deal since Veblen's time, but the association between women and consumption remains strong. Thus, we find the words of a 1929 advertising publication—which declared that "the proper study of mankind is man . . . but the proper study of markets is *woman*"[42]—echoed in a 2003 bestseller on marketing strategy, *Just Ask a Woman*.[43] Though the majority of American women are now employed outside their homes, women still take primary responsibility for homemaking and consumer purchasing.[44] This pattern holds even when women earn more than their husbands; sociologists speculate that the symbolic role of woman-as-consumer has maintained precedence over the reality of changing economic conditions in order to retain the traditional gender status order.[45] The persistence of this linkage may lead women to invest preferentially in stocks they know through their consumer experience.

This would be consistent with the phrase that served as a rallying cry for the amateur investment phenomenon of the 1990s: "buy what you know." The slogan was made famous by former Fidelity mutual fund manager Peter Lynch in his 1989 bestseller, *One Up on Wall Street*. In one sense, "buy what you know" was a populist call to arms, expanding the notion of who could be an investor. Lynch suggested that anyone could "beat The Street" by simply drawing on personal experiences to inform one's own investment choices. And as the case of the purchase of PriceCostco by Ladies with Leverage suggests, retail investors took Lynch's claims to heart, making "buy what you know" a leitmotif for both men and women in this study.

This also suggests why the men in the observational portion of my study focused their investment behavior on sectors of the economy related to their professional experience. Just as consumer products stocks are associated with women in this sample, men showed a marked preference for what the president of ESAP called "boy stocks": shares in firms involved in manufacturing, high technology, and basic energy (oil, natural gas, etc.)—all industries in which men hold most of the leadership positions and make up most of the employees.[46] Indeed, consistent with the pattern observed by the president of Bulls & Bears, all the men in my qualitative sample focused their stock recommendations on industries connected to their personal work experience.

For example, in the all-men's group Portfolio Associates, the dentist persuaded the club to buy stock in a dental supply firm, the engineers recommended high-technology firms, the doctor was responsible for the club's purchase of a pharmaceutical company stock, and the bus driver got the club to buy shares of Quaker State Oil. Similarly, a surgeon who belonged to the Valley Gay Men's Investment Club said he had experienced "a Peter Lynch moment," leading to his recommendation that the club buy stock in a firm he knew through his professional experience: a company that made steel appliances for spinal surgery. The club voted to buy twenty-five shares.

Even on the rare occasions when all-male clubs *did* discuss buying stock in the consumer products sector, the dialogue was framed by the members' professional expertise. For example, when the Valley Gay Men's Investment Club looked at La-Z-Boy in June of 1997, the narrative was constructed around observations of the firm made by Troy, a professional interior designer. After Larry presented the financials on La-Z-Boy, Troy acknowledged that the firm "appeals to people who can afford $400 to $600 for a chair—and they're incredibly loyal customers." However, he added, "it's not Hillsborough, it's Daly City—sneer, sneer." By linking the

firm to a working-class suburb of San Francisco (Daly City)—as opposed
to ultrawealthy Hillsborough—Troy invoked social identity in a way that
was similar to the process that unfolded in Ladies with Leverage during
the discussion of discount retail firms: the men could not (or would not)
"identify" with a firm whose products smacked of working-class tastes.
Thus, the Valley Gay Men's Investment Club, like Ladies with Leverage,
ultimately decided against buying stock in a firm with which the members
did not wish to be identified. But, in an important difference from the all-
women's club, the basis of the men's decision was not consumer experience
but Troy's professional expertise.

On the one hand, men's preference for presenting stocks related to
their work experiences is an issue of credibility and expertise: virtually any
claim is more persuasive when the narrator can claim direct, authoritative
knowledge of a subject.[47] However, there is also an element in this pattern
that suggests stock purchases can be an arena for the social construction
of masculinity, just as women construct femininity through their portfolio
decisions. While it is not clear how much of this gendering of stock purchases occurs at a conscious level, the occasional offhand remark by participants in this study suggested that they were aware of these dynamics to
some extent. For example, when the all-men's group California Investors
voted to buy stock in the temporary employment firm Robert Half International, the decision was based on little more than the presenter's knowledge
of the company as a client of his benefits consulting business. "I don't know
anything about the company except what I read [in their client files]," Jack
said in winding up his brief presentation, "but I like it." When Ken made
a motion to buy two hundred shares, there was a long silence, with some
members looking uncomfortably at the SSG, which was only half-com-
pleted and mostly illegible. Then Ted piped up, "who's got balls here?" and
raised his hand in support of the purchase. Almost immediately all the
other hands went up, and the motion to buy two hundred shares passed
unanimously. In this case, while Jack had a professional connection with
the firm he was recommending, he was up-front about how little he had
to offer in the way of expert insight. Instead, the decision came to be
framed as a challenge to the masculinity of the members.

Ultimately, the logic of gender appropriateness seems to be so ingrained that men in this sample rejected investments in the consumer sector as assiduously as women sought them out. For example, when the
Valley Gay Men's Investment Club looked at the possibility of investing in
the discount retail chain Dollar General, the members decided against it
despite the firm's promising financial prospects. The decision was sealed
by the following dialogue:

Leonard: I don't like retail very much.

Mel: Me too; I don't trust retail.

Larry: Me three.

No reasons for this dislike and distrust were given or requested.

Discomfort with and avoidance of the consumer products sector came across in both the stock presentations and the decisions in all-male clubs. Table 3.2 shows the percentage of presentations in each club that involved consumer products stocks during the yearlong observation period. The percentage of women members in each club has also been included for reference.

The pattern is clear: consideration of consumer products stocks rises in direct proportion to the percentage of women in each club. The all-women's clubs discussed these stocks more often than mixed clubs, and mixed clubs considered consumer products stocks more often than all-men's clubs. Furthermore, mixed clubs discussed consumer products stocks in proportion to the percentage of women members. Thus, the results from both same-sex and mixed clubs indicate that women investors preferentially attend to and recommend stocks in the consumer products sector of the economy.

This pattern extends beyond stock discussions to actual commitments of cash through stock purchases. Table 3.3 (over, page 98) summarizes the stock purchase decisions of each club in terms of the entire range of economic sectors. The number in each cell represents the percentage of total portfolio value allocated to each sector. Industry sectors are the broad economic categories which are used to classify firms and stocks; while there is no single accepted taxonomy, stocks in this study were coded using the classification schemes most commonly employed by the participants, the

Table 3.2

Gender Composition and Stock Presentations in the Consumer Sector

Club	% Women Members	% Consumer Stocks Discussed	Total # Stock Presentations
Portfolio Associates	0	17	8
California Investors	0	20	20
Bulls & Bears	40	29	7
Educating Singles Against Poverty	69	50	6
Asset Accumulators	100	63	8
Ladies with Leverage	100	66	6

ones developed by *Standard & Poor's Outlook* and the *Value Line Investment Survey.* These investment guides are used as the primary information source by 90 percent of the clubs in this sample. In addition, both are in common use in the financial services industry, and are available to the public through libraries as well as online and by subscription.[48] *Standard & Poor's Outlook* categorizes stocks into eleven broad industry categories: energy, basic materials, capital goods, consumer cyclicals, consumer staples, health care, financial, technology, communication services, utilities, and transportation. These eleven broad categories are based on a more detailed breakdown of the market into 113 subcategories that are virtually identical to the *Value Line* schema, which divides the market into 84 subcategories. I was able to directly match over 85 percent of the *S&P Outlook* industry classifications to *Value Line* categories; the remaining 15 percent of the *S&P Outlook* industry classifications were matched to a *Value Line* industry category by a consensus of three research assistants.[49] Inter-rater reliability was .90.

The data in table 3.3 have been divided by club type (all-male, all-female, and mixed), rather than by individual club, to highlight the impact of gender composition on stock selection choices. (Only eight sectors are included because no club had investments in the other two sectors: utilities and raw materials.).

These portfolio choices suggest that patterns of asset allocation across economic sectors reflect a mapping of gender roles onto economic roles, and a logic of gender appropriateness in stock purchases. Investors "buy what they know," but this means different things for men and women—including, notably, women's preference for investing in the consumer sector regardless of their employment experience.

Gender Differences in Investing: Evidence from the Survey Data

In order to see how widespread this phenomenon of gendered asset allocation was among investment clubs, I conducted statistical tests using a sub-

Table 3.3

Sector Allocation by Club Gender Composition in Observational Sample

Club Type	Consumer Products	Basic Energy	Financial Services	Health Care	High-Tech	Industrial Mfg.	Industrial Services	Transport
All-male	4%	5%	11%	13%	55%	5%	2%	5%
Mixed	26%	0%	12%	9%	41%	5.3%	5.5%	0%
All-female	35%	0%	5%	5%	50%	1%	2%	0%

set of the survey data I collected. A group of 578 clubs provided detailed records on their trading and investment patterns. These data were an unexpected windfall, but a logistic regression analysis for response bias did not indicate any significant differences in club demographics or performance between clubs providing trading information and the rest of the sample. In addition, the portfolios included in this study closely match those of the NAIC investment club population as a whole: of the more than six hundred stocks represented in this sample, 70 percent are among the top two hundred stocks owned by NAIC clubs nationwide. This suggests that the data used in this study are representative of the population. Means and standard deviations for relevant variables are listed in table 3.4.[50]

Measures

Dependent Variables

Portfolio data were coded according to the two major dimensions of asset allocation and diversification used in the financial services industry: industry sector and market capitalization. Industry sector was coded using the procedure described for table 3.3 above. Market capitalization was operationalized using the standard financial industry definition of the term: the total value of a firm's outstanding stock, equivalent to the number of shares on the market times the price per share. As with industry sector, there is no single accepted classification for market capitalization, but firms and stocks are usually categorized as small-cap, mid-cap, and large-cap. Both industry sector and market capitalization are considered important measures of diversification; portfolios are considered diversified when they contain stocks from a wide range of economic sectors and a mix of market capitalization levels.[51]

To obtain data on market capitalization, the primary data source was the Standard & Poor's COMPUSTAT database.[52] For a minority of trades,

Table 3.4
Portfolio Diversification in the Survey Sample

	N	Mean	Standard Deviation
Percent female club members	578	63.96%	0.3422
Age of club (in months)	578	50.1208	70.3587
Percentage of members managing their own account	578	64.25%	0.2049
Club size (number of members)	578	15.1152	5.1806

the market capitalization information was not available through COM-PUSTAT and alternate sources were employed, such as the *Wall Street Journal, Investors's Business Daily,* the U.S. Securities and Exchange Commission website, and the Yahoo! Finance website. In these cases, market capitalization was calculated as the product of number of shares outstanding and stock price as of purchase date. In consultation with colleagues from finance departments, I ultimately settled on the following definition of small-, mid-, and large-cap stocks: small-cap stocks were defined as those with less than $500 million in of shares outstanding; mid-cap stocks were those with $500 million to $5 billion in shares outstanding; and large-cap stocks had over $5 billion in shares outstanding.[53]

Diversification on both market capitalization and industry sector was calculated using Teachman's (1980) entropy index, which is used to measure variation among categorical variables. Entropy is measured as follows: $H = -\sum p_i (\ln p_i)$. If the levels of the variable consist of I categories, the proportion of events in the ith category is expressed as p_i. The entropy measure is the negative sum of the product of each proportion times its natural log. The closer the measure gets to zero, the closer the group is to perfect homogeneity; increasing values indicate increasing heterogeneity. I summed the entropy scores for each item on the scale to create an overall group-level measure of informational diversity.

In addition to the two measures of diversification, the third dependent variable—allocation of assets to the consumer products sector—was calculated as the percentage of portfolio value invested in the consumer cyclicals and consumer staples categories. Table 3.5 shows the descriptive statistics for each of the three dependent variables.

Independent Variables

The primary independent variable in this study is the gender composition of investment clubs. I operationalized gender composition by classifying groups as all-female, all-male, or mixed.[54]

Table 3.5
Descriptive Statistics for Dependent Variables

	N	Mean	Standard Deviation
Allocation to consumer products	539	0.3381	0.1986
Entropy by industry category	539	1.409	0.3746
Entropy by market capitalization	445	0.6212	0.2719

Controls

The analysis included a number of control variables known or hypothe-sized to influence asset allocation and portfolio diversification—specifi-cally, individual investing experience, the number of members in each group, and how long the group has been in business. Investing experience is represented in the analysis by the percentage of club members who man-age their own investment accounts. A major goal of investment club partic-ipation is learning to manage a personal investment account, such as an IRA or 401(k), without relying on a stock broker's advice. Thus, if an individual respondent manages a personal account, it is likely that he or she has more investing experience than those whose investments are lim-ited to the club only. Since diversification is commonly cited as essential to protecting investment gains and mitigating risk, a positive relationship would be expected between investing experience and diversification.[55]

Finally, I controlled for club age (operationalized using both a linear and a quadratic term) and club size (operationalized as the number of members). Club age is highly correlated with the value of a club's portfolio. Club size was also included to control for portfolio value and potential effects of group size on decision making. In terms of club size, it is im-portant to note the low levels of turnover within investment clubs (at the time of the survey, fewer than 1.5 percent of groups reported the departure of any founding members). Investment clubs tend to persist with the same group of people, following the life cycle of the members.

Results

Coefficients for this OLS regression analysis are shown in table 3.6.[56] The reference category is all-female clubs; dummy variables were used for all-male and mixed clubs. The coefficients in these models should therefore be interpreted as deviations from the all-female groups. I opted against using mixed groups as the reference category because doing so might ob-scure significant differences between all-male and all-female clubs. Using all-male clubs as a reference group also seemed inadvisable because of the small percentage they represent in the sample.

Consistent with the qualitative findings, the portfolios of the all-male groups in the survey sample were significantly more diversified by industry sector and market capitalization than those of either all-female or mixed groups. The effect was particularly strong for industry sector diversifica-tion. For allocation of funds to the consumer products sector, the regres-sion coefficients, while falling just shy of statistical significance, were in the

Table 3.6

Regression Coefficients for Investment Allocation—Survey Sample

	Diversification by Industry Sector N = 588	Diversification by Market Capitalization N = 444	Allocation to Consumer Sector N = 588
All-male club	0.1139**	0.1390**	−0.0582
	(0.0740)	(0.0323)	(0.0385)
Mixed club	−0.0108	00103	−0.0265
	(−0.0141)	(0.0187)	(0.0181)
% members managing their	0.2081**	−0.0038	−0.0905**
own portfolios	(0.1134)	(−0.0028)	(0.0443)
Age of club (months)	0.0047**	0.0013**	−0.0005*
	(0.8461)	(0.2518)	(0.0003)
Age of club squared	0.0000**	0.0000**	0.0000
	(−0.7059)	(−0.3752)	(0.0000)
Club size (number of members)	0.0166**	0.0004	−0.0021
	(0.2235)	(0.0081)	(0.0017)
Constant	0.8619**	0.3740**	0.4615**
			(0.0392)
Adjusted R^1	0.2153	0.0283	0.0230

Numbers in parentheses represent standard errors. $*p < .05$ $**p < .01$

right direction: that is, consistent with the qualitative data, mixed clubs allocated a smaller percentage of investment dollars to consumer products stocks than all-female clubs, while all-male clubs invested the lowest percentage of their assets in that sector. Notably, investing experience was consistently associated with lower allocations to consumer products investments. This suggests that experience biases investors away from "putting all their eggs in one basket" and toward diversification. Finally, additional analyses showed that the proportions of men and women in an investment group had little substantial effect on investment outcomes.[57]

Some bias may have been introduced into these findings by the unevenness of the distribution of all-women's clubs: there is a cluster of very old clubs (over fifteen years in operation) and a cluster of very young clubs (less than two years in operation). This clustering may be partly responsible for the lack of strong association between women and investment in the consumer products sector. The older women's clubs may be more influenced by traditional gender roles and economic expectations—and thus more inclined to invest in the consumer products sector—but this effect would be hidden by a cluster of younger women's clubs whose members are more accustomed to seeing women with careers, and thus less likely to invest from a consumer orientation. To test this alternative explanation, it would be ideal to have a more evenly distributed sample of women investors and their portfolios; but given the huge influx of women into investing over the past decade, it may be difficult to find a sample that is not heavily weighted toward younger investors.

Performance Effects of Social Category and Informational Diversity

Finally, I used the survey data to examine the relationship between informational diversity, social category diversity, and performance outcomes in terms of return on investment and percentage of assets allocated to investment (as opposed to cash).

Independent Variables

Social category diversity measures heterogeneity on sex and age; both variables have been found to influence investment behavior and performance at the individual level.[58] Among respondents, 63.1 percent were women, and the average age category was forty-five to fifty years old. (Gender was coded categorically, with female = 1.) I did not have access to the race/ethnicity of respondents. Individual responses were aggregated using the entropy calculation described above, then summed to create a group-level index. The eta squared exceeded .20, indicating that aggregation is acceptable. The mean social category diversity among groups in this sample is 6.15 (s.d. = .98).

The measure of informational diversity assessed heterogeneity within the groups in terms of members' sources of ideas about investment in the stock market. Respondents were asked to name their most-used information sources from print media, television, and the World Wide Web; the list of options was gleaned from qualitative interviews and pretesting of the survey. In addition, research in finance indicates that investing experience and income affect where investors get stock market information and how they use it.[59] Thus, respondents were asked about their investing experience (mean = 11 years; s.d. = 6.6) and household income (mean = $58,000; s.d. = $13,000). Individual responses were aggregated using the entropy calculation described above, then summed to create a group-level index. The eta squared exceeded .20, indicating that aggregation is acceptable. The mean informational diversity among groups in this sample is 12.34 (s.d. = 1.04).

As the correlations in table 3.7 indicate, social category diversity and informational diversity are significantly positively related; that is, the more social category diversity in an investment club, the greater the informational diversity. At the same time, the two variables have distinctly different effects on work group performance. Consistent with previous research, informational diversity made a significant positive contribution to performance in terms of rate of return and, to a lesser extent, in the percentage of cash contributions invested. Social category diversity, while it had no significant effect on portfolio returns, did have a significant and large negative effect on clubs' ability to invest their cash contributions. This is consistent with the accounts given in previous research of the effects of social category diversity: that is, the higher proportion of uninvested cash in mixed groups suggests difficulty in making collective decisions, an outcome often found in work groups in which gender, age, or other social category diversity differences lead to conflict that undermines the group's ability to function.

Next, I tested the causal effects of social category diversity and informational diversity on investment club performance using my survey data, controlling for factors known to influence portfolio returns, such as beta (the volatility of the stocks in a portfolio, mean = .55, s.d. = .38), the number of members in the group (mean = 14.72, s.d. = 6.63), and the length of time the group had been in business (mean = 52.10 months, s.d. = 74.84 months). I also measured individuals' gender (63 percent were women, s.d. = .35), age (mean age group category was 45–50 years old), investment experience (mean = 11.31, s.d. = 6.63), and income (mean = $58,000, s.d. = $13,000).[60] The analysis was conducted using OLS regression, with results shown in table 3.8.

Table 3.7
Correlation Coefficients for Diversity and Portfolio Performance

Variable	1	2
1. Information diversity	—	
2. Social category diversity	.27**	—
3. Rate of return	.16**	.02
4. % contributions invested	.06*	−.23**
Mean	12.34	6.15
Standard deviation	1.04	.98

*p < .05   **p < .01   N = 1,245 groups

These results indicate that, even controlling for the effects of group age, size, and portfolio beta, both informational diversity and social category diversity have significant, independent effects on investment clubs' financial performance. The diversity of club members' sources of investing information has a positive impact on the rate of return earned by the club's portfolio, consistent with prior research showing that decision-making groups thrive in complex, rapidly changing environments like the stock market when those groups possess broad, varied information pools. The effect of informational diversity on an investment club's ability to keep investing its cash contributions is positive but not statistically significant. However, the effect of social category diversity on this dependent variable is significantly negative, consistent with evidence from previous studies showing that social category differences impede work groups' ability to function smoothly and make decisions.

Thus, there is support in these findings for both the "value-in-diversity" and "diversity-as-liability" hypotheses, depending on which type of diversity is at issue and what kind of outcome is being measured. The interactions between the diversity measures and club age provide an interesting wrinkle in the data. As shown in previous studies, the value of informational diversity in investment clubs declines over time, eventually having a significantly negative effect on portfolio returns, although the effect on percentage of contributions invested remains nonsignificant; this suggests a homogenization process, in which long experience of working together diminishes the variety of perspectives and ideas among group mem-

Table 3.8
Regression Analyses Predicting Financial Outcomes

	Financial Performance	
	Rate of Return	% Cash Invested
Group age (months)	0.29**	0.21**
Group size	0.08*	0.09*
Portfolio beta	0.11**	
Informational diversity	0.13**	0.04
Social category diversity	0.03	−0.08*
Group age × informational diversity	−0.08*	−0.03
Group age × social category diversity	0.10*	0.09*
Adjusted R^2	0.33	0.26
Overall F-ratio	23.28***	21.53***

*$p < .05$ **$p < .01$ $N = 1,245$ groups

bers. However, time mitigates the negative effects of social category diversity, leading differences of gender and age to have a small but significant positive impact on both portfolio returns and the ability of a club to keep investing its cash contributions. This points up a limitation of the cross-sectional survey data and suggests an intriguing direction for future longitudinal research on work group diversity.

Summary and Implications

My qualitative and quantitative data indicate that a significant component of the "diversity premium" in investment clubs is the way that social category diversity is linked to informational diversity when it comes to generating investment ideas and strategies. Both the qualitative and quantitative data show strong gender differences in investors' sources of information about the stock market, as well as where they choose to put their investment dollars. Moreover, my data show that "gendered investing" is not just one behavior—such as women buying stocks in the consumer products sector—but a whole constellation of related beliefs and practices.

Consistent with these data, a major implication of the study is that notions of identity—particularly gender identity—set the parameters of the mental maps amateur investors use to orient themselves and develop lines of action within the stock market. That is, my observational and interview data suggest that amateur investors view the approximately seven thousand stocks traded on U.S. exchanges in much the same way as consumer brands: as identity markers rather than exclusively as instruments of a financial transaction. This is not to say that investors do not care about profits; rather, in keeping with the two-system view, I argue that retail investors want *both* profits *and* identity reinforcement (or enhancement) from their stock purchases. The importance of identity in this process is underscored by the instances in the qualitative data in which investors declined to buy stocks with promising financial prospects out of a desire to avoid association with the image of the issuing firms; similarly, the qualitative data show investors choosing to buy stocks with dubious profit potential because they perceived association with the issuing firms as identity enhancing.

Given the positive relationship that the data in this chapter establish between social category diversity and informational diversity, it might seem straightforward to explain the diversity premium as the logical implication of well-established research in decision making. On this basis, one might reason as follows:

- Existing research shows that complex problems and complex environments favor problem solvers with the largest amount of information at their disposal.[61]
- The stock market fits the research definition of a complex environment.[62]
- Men and women have different sources of information about the stock market, as well as different ways of interpreting that information.
- Thus, gender diversity in investment clubs means larger information pools from which to make decisions, which leads to enhanced performance.

However, this straightforward causal relationship is rare in naturally occurring groups (as opposed to laboratory groups) for two reasons: too little conflict or too much of the wrong kind. Both problems stem from the double-edged nature of diversity, which creates vulnerabilities as well as potential resources for work groups. Unfortunately, these vulnerabilities can render the benefits of diversity inaccessible.

This account is consistent with the "diversity-as-liability" studies showing that while social category difference can be useful in providing alternative perspectives, it can also produce the kind of destructive conflict that impairs collective decision-making. This begs the question, what enables *some* investment clubs—particularly mixed-gender groups—to benefit from their differences without being bogged down by them? That question will be explored in the next chapter, on group processes.

APPENDIX ◆
**Additional Analyses of Investment Clubs'
Gender Composition and Performance**

My argument, which locates the source of the "diversity premium" in gender differences in information about the stock market, is open to challenge based on selection bias. An alternative explanation of the regression results in table 3.8 would be that mixed-gender investment clubs only *appear* to perform better than others because low-performing clubs break up at a higher rate, thus dropping out of the sample frame. This argument is particularly compelling given the volatility and conflict attendant upon demographically diverse groups. In contrast, one might expect similarity-attraction bonds to hold same-sex groups together in spite of poor performance.[63] A variation on this selection bias argument would propose that the sample could be biased by *high-performing same-sex clubs* dropping out of the sample to pursue investing without the constraints of NAIC rules—and NAIC dues. This would lower the average performance of the remaining same-sex clubs compared with their mixed counterparts. Though the latter hypothesis seems less likely, both were tested in the following small study.

I conducted a phone survey of twenty-four clubs that had stopped paying membership dues to the national investment club organization within the previous two years. At my request, NAIC officers drew from their archives a random sample of such clubs. They provided information on forty-four clubs. The data included only the name of the club, the last name and first initial of each member, and the full name, address, and phone number of the club contact person. It was not possible to determine the gender composition of the clubs from these data sheets, nor was it clear whether the club had dissolved entirely or whether it continued to function outside of NAIC auspices. I addressed both issues as part of a short telephone survey, along with questions about club performance before leaving NAIC (and after, if applicable), and reasons for discontinuing NAIC membership. The performance issue was framed in terms of member expectations: whether the club had performed better, worse, or as well as expected. This seemed to be a better strategy than calculating "objective" performance for two reasons. First, the highly detailed information needed to make such calculations would almost certainly not have been available. Second, my observational data indicated that *perceived* performance often varied from objective performance, and that commitment to remain in the club was influenced primarily by perception.

Since the contact information for most of the clubs was out-of-date (i.e., phone numbers no longer in service), I attempted to locate other club members through directory assistance, using last names and the town where the club contact lived. This occasionally proved successful but did not yield enough responses. Eventually, the phone survey became a mail survey, sent to the club contact person in hopes that even if the address was no longer valid, the letter might be forwarded. Finally, I resorted to searching the World Wide Web by the last names of club members, looking for phone numbers, street addresses, and e-mail addresses. In all, these combined strategies yielded only twenty-four responses from the original sample of forty-four; the other twenty remained unreachable. The twenty-four clubs I was able to contact included seventeen that had disbanded; the other seven continued as going concerns outside of NAIC's auspices. There were fifteen mixed clubs and nine same-sex clubs. All were between two and five years old at the time of disbanding (or at the time I contacted them, for the seven groups that remained in operation); the average club age was three years.

If the first selection bias hypothesis was true, we would expect the sample of disbanded groups to include a disproportionate number of mixed clubs. These clubs would report that they had been performing worse than they expected while they belonged to NAIC and had dissolved for that reason. If the second hypothesis was true, the sample should include mostly same-sex clubs reporting that they had performed better than expected, leading them to continue operations without NAIC membership.

The sample composition in itself would appear to support the first selection bias hypothesis: mixed clubs made up 63 percent of the dropouts (fifteen out of twenty-four). However, as table 3.9 shows, this hypothesis broke down on the performance issue: mixed clubs that broke up did not perform substantially worse than other disbanded clubs. In addition, a significant percentage of these mixed clubs performed *better* than member expectations.

Perhaps more important, none of the clubs that disbanded mentioned portfolio performance as a factor in their decision. Rather, the explanations fell almost exclusively into two categories: lack of member participation and work-related instability, such as transfers or layoffs. The following responses from survey participants indicate the problems the clubs faced.

Club #1 (mixed): "Couldn't get members to spend two or three hours per month to learn the philosophies and charts. Two of us did all the huffing and puffing."

Club #12 (same-sex): "Most of the people in the group didn't have time to do the research or come to the meetings. We did well financially, though, learned a lot, and have no regrets. We all consider it time well spent."

Club #14 (mixed): "Half of the club advanced so far in knowledge [of investing] that the meetings became quite technical—a good

Table 3.9
Performance of Disbanded Clubs Compared with Member Expectations

	Same-Sex Clubs	Mixed Clubs	Whole Sample
Better	11%	20%	17%
Worse	23%	26%	25%
As expected	66%	54%	58%
N	9	15	24

point. The other half of the club fell further behind and eventually lost the ability to understand what was going on. We asked the nonparticipants to drop out, but they wouldn't and we had a legal partnership [so they couldn't be kicked out] . . . So we decided the prudent thing to do was to dissolve the legal organization."

Club #7 (same-sex): "Too busy to attend meetings."

In the majority of cases, lack of time and commitment caused the group to fall apart. As the respondent from same-sex club #12 notes, the group dissolved *despite* members' perceptions that it was performing well. There is also a significant theme of dissolutions related specifically to the group's selection and recruitment networks, as with the mixed groups that broke up because of members' work-related travel or job transfers, or the same-sex group whose social origins clashed with some members' desire to study investing seriously.

Table 3.10 summarizes the reasons for the dissolution of the seventeen clubs that disbanded. The two clubs in the "other" category dissolved for reasons unique in this sample: the same-sex club broke up because it was unable to complete tax-filing requirements; the mixed club was established with a fixed end date of five years, and dissolved as scheduled (at which point the members used their profits to go on a cruise together).

The most significant things to note about this table are that lack of participation was the leading cause of club dissolution across the board, and that mixed clubs were unique in this sample in suffering the effects of work-related instability. Of course, this is directly related to the networks that brought the members together in the first place: clubs that originate in occupational networks are more vulnerable to problems created by layoffs, business travel, and job transfers. As table 3.11 shows, more than half of mixed clubs that broke up originated in occupational networks. In con-

Table 3.10
Reasons for Club Dissolution

	Same-Sex Clubs	Mixed Clubs	Whole Sample
Lack of participation	80%	66%	71%
Work-related instability	0%	26%	18%
Other	20%	8%	12%
N	5	12	17

Table 3.11
Origins of Disbanded Clubs

	Same-Sex Clubs	Mixed Clubs	Whole Sample
Social origins	80%	42%	53%
Work Origins	20%	58%	47%
N	5	12	17

trast, most or all of the same-sex clubs in this small sample came from friendship networks.

The pattern of results in tables 3.10 and 3.11 suggests that mixed clubs may break up at a higher rate because of the added burden of instability caused by their origins in occupational networks. While both same-sex and mixed clubs suffered from lack of participation, only mixed clubs broke up for work-related reasons. In other words, there were more forces working against mixed clubs than same-sex clubs.

The data from the seven clubs that were still active outside NAIC reinforce this point. Every one of them—including three mixed and four same-sex clubs—was based on affective ties such as friendship. While social bonds do not guarantee that a club will survive through good times and bad, affective networks seem to offer more stability than instrumental ties. Members of clubs based on social ties may get laid off or travel on business, but they can still see their friends and neighbors outside of work hours. In contrast, members of work-based groups reported losing touch as soon as they no longer saw each other at work.

With respect to the second selection bias hypothesis, the seven clubs that remained going concerns offer additional useful information. The data do not support the contention that high-performing same-sex clubs drop out of NAIC more frequently than other clubs. Instead, nearly as many mixed as same-sex clubs left NAIC to strike out on their own. Only one of the seven—a same-sex club—considered itself a high-performer prior to leaving NAIC. The other six were doing only as well as members expected—no better and no worse. All said, they left the national organization because they did not wish to pay NAIC dues any longer.[64] They did not say they could do *better* without NAIC; indeed, all seven said they were performing at the same level as they did when they belonged to the national organization.

The right decision grows out of the clash and conflict of opinions and out of the serious consideration of competing alternatives.

—PETER DRUCKER[1]

Getting Ahead versus Getting Along
Decision Making in Investment Clubs ◆ 4

The previous chapter showed how a broad and varied information pool contributes to the "diversity premium" in investment clubs. This chapter will now turn to the question of group processes: specifically, how groups use (or fail to use) information held by their members. Group processes require separate consideration as part of the "diversity premium" because in investment clubs, as in all work groups and teams, the presence of a resource like information does not tell us much about whether and how it will be used. Instead, group processes act as a kind of master switch for the expression of diversity, eliciting its benefits or suppressing them. As a result, work groups and teams often possess more informational resources than they ever use, as research in decision making shows: "examination of information sharing in groups shows that members do far less of it than the 'productive conflict' argument assumes; group discussion tends to focus on what is known by everyone, and uniquely held information tends to be ignored."[2] Thus, the information made available for group decision making is largely independent of the actual range and quality of information held by the individual members. Moreover, this process often occurs with the awareness and complicity of participants.

Why would work groups waste a valuable resource like information? Previous research suggests that informational diversity and its potential benefits are often sacrificed for the sake of preserving interpersonal relationships among group members. Irving Janis's well-known work on "groupthink" suggests an explanation for this phenomenon, positing that "the more amiability and esprit de corps among the members ... the greater is the danger that independent critical thinking will be replaced by groupthink."[3] In other words, the stronger the socioemotional bonds among group members, the more likely they are to suppress diverse or uniquely held information. While sharing uniquely held information can lead to better decisions, helping the group "get ahead" in the instrumental sense, it simultaneously carries the risk of igniting destructive conflict among members, impeding their ability to "get along."

While the "getting ahead"/"getting along" distinction is highly stylized, it has deep and empirically well-established roots in small-group and organizational research, going back as far as the Hawthorne studies in the 1930s.[4] It received the lion's share of scholarly attention in the 1950s, however, through the work of Harvard sociologists such as George Homans and Robert Freed Bales. Research by Bales, in particular, helped establish a model of group processes governed by the tension between task-related or "instrumental" goals, on the one hand, and affective or socioemotional goals, on the other. This model has been supported by subsequent research well into the twenty-first century, suggesting that the pull toward task or goal achievement on the one hand, and socioemotional cohesion on the other, constitutes a fundamental tension in all groups—one that is never fully resolved, but repeatedly adjudicated.[5]

These group processes need not be in conflict with each other, and indeed may be mutually enhancing in some cases. But groups often favor "getting along" over "getting ahead" when it comes to decision making because genuine debate can be costly in terms of morale and performance, leading to more difficult decision making in the future or even the dissolution of the group.[6] As a result, in work groups where members individually hold very different opinions and ideas, the pressure to "get along" or conform tends to suppress the expression of that diversity.

Adding to these centripetal forces in group decision-making processes are the ways in which conformity can be "built into" groups through recruitment and selection. Social structure tends to put people with similar demographic profiles (which also correspond closely with homogeneity of opinion and information sources) in frequent contact with one another, while separating those whose backgrounds are different.[7] In addition, as the similarity/attraction paradigm suggests, individuals prefer to associate with others similar to themselves.[8] Thus, studies of group formation show evidence of "homophily"—preference for demographically and intellectually similar others—in the formation of both voluntary associations and formal organizations.[9] What remains to be better understood are the conditions under which group processes either reinforce or counteract these pressures toward conformity. In other words, what makes some groups able to "get ahead" in addition to "getting along" at least well enough to avoid dissolution? Group processes that permit productive engagement with differences of opinion and information are the second component of the "diversity premium."

The data presented in this chapter will show that the the most profitable groups in the study evolved interaction processes that allowed them to make the most of their information resources—enhancing the quality of their decision making by putting as much information as they had on the table—while keeping conflicts over the discussion and interpretation of that information from threatening the functioning of the group. While such groups were often not very sociable, either during or outside of their meetings, they were able to "get ahead" without undermining their ability to "get along." Thus, the high-performing investment groups in this study were distinctive not only in their financial results but also in their internal robustness to conflict and their resulting ability to adapt to the demands of a complex, rapidly changing environment. These qualities are sought-after in many kinds of work groups and teams, so to permit generalizations from the case of investment clubs, the remainder of this chapter will focus on identifying group processes that encourage "productive conflict," providing the catalyst for the diversity premium.

Ultimately, investment clubs—and any decision-making groups operating within a complex environment—thrive financially to the extent that they can preserve diversity of opinion and constructive controversy while counteracting the forces of conformity. This chapter will examine how investment clubs negotiate this tension; drawing primarily from the richly detailed observational data from my study, this chapter will examine group processes that help or hinder groups in reaping the performance benefits of their resource pools. The variables discussed in the previous chapter set the initial conditions for performance by creating the resource pool from which decisions are made. But these forces are made concrete, and can affect performance, only through group process—the setting in which the tension between "getting ahead" and "getting along" is enacted.

Foundations of Group Process: Selection and Recruitment

In investment clubs, group processes emerge from patterns established by the social pathways, structures, and interpersonal ties that initially drew members into the group. That is, selection and recruitment processes not only create the resource pool available to the group—by regulating who

gets in—but also set up the interpersonal commitments, historical prece-
dents, and default modes of interaction for the many decisions that group
members must make together under conditions of uncertainty and incomplete information. It is in the decision process that the group actuates its
resources—or not. Informational diversity remains a *potential* asset until
activated by the group's willingness to use it.

Thus, one intended contribution of this study to sociological theory
can be summed up in the following proposition: *the process through which
individuals become members of a group influences their subsequent behavior
in that group.* The focus of this chapter will be on decision-making processes, but the proposition could be extended to and tested in other contexts. In a sense, it extends to the microlevel an insight of neoinstitutional
sociology, which foregrounds the role of history in explaining the behavior
of firms and organization fields. For example, Stinchcombe proposed that
organizations are "imprinted" by the circumstances under which they are
created—particularly by historical and technological conditions, which
create path dependencies that endure throughout the organization's life-
span.[10] Subsequent empirical research has supported this contention, extending the notion of imprinting to include founder effects and cultural
practices. Boje, for example, has studied the ways in which a firm's founding story or "creation myth" creates a template that guides present and
future action.[11] Similarly, Baron and colleagues summarized their large-
scale study of Silicon Valley firms and their financial performance by pointing to founder effects as the key causal variable: "a broad conclusion of
this analysis . . . is that *origins matter.*"[12]

My research advances these insights by proposing that "origins matter"
not just at the organizational level of analysis but also at the microlevel of
interpersonal ties within work groups. As part of the broader sociological
agenda to specify the mechanisms of path dependence, or "past dependence,"[13] theorized by neonstitutionalists, I propose that recruitment and
selection are among the most significant forces shaping the lines of action
available to group members. This by no means implies a deterministic role
for those processes; rather, it suggests that we should treat mechanisms of
selection and recruitment as important influences in patterning the interactions that develop among group members.

Modes of selection and recruitment of new members are among the
first decisions that define a group, and as scholars of path dependence
in organizations have observed, such early decisions snowball over time,
delimiting the range of possibilities for action. While this is not an irrevo-
cable process, the decisions made in the foundational period of a group's
existence acquire a momentum such that "decisions that have been taken

in the past increasingly amount to an imperative for the future course of action."[14] Indeed, this section of the chapter could take as its theme Granovetter's observation about the need to account for history when developing sociological theories: "It is important to avoid what might be called 'temporal reductionism': treating relations and structures of relations as if they had no history . . . Built into human cognitive equipment is a remarkable capacity, depressingly little studied, to file away the details, and especially the emotional tone, of past relations."[15] In fact, Granovetter is pointing to two separate issues that develop over time to influence interpersonal relations and structures: their embeddedness in history, and the attachment of "emotional tone" or affective meaning to that history. Both have a profound influence on the development and character of group processes. As illustrations, consider these examples:

- Members of the all-male group California Investors explained an investment decision that made little economic sense—that in fact consistently *cost* them significant amounts of money—by pointing to the group's embeddedness in friendship ties: "we're friends of twenty years' standing, so sometimes we vote for things [stock purchase ideas] just to fly the flag."
- In a similar way, the members of Asset Accumulators pointed to their shared history as teachers in shaping their decision processes as investors, saying: "we have a lot of teachers in the group, so analysis is the bottom line, and you won't get anywhere without doing your homework." This comment points not only to the powerful effect of professional socialization but also to the process expectations developed among these individuals over repeated interactions.

Significantly, participants in the observational part of the study took the initiative in raising these points about the ways in which their patterns of selection and recruitment influenced their group's subsequent decision processes. Far from being a subtext of group interaction, the historical precedent and emotional tone set by the circumstances of members' entree into the group were central to participants' understanding of their investment choices and collective outcomes. Many investment club members I interviewed were at pains to explain their group's stock purchases (and sales) as contingent upon a history of interpersonal relations that often long predated my arrival as an observer. That is, participants understood themselves to be not only *internally* consistent in terms of their individual choices and preferences—which is to be expected, based on the literature of social psychology[16]—but also *interpersonally consistent* in terms of their history with other group members.

In their accounts, the history and emotional tone of their relations arose from the interpersonal ties through which they had been recruited or selected into the group. This could include alliances they had formed through their career choices, such as membership in a professional association or joint participation in a project team; the ties might also have derived from socioemotional contexts, ranging from long-standing friendships to nodding acquaintance as neighbors or friends-of-friends. Over time, participants said, these variations in the interpersonal ties that had drawn them into the group affected how they and their coparticipants processed information and made decisions about investments. That is, participants in the observational part of my study interpreted their group decision-making process as emergent from and contingent upon the nature of the social pathways through which they had entered the group. This suggests a kind of transitivity over time in interpersonal relations, which bears further investigation as a source of the diversity premium. It also implies that the ways in which groups negotiate the dual imperatives of "getting ahead" versus "getting along" are conditioned by an ongoing history and emotional tone initially set in motion by their modes of selection and recruitment.

Illustrations from the Observational Data

For Asset Accumulators, a group that had recruited members through an academic professional association, the history and emotional tone of the members' interpersonal ties served their financial objectives well, establishing a pattern that promoted the profitable use of their informational resources. The result of their shared experience in the American Association of University Women and as educators was a shared stance toward investing—specifically a commitment to rigorous analysis. Not only did this lead them to affirm a highly analytical stance toward investing, but—significantly—to *reject* modes of interaction inconsistent with their relational history. For example, at one point during the April 1998 meeting, members complained—albeit mildly—about the group's businesslike demeanor and lack of social activities:

> *Julia*: We didn't even celebrate our fifth anniversary as a club. We should have something social once in a while.
> *Liza*: I agree; we don't socialize enough.

Despite such instances of friction, the consistency of Asset Accumulators' selection and recruitment processes—no members could be accepted without having first belonged to the AAUW—meant that members were largely *presocialized* to their analytical, all-business approach. This was reflected in the high rates of return on their investments; for several years, Asset Accumulators was among the top-performing NAIC clubs in the nation, with compound annual returns of 36.49 percent.

In Bulls & Bears, as in Asset Accumulators, the legacy of the founders' professional socialization experiences prevailed in shaping group dynamics, but the struggle between "getting ahead" and "getting along" was far more intense and explicit. To illustrate this, recall the comment made by one of the founders after a heated and awkward exchange between Paul, the club president, and a club member whose presentation Paul found insulting in its sloppiness and lack of analytical rigor. Greg, who had founded the club along with Paul and a few others, took Paul aside after this exchange and said, "you know that in real life you would never associate with him [Jeff]." Later, when I asked Greg to expand on his comment, he said that he had intended to help Paul cool off by depersonalizing the situation, reminding him that interactions in the club were "strictly business."

While this "strictly business" framing of group process was consistent with the history and emotional tone of the ties that had drawn members into Bulls & Bears, a similar emphasis on "getting ahead" fell flat in California Investors, whose selection and recruitment processes had left a very different legacy. Thus, when one of the younger members of California Investors tried to persuade the club to adopt more rigorous standards of stock analysis, he encountered intense opposition. In effect, his proposal that investment decisions be subjected to more quantitive scrutiny than they had been receiving put him in conflict with the history and emotional tone set by the friendship ties that were the basis for membership, and that subsequently steered participants into accepting poor investment proposals as a sign of affiliation and loyalty. Mark, the member who argued for this reweighting of priorities in favor of "getting ahead," said that his repeated attempts over the course of six months to argue for a more economically rational decision process were met with such hostility that he would often drive home from meetings "in tears, thinking 'they hate me.' " This put him in the position of having to decide whether to remain in the group and, if so, on what terms. Having attempted to exercise "voice" to effect change, in the terminology developed by Albert Hirschman, Mark was left with a choice of "exit"—to leave the group—or "loyalty," which would mean accepting the group on its current terms.[17] Ultimately, Mark opted for "loyalty," despite his misgivings. His case, and that of other investment club members, illustrates a phenomenon that bears further exploration: the struggle between competing commitments.[18]

Broader Themes in the Observational Data

Early in the ethnographic part of this study, a pattern of association emerged between club performance and interpersonal ties: the investment clubs that had recruited and selected their members based on socioemotional ties consistently turned in the poorest financial performance in my qualitative sample. For example, the members of Educating Singles Against Poverty had met through a church singles group. The women of Ladies with Leverage had met as members of local voluntary associations, including a gourmet club, a book club, and a local charity. California Investors was an exception to this pattern, in one sense, since its members had worked together as insurance executives; but the group was created after the members had retired, based on a subset of acquaintances who had developed social friendships through the country club where they later held investment club meetings. Tellingly, the members described one another as "friends of twenty years' standing," not as former coworkers.

In addition, all three of these clubs held meetings in settings usually associated with social functions rather than business: Educating Singles Against Poverty met in a Mexican restaurant over dinner; Ladies with Leverage met in members' homes over lunch; and California Investors met at the country club over drinks and snacks—members often "warmed up" for the meeting with a round of golf. In addition, all three clubs had at least one purely social meeting—such as a holiday party—per year. The clubs' choices of meeting venues, in and of themselves, set up "competing commitments," situating members within a context (a communal meal, or a sporting event) that could stand alone as an end in itself.

In contrast, clubs in the qualitative study that were not based on friendship ties chose meeting places that reinforced their business agendas. Indeed, all of them met in nondescript conference rooms that offered few distractions or alternatives to the business agenda. Bulls & Bears held meetings in a conference room at the members' workplace; Asset Accumulators met in a conference room at the local public library; and Portfolio Associates held its meetings in a conference room at the brokerage office where the club was founded in 1954.

Table 4.1 summarizes the patterns I observed in modes of selection and recruitment on the one hand, and measures of portfolio performance on the other. Combined with participants' own accounts of their clubs' investment decisions, the data strongly suggested a need to further examine the effects of selection and recruitment processes on group decision-making. I used an iterative process—moving back and forth between the data and relevant literature—to develop an emerging theory about the content of interpersonal ties and their relationship to group performance.

Table 4.1

Interpersonal Ties and Group Performance in Observational Sample

Club Name	Selection and Recruitment Ties	Gender Composition	Gross Internal Rate of Return[a]	% of Portfolio in Cash
Bulls & Bears	Professional	Mixed gender	22.34%	8%
Asset Accumulators	Professional	All women	36.49%	3%
Portfolio Associates	Financial (met through broker)	All men	22.66%	0.2%
Educating Singles Against Poverty	Friendship	Mixed gender	9.44%	27%
Ladies with Leverage	Friendship	All women	11.56%	27%
California Investors	Friendship	All men	12.66%	19%

Note: Since I observed the seventh club, VGMIC, from inception, no performance data were available to track until four months into the study; this did not provide enough data for meaningful measurement of returns.

[a] These internal rate of return figures are "gross" because they are not adjusted for market conditions over the time span of the calculation, as are the performance figures used in the quantitative portion of the study. The performance rates of the lower three groups on the chart look respectable compared with the annual 11% historical average return of the S&P 500, but are quite modest compared with the stock market of 1998, when this study was being conducted and the annual returns of the market indexes were upward of 30%. For example, between September 25, 1998, and September 30, 1999, the S&P 500 gained 32.7%. See http://www.elon.edu/ipe/kleimon.pdf.

Methodologically, my approach is closely related to the "extended case method" employed by Gouldner in his seminal studies of industrial bureaucracy in the 1950s. In this method, researchers revise and expand existing theories based on empirical observations in natural settings.[19] Just as Gouldner used this technique to confront prevailing readings of Weber on bureaucracy, my goal was to employ field data to challenge the current sociological understanding of the types and effects of interpersonal ties at work. Ultimately, I was concerned with issues similar to those that preoccupied Gouldner's research: the ways in which relations within work groups are conditioned by and negotiated in reference to the history of prior interactions among participants, as well as in reference to their ongoing, evolving interactions.[20] Through these means, I developed a conceptual taxonomy that I was able to test using data I collected from my national survey of investment clubs.

Conceptualizing the History and Emotional Tone of Interpersonal Ties

The impact on group processes of mechanisms of selection and recruitment remains among those areas that Granovetter describes as "depressingly little studied." Lack of a strong, ongoing research program in small-group sociology[21] has meant that the legacy of Bales's work has not been realized in the form of a common language or conceptual framework for the qualitative, relational aspects of interpersonal ties. Instead, most recent research has focused on the *structure* of ties among individuals, or on the intensity of those ties (as in "strong" or "weak"). However, there is growing awareness that ignoring what some researchers have called the "content" of interpersonal ties—the relationships underlying the structure—may misspecify or neglect key aspects of these effects.[22]

While there are no current studies linking the content of interpersonal relationships among members to group processes or performance, we know that such relationships influence other aspects of groups that directly affect performance. For example, qualitative aspects of the interpersonal ties in groups are linked to groups' demographic composition: those that emerge from preexisting friendship ties are significantly more homogeneous in terms of gender, race, or age than groups based on other kinds of relationships.[23] Friendships are also, in the main, characterized by homogeneity of ideas, because people from similiar backgrounds often derive information from similar sources.[24] This means that the quality of a relationship—such as whether a relational tie represents a friendship or a business association—affects the size of the resource pools available to decision-making groups. And as a large body of research in social psychology has shown, decision performance increases with the amount of information available to the group.[25]

A second issue impeding the development of the conceptual vocabulary and models we need to study the embeddedness of group processes in intepersonal ties is imprecision in the use of the term "friendship." Several researchers have argued that "friendship" is different in the business domain than in other contexts.[26] "Business friendships" are based not on pleasure but on utility: goodwill and cordiality exist within limits imposed by individual interests, but business colleagues often are not and cannot be friends in many senses of the term (such as emotional vulnerability and self-disclosure). When "business friends" do become "social friends," the results can be detrimental to both the personal careers and the firms of the individuals involved, as recent corporate scandals attest.[27]

Such problems of misspecification may account for some of the difficulties sociology has encountered in developing models of economic behavior that go beyond simple dichotomies such as rational/irrational, or self-maximizing/altruistic. As Uzzi put it, economic sociologists are seeking to develop a "new categorization of motives"[28] for economic behavior, in which individuals are conceived of as neither wholly opportunistic (à la *homo economicus*) nor wholly cooperative, but instead as responsive to the opportunity structures presented by various social contexts.

Within work groups and teams, an important part of the opportunity structure to which individuals respond is the relational content of interpersonal ties with other members. To proceed with this exploration will require enlargement of our current vocabulary in economic sociology, in the direction of more fine-grained description of interpersonal relations for analytical purposes. This need arises in part because the conceptual distinctions commonly used to describe interpersonal relations—such as "weak" versus "strong" ties—do not map consistently onto resources and outcomes attributed to them, suggesting that the causal relationships may be more complex than previously suspected.[29] For example, a recent study shows that weak ties—the arm's length connections among acquaintances that are usually associated with instrumental ends such as finding a job— can also serve as crucial sources of social support, an outcome previously attributed to strong ties among friends and relatives.[30] This suggests that we need to expand our conceptual toolkit and more closely specify the key causal dimensions of interpersonal relationships.

Then the question becomes, if our current conceptual tools are inadequate, how *should* we conceptualize the qualitative content of such ties? The lack of an established vocabulary for defining these concepts presents a challenge. However, the observational and interview data I gathered, combined with the extant literature, suggested some useful approaches to the issue. Following Gouldner's method, with each iteration of conceptual development on interpersonal ties, I searched for coherent patterns in the data and compared them with those discussed in existing research.

"Instrumental" and "Affective" Relationships at Work

The most useful conceptual taxonomy I found in the research literature defined interpersonal ties in terms of either "utility" or "personal" relationships.[31] I found this schema compelling in part because of its groundedness; unlike studies that draw their terms from a priori theoretical distinctions, these terms were derived directly from interviews with managers, who indicated that they conceived of distinct boundaries in their relationships at work along utility-versus-personal lines. In utilitarian relations (which the study sometimes described as "instrumental") the connection among actors was conceived as a means to an end: while the relationships could be experienced as positive and satisfying, they did not have great intrinsic value and were characterized by low psychological attachment. Such relationships were unlikely to outlive their task-related purpose. In contrast, personal relationships (occasionally termed "affective" ties in the study) were perceived as having intrinsic value apart from their task-relatedness, and commonly persisted in the absence of a business connection among the individuals.

The underlying conceptual distinction expressed in the utility/personal taxonomy is echoed in a number of other studies, though they employ different terminology. For example, Renzulli, Aldrich, and Moody use the term "instrumental" in their study of entrepreneurs to describe links to coworkers or other business associates who provide "support necessary for economic achievement."[32] This is in contrast to friendship and kinship ties, which the authors define as providing primarily social and emotional support. A similar distinction was made by Gomez-Mejia, Nunez-Nickel, and Gutierrez, who contrasted "utilitarian" with "affective" interpersonal ties in their study of family businesses in Spain. The authors characterize affective ties in particular as "more likely to be based on emotions and sentiments . . . prone to depart from economic rationality . . . [and] governed by underlying informal agreements based on affect rather than on utilitarian logic or contractual obligations." Consequently, the authors note, "both parties may attach value to the relationship that goes beyond the economic value created by the transaction."[33] The importance of issues such as status and seniority (and of other ascribed characteristics) helps define the dividing line between affective and instrumental ties.

In summary, I found that common themes in previous treatments of interpersonal ties at work included the delineation of two basic categories of relationship: one based on a shared utilitarian or business interest and the other representing socioemotional relationships, which can compete with or add layers of meaning to ties among coworkers. The former are governed by task-related priorities; this means that individuals see their primary purpose in working with others in the group as goal accomplishment.[34] This does not imply that work group members linked through business interests cannot experience social attraction to one another, but rather that their *primary* reason for the association is utility. In relationships characterized as socioemotional, on the other hand, "emotional rather than rational criteria govern the terms of the exchange."[35]

While this model was a good fit for the themes emerging from my qualitative data, I found the terminology used in previous literature problematic for two reasons. First, there was no consistent common language to describe the qualitative content of interpersonal ties. Second, terminologies that had been proposed in earlier studies seemed insufficiently precise. For example, the utility/personal distinction was vulnerable to the same kind of problems that vex the term "friendship" in the organizational behavior literature: since the words "friendship" and "personal relationship" are both used loosely to encompass a wide range of interpersonal ties, they are difficult to operationalize in a meaningful, causal sense. For example, playing golf with one's boss for the purpose of information exchange or career advancement might be described as "personal" or "friendly" because it took place outside the office or working hours; but the interaction could still meet the criteria for a utility or instrumental relationship as defined above. The golf-with-the-boss example also makes clear why the relational content of interpersonal ties is distinct from dimensions such as the "strength" or "weakness" of the ties: interacting with professional colleagues outside a formal business setting may strengthen a relationship without altering its basic utilitarian character. In other words, working relationships can be strong without evolving into social friendships that would survive outside a context of shared business interests.

To advance the larger aims of this study, including its intended contributions to economic and organizational sociology, a different terminology is needed: one that can provide greater operational specificity than the terms currently in use while also offering consistency and integration with the variety of terms used across studies. I ultimately chose the terms "instrumental" and "affective" for two reasons. First, the distinction is longstanding and well known within the field, employing terms dating back to Bales's work at Harvard in the 1950s. Second, the relatively few studies since that time that touch on the content of interpersonal relations employ either the term "affective" or "instrumental," facilitating the integration of the taxonomy with prior research. Table 4.2 summarizes the defining characteristics of instrumental and affective ties. It should be noted that the distinctions are perceptual rather than outcome-based. That is, they

Table 4.2
Characteristics of Instrumental and Affective Ties

Instrumental	Affective
Low intrinsic value of relationship outside of task setting	High intrinsic value of relationship; would persist outside utilitarian context
Low psychological attachment among actors	High psychological attachment among actors
Provides utilitarian support, including economic and information resources	Provides socioemotional support, potentially economic or utility gains
Governed by mutual utility, contractual obligations	Governed by norms of social obligation, including reciprocity and ascribed characteristics such as status or seniority

are derived from actors' perceptions of the relation and their motives for involvement, rather than from the results of those associations.

Affective and Instrumental Ties across Organizational Domains

It is important to understand that affective ties are present not only in investment clubs and other voluntary associations, or for that matter limited to family businesses, entrepreneurship, or firms outside the United States. Rather, such organizations can be viewed as instantiations of a more general phenomenon of business relations being embedded in webs of affective relations—a phenomenon that may be more prevalent than the current literature would suggest, as implied by the evidence from Wall Street pension fund managers and recent corporate scandals. It is also important to note that individuals can have rational and businesslike motives while still operating within a context of affective ties.

The significance of relational content—instrumental or primarily affective—is the way in which it may impose competing commitments on participants. For example, social friendships among executives and members of their board of directors can impede the board's ability to make sound business decisions when directors put friendship ahead of the best interests of firms and shareholders.[36] Such conflicts between friendship or family obligations on the one hand, and work groups' financial goals on the other, have been documented in the organization studies literature since the 1950s.[37] In such cases, interpersonal ties can represent competing commitments for individuals that undermine their groups' ability to make profitable decisions.

The phenomenon has been observed in a wide variety of settings, from corporate boards to family businesses and entrepreneurial ventures. For example, one ethnographic study from the 1980s followed the transformation of a family-owned office supply firm into a public company. In Weberian terms, the firm shifted from a culture steeped in traditional practices and forms of authority to one based on rational/bureaucratic norms. This transition revealed a host of commitments that competed with the economic interests of shareholders and customers: "What was okay in the once family-operated corporation was not okay when ownership switched to a dollars-and-cents driven conglomerate. It was no longer okay, for example, to *send the boys to Hawaii or pass along a case of wine to a manager's wife*."[38] Such historically sanctioned practices, embedded in the family ties and family culture established by the founders, became a major liability for the firm, limiting financial performance and producing massive upheaval. The attempt to disembed the firm from its founding networks and the commitments they created resulted in takeover by another company, five CEOs in two years, and the loss of a dozen top salespeople. The fifth and final CEO—recruited from outside the company and its founders' networks—was hailed as "a savior" in large part because of his efforts to remove the vestiges of nepotism and the ingrained habits of employees who treated the firm as a personal fiefdom, with their relationship entitling them to enrichment at company expense.[39]

This story is similar to the one presented by sociologists Alejandro Portes and Julia Sensenbrenner in their study of Ecuadorian entrepreneurs.[40] The entrepreneurs' financial successes were occasioned in part by a change in their personal associations, which resolved some of the obstacles to financial accumulation posed by competing social commitments. Many of the entrepreneurs had converted from Catholicism to Evangelical Protestantism, which allowed them to separate their business activity from the context of affective, familial bonds and obligations. In other words, they found in their adopted faith an ideology that resolved the competing commitments they had experienced as Catholics: the Protestant church gave moral legitimacy to the pursuit of profit without a concomitant duty to "share the wealth" through the employment or financial support of extended family members.

Even Wall Street is affected by the embeddedness of business transactions within personal relationships. As the interview study of pension fund managers showed, maintaining friendships was "often more important than the bottom line" in investment firms.[41] In addition, most of the corporate scandals that struck Wall Street during the postboom era can be traced to business deals embedded in a history of friendship ties among the transaction partners. For example, in 2002 and 2003, Ford Motor Company chairman William Clay Ford Jr. was the subject of an investigation by the U.S. Congress for receiving an "improper allocation" of stock in the Goldman Sachs Group—stock purchase rights that investigators claimed belonged to FMC shareholders.[42] It came out in the investigation that Ford had been granted those stock purchase rights by Goldman's (then) president John L. Thornton, a friend of Ford's for thirty years, since they attended prep school together at Hotchkiss. As one of the investigators—House Financial Services Committee chairman Michael G. Oxley (R-OH)—concluded, the "corrupt practices" exposed in the Ford case suggested that "There is no equity in the equities markets."[43]

This is not to say that all friendship or family ties compete or interfere with the business objectives of a work group or organization. Indeed there is a great deal of literature on the benefits of developing friendly social relationships with business associates, both for personal career advancement and for the advancement of interfirm relations.[44] However, those studies focus on outcomes for individuals and firms; in contrast, this study examines the consequences for *work groups* of friendship and other kinds of interpersonal ties among group members.

Evidence from the Survey Data

To test the conceptual distinction I propose, I used the data from my national survey of investment clubs to examine the effect of relational content on work group performance. To conduct these analyses, I operationalized the affective/instrumental distinction by asking individual investment club members to respond yes or no to the following statements: (1) "I socialize with most of the other club members outside of meetings"; (2) "If not for club meetings, I would rarely see most of the other group members"; (3) "Most of the conversation during group meetings concerns investing and other club business"; and (4) "A substantial part of group meetings is spent talking about personal news, social events, family and so on."[45] Respondents who answered yes to questions 1 and 4, *and* no to questions 2 and 3, were classified as having predominantly affective ties to other group members. Respondents who answered yes to questions 2 and 3, *and* no to questions 1 and 4, were coded as having primarily instrumental ties to the others in the group. Other patterns of responses were coded as "mixed." The 11,138 individual responses were aggregated to the group level by calculating the percentage of respondents in each category of tie content, such that the average *club* was found to have 51 percent of members classifying their relationships to the others as primarily instrumental, 44 percent classifying their ties to the group as primarily affective, and 5 percent mixed.[46] Finally, I created two interaction terms (tie type × group age) to account for the possibility of change over time in the impact of affective and instrumental ties, respectively.

Table 4.3 shows the correlation between the percentage of an investment club's members who identified the ties that brought them into the club as primarily instrumental or affective in character. The pattern of association in the survey data corresponds to that in the qualitative study, with affective ties associated with declines in investment returns and instrumental ties associated with increasing financial returns; both coefficients are significant at the .01 level.

Next, using OLS regression, I analyzed the causal relationship between tie content and financial outcomes in investment clubs. I operationalized investment club performance, social category diversity, informational di-

Table 4.3
Correlation Coefficients for Tie Content and Portfolio Performance

Variables	Mean	S.D.	1	2
% affective ties	44.14	26.58		
% Instrumental ties	50.83	25.87	$-.55^{***}$	
Internal rate of return	-20.80	19.88	$-.17^{**}$	$.15^{**}$

$^* p < .05$; $^{**} p < .01$; $^{***} p < .001$ $N = 1,271$ groups

versity, and controls (such as portfolio beta and group age) as described for the regression analyses in chapter 3. Table 4.4 (over, p. 130) shows the coefficients for this analysis:

As the coefficients indicate, there is a significant causal relationship between the content of interpersonal ties among investment club members and the financial performance of the portfolios they select. The larger the proportion of friendship and other socioemotional ties within a group, the worse its portfolio performs; the larger the proportion of relationships based on professional, financial, or academic ties, the better the group performs.

What might account for this connection between interpersonal ties and portfolio outcomes? That is, through what group processes do the history and emotional tone of relations among group members manifest themselves? Answering this question necessitates a return to the qualitative data for insight on the microlevel processes through which the diversity premium is realized—or not.

Decisions and Dissent

When investment clubs make decisions about whether to buy or sell stocks, they are entering socially risky territory. This is in part because discussion and voting may expose conflicts within the group. But there is an even more socially perilous aspect to the process, in that it necessitates a confrontation between the individual who makes a proposal to buy or sell a stock and the other members of the club. Because preparing presentations generally involves a minimum of several hours of work—gathering financial information and making calculations—voting against a proposal means disappointing, and possibly antagonizing, the presenter. The process is made even more confrontational by the use of a show of hands to take votes. This practice, which the vast majority of clubs employ, means that individuals who vote against proposals cannot do so anonymously; their relationship with the presenter may be hurt by a "no" vote.

Table 4.4
Effects of Tie Content on Investment Club Performance

Independent Variables	Financial Performance	
	Rate of Return (%)	Cash Invested
% Affective ties	−.15*	−.19*
% Instrumental ties	.24*	.17*
Group age (months)	.66**	.36**
Group size	.11*	.11*
Portfolio beta	.08**	
Informational diversity	.12**	.02
Social category diversity	−.05	−.07*
Group age × % affective ties	−0.43**	.03
Group age × % instrumental ties	−.39**	.08*
Adjusted R^2	.41	.30
Overall F-ratio	33.28**	31.53**

*$p < .05$; **$p < .01$ $N = 1,245$ groups

Moreover, such votes are required at least once—and often several times—in the course of each club's monthly meeting. Each vote is a "moment of truth" in which individuals must weigh not only the facts presented to them but also whether and how to express their views. In taking a position on the proposal(s) offered them, club members confront the tension between "getting ahead" and "getting along." Some proposals are financially sound and do not force this choice. But investment decisions are judgment calls first and foremost; there are no certainties in the stock market, so there is plenty of room for disagreement, even on a proposal that has been prepared with care.

Given this context, the voting records of clubs in the qualitative study are particularly revealing. Of greatest interest are the proportion of decisions that pass unanimously and the proportion that fail to pass altogether. Since there is so much judgment involved in stock decisions, a high degree of unanimity is unexpected; the proportion of unanimous decisions is also a good indicator of group conformity and the importance clubs assign to social cohesion. And since dissent—particularly the failure of a proposal— is extremely socially threatening, the proportion of failed votes is a good indicator both of a group's commitment to the task and of the leeway allowed dissenting opinions. Measures were operationalized in the following way: if a club voted on ten proposals and five passed unanimously, the measurement of unanimity was 50 percent; if two of the ten votes failed to win a majority, the failure rate was measured as 20 percent.

Table 4.5 shows the voting record for six of the seven clubs in the observational sample.[47] The columns show how many votes each club took on proposals to buy or sell stock over the yearlong observation period and, of these, how many votes passed unanimously and how many failed outright. The selection and recruitment pathways of each club are included for reference.

The results indicate that high-performing clubs sustain a great deal more dissent than low-performing clubs. The vast majority of votes in low-performing clubs are unanimous: so when a member's proposal to buy or sell a stock comes up a for a vote, the result is usually all in favor. In contrast, members of high-performing clubs are much more likely to openly debate each others' ideas; far fewer of their votes pass without dissent. The column showing the number of failed votes indicates that while low-performing clubs almost never allow members' proposals to fail, high-performing clubs do so routinely.

If low-performing groups were not debating investment ideas, how were they spending their two-hour meetings? As part of my observational study, I timed group meetings with a stopwatch, tracking the minutes spent on investing-related matters (such as the status of the group's portfolio, stock purchase or sale proposals, and brokerage arrangements) versus time spent on social topics (such as members' personal lives and club social events). In addition, I tracked the amount of cash each group kept in its portfolio each month, and averaged that over the yearlong observation period. Table 4.6 shows how six of the seven clubs in the observational sample allocated their meeting time and investment assets.[48]

Table 4.5
Decision Record for Clubs in Observational Sample

Club Name	Selection and Recruitment Ties	Unanimous Votes	Failed Votes	Total # Votes
Bulls & Bears	Professional	40%	20%	5
Asset Accumulators	Professional	75%	25%	4
Portfolio Associates	Financial (met through broker)	13%	42%	18
Educating Singles Against Poverty	Friendship	75%	0%	4
Ladies with Leverage	Friendship	100%	0%	6
California Investors	Friendship	63%	6%	16

Table 4.6
Time and Asset Use in Observational Sample

Club Name	Selection and Recruitment Ties	Performance	% of Discussion Spent on Stocks	% of Portfolio in Cash
Bulls & Bears	Professional	High	53	8
Asset Accumulators	Professional	High	63	3
Portfolio Associates	Financial (met through broker)	High	54	0.2
Educating Singles Against Poverty	Friendship	Low	25	27
Ladies with Leverage	Friendship	Low	43	27
California Investors	Friendship	Low	41	19

I found that low-performing clubs spent, on average, less than half their meeting time on stocks and kept large reserves of idle cash in their portfolios—a significant drag on portfolio performance—not as a matter of strategy but as a consequence of not making investment decisions. In contrast, high-performing clubs spent more than half their time on stock presentations and discussions, and were nearly fully invested.

Group Processes That Work . . . and Those That Don't

To specify the processes through which investment clubs managed the tensions between "getting ahead" and "getting along," the following case studies from the qualitative data illustrate how different groups handled the information available to them in making investment decisions. As the four case illustrations show, the high-performing clubs in the qualitative study were able to make the most of their informational diversity by constraining club discussions within the boundaries of a legitimate, depersonalized discourse—their investment philosophy. In contrast, the low performers developed strategies for avoiding debate (and thus conflict) altogether.

Asset Accumulators and "Three Strikes, It's Out"

In September 1997, Jill proposed that the club buy shares in Rotech—a medical services firm. She handed out a sheet she had prepared giving the financial analysis of the firm: price, price-earnings ratio, return on invested capital, and so on. As she began reading this information aloud, Josie interrupted her, noting that two of the key indicators of financial health were down. In terms of the club's investment philosophy, Josie said, Rotech "is already a 'no.' " Jill resumed reading her report, but when she mentioned Rotech's heavy debt, Molly interrupted her again. Combined with the other two financial problems, Molly said, Rotech's debt clearly did not meet the club's standards: "three strikes—it's out," she said. When the proposal was put to a vote, it failed 2 to 10—the only time a vote failed in Asset Accumulators during the entire yearlong observation period.

Most of the time, when members pointed out financial problems in a stock presentation, the proposal never came to a vote; rather, it "fell off" the table when no one made a motion to buy or sell. This strategy—unique in the ethnographic sample—took weak ideas out of the running without creating social tension. At the same time, social considerations did not keep ideas on the table when they were fundamentally flawed. For example, Berry was the acknowledged leader of Asset Accumulators; the other members described her in interviews as "our guiding light." This was in part because of her long and successful personal investing experience and her participation in another investment club prior to joining Asset Accumulators. Still, three of her four stock presentations never even made it to a vote. (The fourth one passed unanimously.)

Portfolio Associates and NACT Communications

In March 1998, Dave proposed that the club buy stock in a start-up telecommunications firm called NACT. He provided extensive financial information and noted that the firm was being strongly endorsed by the financial press. It was also a takeover candidate, which meant that the stock would probably go up in anticipation of the buyout. But despite the positive tenor of the presentation, three members picked up immediately on flaws in the financial picture. Barney remarked that the quality of the presentation concerned him: "we're falling short of our mission (as a club)— we need data and analysis." Dave, taking offense, responded "you're being kind of picky—I worked hard on this!" Rather than backing down, Barney pursued his point, saying, "well you haven't succeeded in communicating the data to me!"

Though this peak of social tension passed, it was replaced by increased factual probing of the weaknesses of the proposal. For example, the club president noted that the presentation had simply ignored several years' worth of negative data. Another member asked how the club could be sure that NACT's profits would continue to rise. Several other members pointed out that the graph of projected profits was misleading, making a difference between earnings of one cent and two cents per share look equivalent to the difference between one dollar and two dollars of earnings per share.

The proposal came to a vote and failed 3 to 9. Following the vote, Barney underscored the "moral" of the story for the whole club: "We have a philosophy to uphold—if you don't want to invest based on fundamental analysis, you can cash out." The debate pushed aggressively at the boundary between getting ahead and getting along, emphasizing the former to the point of discomfort. Though the tension stopped short of provoking dissolution, some members left this meeting shaking their heads somberly; one was overheard muttering "this used to be fun."

ESAP and Avoidance

In May 1997, Bert voiced some reservations during a presentation on a proposed purchase of stock in Viking Office Products. Viking was in the midst of takeover negotiations, and its future was somewhat uncertain. "We shouldn't get involved in such a complex situation with so many other stocks to buy," Bert said. "We don't need the risk." He suggested that the club wait until the merger was complete and look again in a few months. The other members did not agree, and continued with their review of the firm's financials. When the matter came to a vote, Bert did not vote against the proposal—he simply recused himself. Five months later, a different member—Sheila—abstained from voting on another stock, meaning that the vote was recorded in the minutes as passing without objection. In this way, conflict was rendered not only invisible but—in an important distinction from Asset Accumulators—unavailable for acknowledgment or discussion.

Of ESAP's four decisions, only one was *not* unanimous, and that involved one "no" vote by the most socially isolated member of the group. Of the other three votes, two involved suppression of debate and diversity: members who disagreed with the majority abstained from voting. Thus, unanimity did not reflect true consensus but an attempt to mask dissent. Even the unanimity of the fourth vote was somewhat suspect, in that it was taken verbally rather than by a show of hands: everyone in favor said "aye" all at once; no one spoke up when the president called for "no" votes. The whole process happened so quickly that it was impossible to tell if anyone had abstained. This is consistent with the research definition of "getting along" as a set of passive, avoidant "inactions."[49]

California Investors and the Stop-Loss Policy

The members of California Investors developed an automated method for avoiding conflict: they structured their decision process so that the most highly contentious decisions were taken out of their hands. The issue was when to sell stocks—one of the most difficult decisions for all investors, because it often involves taking a loss. As numerous economic studies have shown, people hate realizing losses on their investments and will hold on to poorly performing stocks almost indefinitely.[50] One member echoed this finding during one of the many debates about the club's selling practices, saying, "selling is such an emotional issue; we need to guard against our emotions."

This member was defending the club's attempt to guard against emotionally charged conflict through its practice of "stop-loss" selling: an automated process that the club adopted several years ago to avoid its most heated debates. "Stop-loss" selling means telling a broker to sell one's position in a stock when the price falls below a selected threshold. In the case of California Investors, the members had put a stop-loss order on all the stocks in their portfolio, so that they would sell automatically if they ever dipped 20 percent below the purchase price.

In process terms, this meant that stock could be sold without discussion or a vote. Once members had agreed on the policy, the rest was out of their hands. Without this policy, the members would have had to go through the whole process of proposing the sale, debating the proposal and voting on it with all the attendant social risks. As several members pointed out, this would have created nearly insoluble conflict because there was so much diversity of opinion about investing within the group. As the club treasurer said to me on three or four occasions, "We have no consistent investment philosophy."

The club's stated motivation for the stop-loss policy was to "protect gains" by selling before a stock's price dipped below the amount originally paid for it. In practice, however, the club lost a tremendous amount of money through this strategy. Often, California Investors was "sold out of" a stock when the price dropped on one of the many steep—but temporary—market corrections of the past year. Usually, the stock recaptured its losses the following day and then surged on to new highs. This left the club members in the position of buying back the stock at the next meeting for more than they had paid for it originally, plus transaction costs on both the sell and buy sides.

The club's history with Intel stock demonstrates the financial consequences of the stop-loss policy: California Investors bought one hundred shares of Intel in December 1996 and sold on stop-loss a year later (December 1997) for a gain of $256; the next month (January 1998), they bought back those one hundred shares, only to be "stopped out" three months later (April 1998) for a loss of $460. Instead of protecting its gains, the club's strategy locked in losses. Had the club simply bought the stock in December 1996 and held on through April 1998, it would have had a net gain of $200 rather than a net loss of $204. Counting three sets of brokerage fees, it actually lost more than that. Members of the club were aware that their strategy was not working; as the club president said, "we have a history of selling at the bottom." But as the members of California Investors saw it, automating the tough decisions was the only way to preserve the club.

Discussion

The case data suggest that investment clubs use fundamentally different decision-making processes based on path dependencies created by their modes of selection and recruitment; the effects are particularly strong when it comes to handling differences of opinion. In this small sample, the clubs based on what I have called instrumental ties among members institutionalized mechanisms for channeling dissent in productive ways: they established norms about evaluating member proposals in terms of a shared investment philosophy, providing an impersonal standard against which all proposals can be evaluated. In fact, among the most profitable clubs in the qualitative study, all used NAIC guidelines as the basis of their investment philosophy. This says less about the validity of the NAIC stock analysis method than it does about the value of having a clear, shared, impersonal standard against which members can evaluate each other's work.

It is also important to note that these cases point to a special issue facing mixed clubs in decision making: they are vulnerable to a gender-based conformity process in which women defer to men. This is part of the more general phenomenon of status processes in groups, in which lower-status group members participate in and influence decisions less than high-status members.[51] In ESAP, for example, all four stock purchases were instigated at the suggestion of the three men in the group. Women did the research on these suggestions and made the presentations as well, but never made a motion to buy; that task was performed by the men in the club. In other words, men both proposed and ratified all the clubs' decisions, while the women did the data-gathering work.

In contrast, women had a much greater leadership role in Bulls & Bears—even though there were fewer of them than in ESAP, where women made up two-thirds of the membership. Of the four women members of Bulls & Bears, three contributed a stock to the group's portfolio: in each case, the woman developed the idea, did the research, gave the presentation, and made the motion to buy. Since the fourth woman was new to the club, her failure to propose a stock purchase may have reflected her tenure rather than her gender. In addition, all of the six men in the club contributed stock purchase ideas that passed.

Based on this small sample, it remains to be shown whether mixed clubs in the aggregate can sustain more diversity of opinion than same-sex clubs. To do so, they must work against status dynamics that tend to suppress women's participation. One explanation for the persistence of the diversity premium in spite of this countervailing force may be found in the transitivity of the history and "emotional tone" (as well as roles and norms) of the interpersonal ties through which members were selected and recruited into the club.

For instance, organizations like ESAP, which emerge from prior social ties, may be more likely to fall into traditional patterns of male-female interaction, in which men lead and women follow.[52] In contrast, groups like Bulls & Bears, which emerge from instrumental ties, may be less likely to employ a gendered division of labor. After all, in the setting from which they emerge, men and women work together as peers. The network factor might explain two things: why not *all* mixed-gender clubs perform well and why *most* of them still do better than same-sex clubs. The hypothesis suggested by this analysis is that while some mixed clubs emerge from affective networks, so many more are based on task relationships that in the aggregate the mixed clubs do not fall prey to traditional gender dynamics and thus maintain their edge over all-female or all-male clubs.

Further support for this explanation is provided by recent research in organizational demography, showing that people who are in the minority in terms of social category are often *expected* to hold information or opinions that differ from those of majority members. One such study found that when group members observe social category diversity in others, it "primes" them to receive differences of opinion that might otherwise cause destructive conflicts. In other words, gender diversity (or other types of social diversity) can "trigger expectations that deep-level diversity [such as informational differences] will be present, making group members less surprised when differing perspectives emerge."[53] Conversely, majority group members are not expected to hold divergent views or information compared with other majority members. The implication is that in clubs like Bulls & Bears, where women are slightly in the minority, women would have more influence voicing uniquely held information, whereas in majority-female groups like ESAP, information and opinions from women would carry less weight. This creates a kind of synergistic effect between social category diversity and informational diversity, through which the former can in some situations enable groups to benefit from the latter, yielding the "diversity premium."

Future Research

The evidence presented in this chapter suggests that decision-making groups "get ahead" to the extent that they can withstand the numerous forces pushing members toward conformity of opinion. Selection, recruitment, and group composition may stack the deck in favor of homogeneity of opinion, but group processes determine how the cards are played. The result can be a flourishing of "productive controversy" and profitable decision-making, even where demographic diversity is low, as in Asset Accumulators—an all-women's group in which members were all in the same profession (teaching) and age cohort. On the other hand, ineffective group processes can result in wasted resources and poor performance, as in the case of ESAP, where conformity and stereotyped role behaviors suppressed the potential benefits of the members' gender and informational diversity. The findings are suggestive for future research on work groups and teams, as well as on the broader issues of social capital and social liability.

The intended theoretical contribution of this part of my study is to show that interpersonal ties work not just in terms of strength or weakness, or structural holes, but through what Granovetter calls the "history and emotional tone" of relations. These qualitative aspects of interpersonal ties can assert themselves in the ways illustrated above, forming the basis for alliances or enmities that may be exogenous to the group's task but can nonetheless influence the outcome.

A signal characteristic of these aspects of interpersonal ties is the way in which they can create "competing commitments," in which individuals find themselves having to choose between preserving relationships within the group or advancing the group's instrumental agenda. This can result in the kind of "rubber-stamping" of decisions that characterized many of the investment groups based on friendship ties, in which investment proposals were not subjected to appropriate levels of scrutiny in terms of profit potential; instead, members made their evaluations in terms of the likely impact of their comments and votes on their relationships with other group members.

The findings from investment clubs invite us to reengage problems that were once central to sociological research but have since moved toward the margins of the field, such as the tensions between task achievement and socioemotional bonding in work groups, or the qualitative aspects of interpersonal ties among team members.[54] Two findings with particular relevance to the sociology of work and organizations stem from the proposed conceptualization of interpersonal ties as either primarily instrumental or primarily affective in "relational content":

- Different types of relationships among work group members have a significant effect on group-level outcomes such as performance. The greater the percentage of instrumental ties among individuals, the better the group is at using its resources effectively and turning a profit. In contrast, affective ties among work group members come with built-in liabilities for goal achievement, creating obligations and motives that can conflict with individuals' commitment to the group's task objectives. This observation underscores the need for researchers to develop more finely grained analyses of interpersonal ties in work groups, taking account of the nature of relationships among actors rather than just the structure or intensity of those relationships.

- The qualitative aspects of interpersonal ties have quite different effects depending on the level of analysis at which outcomes are measured. In relation to the existing literature, one of the most significant findings of my research is that friendship ties—which have been shown to have positive effects at the level of individual career advancement or interfirm relations—may have a negative effect on outcomes at the intrafirm or work group level. While individuals and firms may benefit from mixing business and socioemotional relationships, such affective bonds can undermine performance in work groups by representing competing commitments, creating obligations and loyalties that conflict with utilitarian objectives such as task performance. What is synergistic at the individual and interfirm level may be ineffective for work groups. This finding is particularly relevant for the social capital literature, which has often emphasized the positive aspects of affective relationships at work—an issue that will be addressed in more detail in chapter 6.[55]

It is important to restate that asserting the causal role of relational content in interpersonal ties does not duplicate the "weak/strong" taxonomy made famous by Granovetter.[56] For example, a relation of a primarily social character may vary from weak—as with nodding acquaintances—to strong, as with best friends. By the same token, an interpersonal tie that is understood by interactants as primarily instrumental in nature can also be weak—as in the brief transactions between a street vendor and a regular customer— or strong, as with the relation between lawyer and client in a drawn-out court case.

Ultimately, this chapter proposes not only that the history and emotional tone of relations among group members are consequential for investment club outcomes but also that these qualitative aspects of interpersonal ties deserve more broad theoretical consideration as causal variables in models of group performance. The evidence presented here suggests that the qualitative content of relations among group members enters into their decision-making and problem-solving processes, whether or not that influence is acknowledged. While such factors have received less attention in recent years than they once did from organizational researchers, the spate of corporate influence scandals that arose in the early part of the twenty-first century reminds us that such social processes continue to thrive despite the elaboration of structures and rhetorics of bureaucracy and disinterested professionalism. Indeed, one advantage of studying investment clubs is that, because they exist in a liminal space between the modern business world and the traditional world of affective associations, they allow us to observe more clearly the conflicting currents that often run unacknowledged through economic and organizational phenomena.

APPENDIX ◆
Additional Analyses of the Effects of Interpersonal Ties

This evidence presented in this chapter suggests that affective and instrumental interpersonal ties among members have significant effects on financial performance in investment clubs. However, there are a number of alternative explanations for these effects that must be addressed. This appendix details the additional tests I conducted, using the data described in the appendix to chapter 3.

I conducted additional analyses to explore the possibility of selection bias in the findings discussed in this chapter. Two alternative explanations suggested themselves. The first was that performance might be driving selection and recruitment, biasing interpersonal ties in the group toward greater instrumentality. That is, individuals linked through instrumental ties might preferentially seek out membership in high-performing investment clubs, so that performance drove utilitarian construal of relationships rather than instrumental ties themselves causing high performance. A second alternative account would involve selection bias in the sample of investment clubs chosen for this study. This would occur if low-performing organizations based on instrumental ties drop out of the population at a higher rate than low-performing organizations based on affective ties. I tested both possibilities and found that the data do not support either contention.

In the first case, there are several reasons to expect that performance does *not* create the type of interpersonal ties formed among work group participants. As discussed above, most investment groups in this sample were formed very recently as of the date of the survey; 21.7 percent were under a year old, and 50.1 percent were under two years old. Given that most individuals in these groups joined at the time of inception, they could not have known in advance what the performance of the group would be. In addition, if performance did drive the selection process by which more instrumentally oriented individuals chose their groups, one would expect that there would be more movement into and out of groups as performance results became clearer, and that lower performance would be associated with smaller group size. Yet the data show that there is very little movement of members into or out of groups. As a final check, I regressed organizations' financial performance on the rate at which new members entered the club, controlling for the departure of previous members. The causal relationship was negative and significant, though modest in size ($-.11$, $p < .05$). It suggests not only that high performance does *not* drive recruitment but also that the lower the financial performance in an investment club, the more new members it attracts, and these new members are not replacing others departing as a result of low performance. This economically counterintuitive result may occur because work groups in which participants are instrumentally oriented toward one another are less socially pleasant—and perhaps less attractive to new members—than their lower-performing counterparts. These trade-offs between socioemotional benefits and optimal task performance have been observed repeatedly in small-groups research and will be discussed in greater detail in the subsequent chapters.[57]

In the second case, I used the data set described in the appendix to chapter 3 to test the possibility that my sample might be biased by a higher propensity to disband among low-performing clubs based on instrumental ties. Of the seventeen disbanded groups, 53 percent were based on affective ties; 47 percent were based on instrumental ties. Groups based on affective and instrumental ties also broke up for different reasons. Lack of participation or member commitment was the primary reason for disbanding for all clubs in the sample, with clubs based on instrumental ties facing an additional set of problems not mentioned by the other organizations: work-related instability because of layoffs, business travel, and job transfers. For example, one high-performing group composed of U.S. Navy officers had to disband because most were transferred out of state or overseas as part of their military obligations. The following responses from survey participants indicate the types of problems the clubs faced:

Club #3 (instrumental): "The main reason and probably the only reason is that we were [are] all in the military [navy] . . . I don't feel we broke up for lack of interest or lack of participation. It was just the fact that we all had to go separate ways." (Members were transferred to other states.)

Club #15 (affective): "The meetings became more social than educational, with extensive spreads of snacks and drinks . . . The club broke up because of differing philosophies. Some didn't want to study but wanted to buy impulsively or on someone's recommendation. Others were more serious. Most found little time to research and present a stock at a meeting."

Club #8 (instrumental): "The club was organized at our place of employment. Most of the members traveled a lot and were unavailable for club meetings."

None of the disbanded clubs reported that performance was a factor; in fact, a number of instrumentally based clubs reported disbanding in spite of members' perceptions that the group was performing well. These data suggest that there is little reason for concern about the possibility of selection bias via increased rates of disbanding among low-performing clubs based on instrumental ties.

*At the risk of shocking sociologists, I should be inclined to say
that it is their job to render social or historical context more
intelligible than it was in the experience of those who lived it.
All sociology is a reconstruction that aspires to confer intelli-
gibility on human existence, which, like all human existences,
are confused and obscure.*
—RAYMOND ARON[1]

Aftermath and Implications

SECTION THREE

The creation story of contemporary economic sociology begins in the 1950s, when sociologist Talcott Parsons made a verbal treaty with the economists whose offices adjoined his in Harvard's Littauer Hall—a division of epistemological territory in which sociologists got "values" and economists got "value"; economists got "the market" while sociologists got the social relationships in which markets are embedded.[2] But within a generation, sociologists began to chafe at these boundaries, leading to breakthrough work that encroached on economists' reserved areas of inquiry by proposing alternative, *sociological* accounts of markets and value. For example, Harrison White asserted that markets are not merely embedded in social relations; they *are* social relations.[3] Other sociologists countered economists' unitary conception of value by arguing that in modern economies there are always multiple metrics of value available, and that the study of markets requires us to account for conflict and change in the ways actors adjudicate among these metrics.[4]

The present study contributes to this expansionist movement in economic sociology in several ways. First, it lends support to White's contention that economy *is* society—thus the assertion earlier in this book that investment clubs are "markets in microcosm." The claim is that all investing is a social undertaking, whether it occurs between brokers and clients, among neighbors, on trading floors, in networks of institutional investors, or within investment clubs. By approaching investor behavior from an interactionist framework, employing the techniques of "sociological miniaturism,"[5] this study can shed light on what the oft-used term "embeddedness" really means in practice.

For example, the data from investment clubs support previous work showing that markets are rarely a matter of "spot" transactions in which strangers engage in one-time exchanges. Rather most commerce, even in a world in which computerized buying and selling is common, still involves highly personalized interactions in which status, trust, and reputation matter as much as—if not more than—prices.[6] In settings such as eBay, for example, where trade is conducted in conditions that closely approximate an ideal-typical spot market (i.e., strangers who are unlikely ever to meet in person engage in what are usually one-time transactions), a seller's good reputation increases the sale price of an item by an average of 7.6 percent.[7] In the context of the stock market, I argue, how individuals spend their money is intimately linked to their position in the social cartography (as defined by coordinates such as gender), which gives them distinctive perspectives on the market and other investors.

Second, by identifying several previously undertheorized social forces that shape investors' decision making, I show that financial measures vie with identity-based metrics to create a complex environment composed not of rational or irrational motives but of *competing* logics of exchange. Further, I show that it is through storytelling that these contests are conducted and lines of action established. In this way, I seek to bring the insights of social psychology, symbolic interaction, and other modes of "miniaturism" to bear on the study of investor behavior. I intend this to further understanding of the social underpinnings of financial markets.

Like any study, this one is imperfect and limited. The bulk of the research took place during the unusual conditions that characterized the U.S. stock market during the late 1990s. It could be, for example, that phenomena I observed—such as the importance of stories to investment decisions—arise only during times of great market volatility. (Though it must be said that many finance scholars believe that "excess volatility"—that is, price fluctuations that greatly exceed actual changes in the fundamental value of securities—is now a permanent feature of the stock market.)[8] Second, the full scope of the investment club phenomenon is unknown, and probably unknowable without undertaking a multimillion-dollar research program.

However, the object of this study has been *exploratory*, acknowledging that the market system is extremely complex and that much remains to be understood. In recognition of this, I have adopted the strategy outlined by Jane Jacobs in her classic study of a complex system, *The Death and Life of Great American Cities*. Following her method, I have taken a "microscopic or detailed view" of a system and have worked "inductively, reasoning from the particulars to the general, rather than the reverse," and focusing on processes and " 'unaverage' clues involving small quantities, which reveal the way larger and more 'average' quantities are operating."[9] Thus, this study is not intended to be the definitive word on investment clubs, amateur investors, or financial markets, but rather the beginning of a research conversation enriched by increasing convergence and cooperation among disciplines.

Specifically, I designed this research to explore three questions about the investment club phenomenon—questions I hope will offer a productive basis for future research:

1. What forces gave rise to the surge in the ranks of amateur investors during the 1990s?
2. How did these investors understand their own motives and behavior, and what were their "theories of mind" about other participants in the market?
3. What is the likely impact of this rapid change on the culture, politics, and economy of the United States?

Having addressed the first question in chapters 1 and 2 of the book, and the second question in chapters 3 and 4, I will now turn to the third question by reviewing the results of a follow-up study I conducted with the participants in the ethnography I originally undertook in 1998.

When I returned to the San Francisco Bay Area in February 2004, I did not know whether any of the seven groups I had studied six years earlier would still be in operation, given the steep decline of the U.S. stock market that began in April of 2000. To my surprise, I found that four of the groups were still going strong—battered, but not bowed, by the bursting of the high-tech bubble. I was even able to interview most of the members of the three groups that had disbanded. My primary goal in reconnecting with them was to understand what they had learned from the past few years of stock market decline, as well as to gather their reflections on investing during the frenzied market of the 1990s. A second major goal was to explore their group dynamics, particularly to find what led some to stay together and others to disband—and whether that outcome was connected to their financial gains or losses. Consistent with the small-scale study of disbanded clubs I had conducted in 1998, I found that performance was loosely connected, if at all, with a club's survival. Of the four groups that remained in business, all had lost substantial sums of money compared with their cash outlay—most estimated the loss at between one-third and one-half of the club's precrash portfolio value. Perhaps tellingly, few of them kept detailed enough records for me to confirm these figures independently; maybe not knowing exactly how much they lost was part of what enabled them to survive.

Another effort to dissociate commitment to the club from its financial situation came from the members of the three clubs that had disbanded. All vehemently denied that money had anything to do with their decision to split up, citing other factors—such as fragile network ties—instead. This was consistent with the data from the small sample of disbanded clubs I had studied in 1998, though my 2004 interviews yielded much richer data on the internal workings that lead members to dissolve their groups.

Table III.1 summarizes the status of the seven clubs at the time of the follow-up study. For the groups that remained intact, I was able to use their current records to calculate their annualized internal rate of return—the standard performance measure for NAIC clubs that I have used throughout this study. For disbanded clubs, I spoke to the treasurers and either obtained the last accounting statement or used the treasurer's best estimate of the group's returns. While the estimates are obviously less reliable than the accounting statements, the goal of this section will not be to document rates of return with precision, but rather to explain what lies

Table III.1

Club Survival and Performance

Club	Still Together?	Compound Annual Return from Inception through 2/04 or Date Disbanded
Portfolio Associates	Yes	24%
Valley Gay Men's Investment Club	Yes	16%
Ladies with Leverage	Yes	3%
California Investors	Yes	–2%
Bulls & Bears	No	30%
Asset Accumulators	No	22%
Educating Singles Against Poverty	No	9%

behind the numbers: the story of what these clubs had been doing for the previous six years.

The events leading up to these results are recounted in chapter 5. In chapter 6, I discuss the impact that investors like these have had on public policy, civil society, and the behavior of publicly traded firms. For example, during the 2000 presidential campaign, advisers to George W. Bush unveiled a proposal to allow Americans to invest a portion of their Social Security benefits in the stock market—based largely on the mass movement into investing during the 1990s, which was driven in part by participation in investment clubs. Bush and his campaign staff argued that as the majority of Americans had recently become investors, both their expectations and their financial savvy had increased, necessitating a change in the federal retirement insurance program. As one member of the Bush staff said, "People have an understanding of how markets work, and are used to securing a higher return on their savings."[10]

While this proposal never got off the ground—despite the repeated efforts by the Bush administration—it did generate a new set of terms to describe what it means to be American in the twenty-first century. When the majority of registered voters (as opposed to the adult population as a whole) became investors, the *New York Times* coined the term "shareholder democracy."[11] More recently, President Bush adopted the term "ownership society" to describe the electorate. Both phrases have come into everyday use outside of policy circles, and both imply a new conception of what it means to be an American. In previous eras, the prototypical citizen was a landowner—Jefferson's "yeoman farmer"—or the small-business owner conjured up by the maxim attributed to Calvin Coolidge: "the business of

America is business." In the twenty-first century, however, the prototypical American is defined by his or her stock portfolio.

This has significant implications for civil society and recent claims that Americans have withdrawn from civic engagement. If, as Robert Putnam famously suggested, most of us are now "bowling alone," we are certainly not investing alone. One of Putnam's chief metrics is the shrinkage of participation in clubs: he claims that attendance at club meetings has decreased by 58 percent in the past twenty-five years.[12] Is the popularity of investment clubs the exception that proves the rule, or do these clubs represent a challenge to Putnam's thesis? These questions will be addressed in more detail in the final chapter of the book.

The book concludes with implications and new directions for research in economic sociology. The model sociology offers for understanding economic behavior (including socially responsible investing and other forms of what I have called "identity investing") foregrounds the role of processes—that unifying theme among systems of organized complexity. In particular, economic sociology proposes that processes of social interaction are central to the understanding of exchange. This means that any account of economic behavior must acknowledge that the assessment of value is itself a kind of process—an emergent characteristic of particular interactions, which evolves out of the simultaneous processes of formulating one's own strategy and aims while attempting to anticipate the strategies and aims of others. The final section of chapter 6 links the data and theories used in the previous chapters to show how this study contributes to a more detailed specification of valuation and exchange processes; it concludes with a new model of competing modes of exchange, to be examined in future research.

*For men to plunge headlong into an undertaking of vast change,
they must be intensely discontented yet not destitute, and they
must have the feeling that by the possession of some potent doc-
trine, infallible leader or new technique they have access to a
source of irresistible power. They must also have an extravagant
conception of the prospects and potentialities of the future. Finally, they must be wholly ignorant of the difficulties involved in
their vast undertaking. Experience is a handicap.*
—ERIC HOFFER[1]

Reflections on Investing in the 1990s ◆ 5

The Uses of Disenchantment

In reconnecting with the participants in my observational sample, the most
surprising finding was that all of them were still investing. Though they
recognized that much had changed since the 1990s, many said they had
no choice but to keep buying stocks. As Troy of Valley Gay Men's Investment Club put it, "Where else are we going to put our money? In the
mattress?" Among the groups that remained intact as of 2004, their patterns of investment decision-making were similar to those I had observed
in 1999. For example, the members of Portfolio Associates continued to
bicker amicably after amassing over $1 million in stock holdings; of the
twelve members, seven had withdrawn more money than they had invested
over the fifty years the club had been in business. The men of Valley Gay
Men's Investment Club had experienced some turnover, but five of the
original members remained, six new ones had joined, and most of the
stock purchases I had observed them making six years before were still in
the portfolio, including Dollar General, Amgen, Lear, and Medtronic.

California Investors was in many ways unchanged. One member had
died, and two new ones had joined, but otherwise it was the same group,
meeting in the same country club, making the same jokes at each others'
expense, and using the same investment strategies. The group continued
to use stop-loss orders as a way of automating sell decisions, and they
continued to use their business connections as their primary source of data

about stocks. In reviewing the portfolio, instead of requesting a formal financial analysis like other clubs, California Investors relied on its members' social capital for information. For example, when it came time to review the club's holdings in Caremark—a pharmaceutical services company—the club president turned to one of the members and said, "Stan, you just played golf with the chief information officer of Caremark. Can you give us any insight on what's going on with that company?"

Similarly, I found that the members of Ladies with Leverage were still evaluating stocks through the lens of their consumer experience; on the day I attended their meeting, the firms under consideration included the restaurant chain Macaroni Grill and the clothing retailer Chico's. Karen dismissed the restaurant by noting that the food was mediocre. However, the entire group nodded favorably at the mention of Chico's, with Tanya adding that she owns the store's entire travel wardrobe. As soon as the conversation turned to travel, the investment discussion was derailed by Connie's observation that LWL "must be doing something wrong, because my friend's investment club has their annual meeting at the Ritz Carlton spa, and they write it off as a business expense on their taxes." Karen and Georgia reminded the club that the members had originally planned to go to Paris when they "cashed out" of their investments, "even if we have to go in walkers!"

But some things *had* changed: the stock market had been down or flat since April 2000, and a string of scandals had cast doubt on the trustworthiness of corporate accounting and stock brokers. When I asked current and former investment club members how they were able to continue investing—alone or in their groups—following these upheavals, I found a surprising frankness and resiliency. Virtually all the participants I interviewed expressed resignation about and even a sense of *complicity* in the decline of the bull market. As Greg of the disbanded club Bulls & Bears put it:

> I knew it was a sham back then. I was just riding it as long as I could. I remember being so surprised that a start-up like Iomega was valued more highly than General Motors; there's no way a start-up could be worth more than GM on the first day of trading. I knew there was cheating going on in the whole market, how some people got in on IPOs and some did not, and I knew I was only a two-bit player, because I had to buy stock on the open market. I knew there was favoritism among boards of directors. It was all a sham when people said, "It's a new era, things are different now." I never believed it. And the scandals haven't damaged my trust in the system

because I never trusted it to begin with. So some people got special deals from mutual fund managers—so what? I work at [a major defense contractor]: we see special deals all the time!

Cate, also of Bulls & Bears, gave a strikingly similar account in a separate interview, unaware of Greg's remarks. She said that during the 1990s, "We sort of knew the books were cooked; I kind of saw it coming." But unlike Greg, who pulled his money out of the stock market for a few years after the market downturn (he started investing again in 2002), Cate says she "never considered getting out of the market; I still believe in the business models, even though the top management is corrupt."

The notion of corruption in upper management was a matter to be taken for granted, according to most of the participants in my study. While one or two expressed shock at the revelations uncovered by the Enron trial and Elliott Spitzer's prosecution of mutual funds, the majority shared the view of Karen, a member of Ladies with Leverage who remarked: "My experience in the work world taught me that businesspeople cheat all the time, so the scandals didn't come as a surprise. But in the 1990s, people weren't looking that closely at the veracity of the numbers, either, because it was all good news. That's just human nature—why look a gift horse in the mouth?" In fact, Karen's position—that investors in the 1990s were in some way responsible for the bubble by failing to look closely at the stocks in which they invested—was echoed by several other participants. Frank of Valley Gay Men's Investment Club said that when the members were confronted with facts or reliable data on the stocks they owned, or were considering for purchase, "we would discount the data and manipulate it to fit our needs." Similarly, Dan of California Investors summed up the attitude of his group toward analysis during the 1990s as "Don't confuse us with the facts, because we already have our minds made up."

Yet while all the participants continued to invest in the stock market, the changes in the market environment of the previous few years had brought discernible alterations in their behavior. Initially, most said, when the stock market began its freefall, they simply froze, like deer in the headlights. Unsure what the declines in stock valuations meant, or how long they would last, the majority of participants in this study entered a state of temporary paralysis in which they neither bought nor sold. This was followed by a more conservative turn: a few began investing in real estate, but most simply focused on investing in "bigger, safer firms"—especially those that paid cash dividends. As Stan of California Investors put it, "I love cash dividends; you can't fudge a cash dividend." This "show me the money" response was echoed by the members of Valley Gay Men's

Investment Club as well as the defunct Bulls & Bears, whose members continued to invest on their own. Like Cate of Bulls & Bears, none of the people I interviewed saw ceasing to invest in the stock market as an option. As Connie of Ladies with Leverage put it, unwittingly echoing Troy of the Valley Gay Men's Investment Club, "We have no alternative to putting money in the stock market. Where else are we going to put it—under the mattress?"

Several participants also noted their increased reliance on professional money managers, but only those with whom they had long-term, face-to-face relationships. For example, Janet of ESAP turned her investments over to a professional money manager, but only because he was her nephew. Greg of Bulls & Bears, who took all his money out of the market for two years, said he only trades "based on the recommendations of people I know personally"—a major shift from his reliance on analysis of firms' financial data during the 1990s. Greg and virtually all the other participants I interviewed had lost trust in traditional financial advisers, including mutual fund managers and brokers. As Carla of ESAP put it, "I don't know whom to trust. I'm not sure if NAIC's system is wrong, but their system assumes that you can trust firms' financial statements, and I have no idea what to do now that we know you can't trust anything firms tell you."

Such comments resound as a coda to remarks made by Federal Reserve Board chairman Alan Greenspan during his June 1999 commencement address at Harvard University: "Trust is at the root of any economic system based on mutually beneficial exchange. In virtually all transactions, we rely on the word of those with whom we do business . . . If a significant number of businesspeople violated the trust upon which our interactions are based, our court system and *our economy would be swamped into immobility.*" With his usual prescience, Greenspan accurately assessed the psychological impact of the degradation of trust in financial markets almost a full year prior to the dot.bomb debacle and the discovery by the public that much of the market boom had been built on accounting fraud and other deceptions.

My data suggest that the results have gone beyond a temporary paralysis to create a longer-term attitude of resignation toward corruption in financial markets. While the investors I studied continue to put their money into U.S. stocks, they appear to be doing so based not on the generalized, impersonal trust in the "system" that Greenspan says is necessary for the economy to function. Rather, they invest by default—out of a sense that they lack good alternatives—and via close personal ties that limit the information and investment opportunities available to them.

Fear and Self-Loathing after the Boom

Despite the apparent failings in the market system, the most intense re-
criminations voiced by the participants in this study were reserved for
themselves, rather than for corporations or financial managers. Several
participants used the word "delusional" to describe their thinking during
the bull market. Others used phrases that hinted at a sort of temporary
insanity: "We thought we were brilliant." "We were living in a fool's para-
dise." Still others judged themselves in terms reminiscent of an old-time
revival meeting. Cate of Bulls & Bears said, "We got greedy—it was too
easy for us. We forgot the basic principles." Frank of Valley Gay Men's
Investment Club put it even more bluntly: "We were money whores back
then—we would buy anything that would make us a buck."

And in the classic mode of redemption narratives, these confessions
of error and decadence were followed by a recommitment to the fundamentals—the Old-Time Religion of investing in undervalued firms and
expecting modest profits in return. In this light, the financial losses that
the participants experienced, in both their club portfolios and their personal investments, were interpreted as just punishment for straying from
the path of fundamentalism. In fact, participants continually spoke of
their experiences in the market downturn using terms that would be familiar in any tale of sin and redemption: "I'm still a fundamentalist," said
Berry of Asset Accumulators. "We never lost faith," said Skip of Portfolio
Associates.

Perhaps the most eloquent expression of this quasi-religious faith in
the market system was provided by Stan of California Investors. When I
asked the group when they knew the bull market of the 1990s was over,
Stan launched into a soliloquy worthy of a Frank Capra movie:

> I don't agree that the bull market ended. I don't believe there ever
> was a bear market. The bull just slowed down for a few years. I be-
> lieve in the optimism of the people—people are going to create
> things and want things for themselves and their children, and that's
> going to keep the big wheel turning. And if you think it's over,
> you're making a big mistake.

Like Cate of Bulls & Bears, Stan's faith in the market experience was born
of his ability to use the economic system to bootstrap himself out of difficult circumstances and into financial independence. While Cate began her
American Dream as a secretary sharing a house with three other women,
Stan began in early childhood, as the eldest of eight children in a working-
class Italian immigrant family. He said he became interested in money

when he was seven years old, working as an altar boy: after serving at a funeral, he received a 50-cent tip from a Protestant mortician; at a second funeral, he received a whole silver dollar from an Irish Catholic mortician. "The feel of the money in my hand was very powerful," Stan said. "I learned that the buck is the common denominator—it's the ticket to mobility and freedom for all these different groups of people." After working his way up to $20 and $100 tips in the 1950s, working as a valet car attendant and as a golf caddy, Frank became an investor. These experiences created a passion for capitalism:

> I learned that there's nothing out there that you can't be part of—
> that's the American Dream. Here, even at the earliest age, you can
> be part of the Dream. It's easier than you think. If you think you
> can, you can. My mother always said, "The turtle only gets ahead by
> sticking his neck out."

This same set of beliefs led him to join California Investors, even after retiring from a successful career in real estate development. While he acknowledged that it is difficult to get reliable information about the market—"You can only believe half of what you see and none of what you hear, and there's a lot of mistrust of the media out there"—his basic faith in the market was grounded in face-to-face interactions such as those in his investment club. He had to join, he said, "because you can only learn so much as an individual; we can't know it all. You have to rely on more opinions than your own."

Like Stan, all the participants in the qualitative portion of my study were surprisingly positive about their experiences in investment clubs. Even if they were part of a club that had disbanded, even if they had lost money, everyone I interviewed said they had learned a lot from their participation and had no regrets about it. For example, Carla of ESAP said that despite her doubts about the NAIC method's effectiveness in a market plagued by dishonest information, she was still very satisfied with her investment club experience: "I got a tremendous amount out of the club; I started out not knowing even what a stock was, and it got to the point that I felt able to manage my own finances." Paul of Bulls & Bears echoed these sentiments, saying that as a member of the club, he "learned to do analysis, and to identify firms that weren't popular or high-profile, but which were 'sleepers' in terms of returns—like the aftermarket auto parts firm that turned out to be one of our best performers. When I heard the presentation on it, I thought 'ugh, that's not interesting,' but it turned out really well."

Finally, when I gathered the women of Asset Accumulators for a reunion/interview, four years after the club's breakup, their reflections on investing in the 1990s spontaneously turned to their positive feelings about the NAIC investment club experience:

> *Keiko*: I'm glad I was in a club. I can't stand to lose money and
> most of my personal savings are in fixed-income investments,
> so I would never have participated in the bull market without
> the club.
>
> *Tara*: I would have wanted to invest, but I needed a vehicle.
>
> *Renee*: We gained a whole new vocabulary, and learned about all the
> resources available to us as investors.
>
> *Tara*: My husband wanted to sell everything when the market when
> down, but I convinced him to hold on to our stocks. And he
> trusted me because I'd been meeting with Asset Accumulators
> for ten years and he thought I must know something! He would
> have sold everything if I hadn't convinced him otherwise; and
> now the stocks are going up again. Now investments are my area
> of expertise at home.
>
> *Liza*: It was empowering to be in a club.
>
> *Nora*: We'll take that education with us wherever we go.

Group Dynamics

The high level of satisfaction participants expressed with the investment club experience begs the question: why did three of the seven groups disband? This is particularly puzzling since two of those three groups—Bulls & Bears and Asset Accumulators—were among the highest performers in my sample and in NAIC's national rankings. By the same token, it is worth asking why the remaining groups stayed together, particularly since two of them—California Investors and Ladies with Leverage—were doing so poorly from a financial standpoint.

All the groups insisted that their decisions to disband or remain intact were not driven by money. The reasons they *did* cite for their decisions provided some of the most interesting data in this follow-up study. Among the common themes were issues of stability in social networks: all three of the groups that disbanded cited work-related transience as the primary cause of their breakups, while the four clubs that remained intact involved members who were geographically and physically rooted in their communities, and thus able to maintain a long-term commitment to group membership. However, the ability to maintain group membership does not equal willingness to participate, particularly when the financial incentives decrease as dramatically as they did following April 2000. I will address

the participants' explanations for this resilience in commitment after reviewing the fates of clubs bound by more fragile ties.

When I interviewed the members of Bulls & Bears about their 1999
breakup, both Greg and Tim—founding members who held officer positions while I was studying the group—said that the dynamics of being
based at work created a vulnerability in the group's cohesion. Greg said,
"good people left because they were smart and got promoted out of town."
In fact, this happened to founding member Paul, who was president of
Bulls & Bears at the time of my study and was transferred to his firm's
Colorado office shortly thereafter. Tim was quick to add that "nobody
bailed out because they didn't like the club," despite conflicts over how to
analyze stocks. All the members, Greg noted, cashed out at a profit.

Similarly, the women of Asset Accumulators said that while they found
the market downturn discouraging, that in itself did not dissolve their ten-
year bond. Rather, they claimed that the club split up in 2002 because of
members moving away—either retiring out of state or taking new jobs
elsewhere. When I suggested that declining profits in the stock market
might have affected their decisions, they vehemently disagreed. "Everyone
got a few thousand out of it, profit above and beyond preserving initial
capital," Renee said. Keiko added, "No one was thinking 'I could cash out
and put money elsewhere.'"

Even the members of ESAP, who made very little on their investment
in the club, argued that finances did not drive the club's breakup. Rather,
they cited the pressures of work and family commitments as creating a
centrifugal force that spun members away from the group. As Janet, the
former president of the club, put it, "The breakup of the club was really
driven by instability—people moving away, Shelley having to care for her
aging father out of state. There's a built-in instability with singles. We move
around a lot."

These insights are reminiscent of findings in the collective action literature indicating that a vital precondition for success in social movements
is stability in the network of participants.[2] In the absence of this stability,
it is very difficult to build the kind of social capital necessary to achieve
lasting group bonds. Janet's observations also echo the findings of my 1998
study of a small group of investment clubs that had disbanded in the previous year (see chapters 3 and 4), most of which cited work-related instability—including travel and transfers—as the primary reason for their
breakup. This explanation was particularly common among mixed-gender
investment clubs—perhaps not surprisingly, since so many of them were
formed by people who knew each other through work. While this vulnerability among mixed groups might appear to bias the performance findings,

it seems that neither high performance (as in Bulls & Bears) nor social bonds (as in ESAP) can override the destabilizing forces of occupational mobility. Mixed clubs appear to have a higher mortality rate regardless of their financial performance.

One implication is that diversity may be inextricably and reciprocally linked to instability. On the one hand, as these follow-up data show, the same social forces that bring people together in mixed-gender groups (work and school) also create the pressures that drive associations apart. On the other hand, instability in networks may be necessary to preserve diversity within them, since long-standing relationships tend to become more homogenous over time.[3]

In contrast, the absence of these centrifugal forces may help groups preserve their networks and social capital, net of financial performance. Of the four groups that remained together after my study concluded, only two really prospered financially: Portfolio Associates and Valley Gay Men's Investment Club. However, *all* four shared an important commonality: their members were firmly rooted in one geographical area. For three of the clubs, stability was enhanced by all or most of the membership being out of the workforce: most of the members of Portfolio Associates and California Investors were retired, and the women of Ladies with Leverage were homemakers with grown children. In the case of Valley Gay Men's Investment Club, the group was rooted in one of the world centers of gay culture, and in effect benefited from the institutional support of that culture.

Indeed, from its inception, sexual orientation had far greater salience for the club's members than the stated goals of learning about investment. As Frank, the club's treasurer and one of its founders, relates the story, the group's first meeting was held in the basement dungeon of a "leather queen" in the Castro district of San Francisco. The original plan was to call the group DISH—Developing Investment Strategies for Homosexuals—and the first meeting was announced in the classified section of a gay weekly newspaper, the *Bay Area Reporter*. Over one hundred men showed up, according to Frank, "thinking that DISH was some kind of new fetish group or a pickup venue." Ultimately, in order to function as an investment club, the group had to rename itself (literally spelling out "Investment Club" in the process) and meet in venues more conducive to doing business. Still, as a gay men's association in San Francisco, the members enjoyed a kind of stability and institutional support for their group that are unusual among employed people in their thirties and forties in a major metropolitan area. Most of the men in the group had moved to the city from out of state, in large part to find a cultural and political haven; thus, their attachment to the area, and commitment to stay there, were greater than if they had moved there only for work or economic reasons. This lent a stability to the investment club that more transient groups lacked.

But institutional support and geographic stability among the investment clubs that remained intact still leaves open the question of why members kept coming to meetings, particularly in those groups that were losing money hand over fist. Most readers would not find it problematic or mysterious that high-performing groups like the Valley Gay Men's Investment Club or Portfolio Associates remained intact. Combine stability of membership with a profit motive, and there would seem to be very little to explain. As Barney, the treasurer of Portfolio Associates, put it, "we're running our own mutual fund here." Mike added, "a huge aspect of our success is that we treat this as a real business; if I were to quantify this group dynamic, I'd say our association is 95 percent business and 5 percent social."

However, explaining the robustness of low-performing groups like California Investors and Ladies with Leverage presents a bit more of a challenge. When investment clubs lose money, why do members choose to remain in the group, especially when—as in these two clubs—the members staunchly maintain that they are in it to make money? Their commitment is particularly puzzling given that the members are not only losing money on the stocks the club already owns but are also continuing to "throw money down a rat hole" (in the words of Brad, the treasurer of California Investors) with each month that passes. Members of his club were contributing $150 per person per month, while the Ladies with Leverage were each paying $100 per month—money that was either spent on new stock purchases (often money-losing ones) or directed to the group's cash account, where it languished at passbook interest.

This left me with two questions, which I posed to the participants in my follow-up study:

1. Why would individuals who truly wanted to invest do so through a group that was consistently losing money? They could have joined more financially successful clubs, or groups like AAII (the American Association of Individual Investors) that provided the educational benefits of investment clubs without the group setting, monthly meetings and monthly contributions. Given all the alternatives available, why choose one that seemed to have such low payoffs?
2. If, on the other hand, the primary motive of the investors who stuck with losing clubs was to enjoy the social contact the meetings provided, why not choose a less costly and demanding means

of fulfilling those needs? A book club, for example, rarely demands $100 per month in cash outlays. Even if the sums of money were inconsequential to participants, why didn't they simply use it to finance a group dinner or some other activity that required less effort than the investment club?

In other words, if an individual wants to learn about investing *or* enjoy a regular social event with friends, why remain in a group that is both costly and frustrating (in terms of the declining portfolio value) when there are so many attractive alternatives available?

Investor Tribalism

In this way—through members' strong commitment to groups that were failing to meet their stated financial objectives—investment clubs posed the kind of empirical and theoretical puzzle at the heart of sociological inquiry: the difference between *reasons* for action and the *consequences* of action. The great social theorist Robert Merton called this the distinction between "manifest and latent functions" of social behavior.[4] The sociologist's job, according to Merton, is to ferret out those latent functions, which "clarifies the analysis of seemingly irrational social patterns" and "directs attention to theoretically fruitful fields of inquiry." He cites, for example, the Hopi rain dance as a practice that can be dismissed as "irrational" or "superstitious" based on its failure to attain its manifest purpose of influencing the weather. This labeling represents a kind of intellectual laziness, Merton argues:

> It is simply a case of name-calling; it substitutes the epithet "superstition" for an analysis of the actual role of this behavior in the life of the group . . . But with the concept of latent function, we continue our inquiry, examining the consequences of the ceremony not for the rain gods or for meteorological phenomena, but for the groups which conduct the ceremony. And here it may be found, as many observers indicate, that the ceremonial does indeed have functions— but functions which are non-purposed or latent. Ceremonials may fulfill the latent function of reinforcing the group identity by providing a periodic occasion on which the scattered members of a group assemble to engage in a common activity.

Amateur investors, such as the members of investment clubs, can easily be written off as "irrational" and even "superstitious." In some of the economics literature, they have a status similar to that of "primitives" in the anthropology of a century ago. Rather than fighting that characterization, a more productive sociological response might be to take seriously the proposition that investment clubs are actually ceremonial gatherings, and to examine them as such. Having ruled out financial gain as a function of the group, the task is simply to figure out what the "natives" *are* accomplishing with these ritual gestures.

Any reference to ceremony or ritual in a sociological text must ultimately lead back to Durkheim, one of the founding fathers of the discipline, whose *Elementary Forms of the Religious Life* created the template for sociological understanding of group behavior. Durkheim's study, conducted at the beginning of the twentieth century, proposed that one of the best ways to understand "modern" humans was to examine the behavior of what was then considered the most "primitive" group available for study: that of Australian aboriginal cults that worshipped animal totems, such as the kangaroo or the wallaby. He argued: "At the foundation of *all systems of belief* and all cults there ought necessarily to be a certain number of fundamental representations or conceptions of ritual attitudes which, in spite of the diversity of forms which they have taken, have the same objective significance and fulfill the same functions everywhere."[5]

In his search for these "fundamental representations" or "elementary forms," Durkheim identified a number of building blocks essential to the creation and survival of groups. These included regular meetings and shared activities—notably eating and drinking, ritual sacrifice, and enactment of totemic behavior. Totems are the sacred beings or objects that form the object of the group's attention: sacrifices are made to the totems, and individuals identify themselves as members of a group through imitation of the group's totem. Thus, Durkheim observed that members of the aboriginal kangaroo cult actually jumped around like kangaroos and ate like kangaroos during ritual gatherings: "A man of the kangaroo clan thinks and feels he is a kangaroo, he defines himself by this quality and it marks his place in society."[6]

Organizing society and marking the place of individuals within it, Durkheim argues, are the ultimate purposes—what Merton would call the "latent" functions—of group life, no matter what a group's stated motives. Totems, for example, may ostensibly be worshipped to gain the energy or goodwill of the sacred; but whether or not that energy transfer is successful, the totems become the basis for differentiating individuals into clans. The accomplishment of any manifest goal is beside the point: "The real reason for the existence of the cults, *even of those which are the most materialistic in appearance*, is not to be sought in the acts which they prescribe . . . So we have here a whole group of ceremonies whose sole purpose is to awaken certain ideas and sentiments, to attach the present to the past or the individual to the group. *Not only are they unable to serve useful ends, but the worshippers themselves demand none.*"[7]

While investment clubs are not cults in the religious sense of the term, they are certainly systems of beliefs that share many of the "elementary forms" of group life that Durkheim identified. Indeed, modern instantiations of group life were precisely what Durkheim was trying to explain; and as he stated elsewhere, he expected business and economic associations to fill the vacuum left by declining religious observance in organizing modern social life in the West.[8]

Investment clubs, as groups based on a set of beliefs about self, money, and markets (see chapter 2), have much in common with the aboriginal groups Durkheim studied. They have regular meetings and shared activities—most notably the process of investing together. Moreover, the least financially successful groups share the greatest number of characteristics with the ritual societies Durkheim described, including sharing food and drink (the least profitable clubs met over meals, while the most profitable ones did not eat or drink together) and engaging in behavior imitative of totemic figures. These were the groups that could not explain why they made many stock purchases, except to note—as both ESAP and Ladies with Leverage did—that often they bought stocks just so they could feel like investors and continue to be a club. The same groups were also inclined to invest according to the dictates of certain advisers, whose recommendations they accepted as oracular. Names such as Bob Brinker, host of a popular radio show on investments, or Louis Rukeyser, late of the PBS program *Wall $treet Week*, came up repeatedly in this context.

Similar observations about the homologies between religions and financial markets have been made by other scholars in other contexts. For example, in her ethnography of the Shanghai stock market, Ellen Hertz notes that "financial analysis functions as a modern form of that universal human behavior anthropologists call 'divination.' "[9] And in a review of economic history, Keith Hart extends the analogy by arguing that "economics has become the religion of our secular scientific civilization . . . Durkheim would see economists as the upholders of what is sacred in capitalist society."[10]

But among the most important contributions of the aboriginal analogy to this project is the light it sheds on the apparently irrational behavior of individuals who remain committed to investment clubs that lose money year after year. In this view, the ongoing process of contributing $100 or $150 per month to a money-losing enterprise can be understood as a sacrificial rite—a shared act of renunciation whose purpose Durkheim defines as "communion."[11] Put another way, these individuals pay—ritually sacrificing their dollars—to keep the group alive. As Brad of California Investors said, "If we have money, we're going to invest it. It doesn't matter which way the market is going. If you don't spend the money, the club becomes stagnant and dies."

As for spending $150 per person per month to keep the club alive, Brad could not provide a rationale. But some insight might be provided by another exuberant display of expense: the potlatch ceremonies of Pacific Northwest indigenous tribes. A potlatch involved extravagant feasting and gift giving followed by equally impressive displays of destruction: at the end of the gathering, all the remaining food and goods would be destroyed, often in a bonfire. The "symbolic logic of consumption and waste"[12] was that such displays cemented relationships and social status, creating the sense of communion that Durkheim defined as essential to group life—and which, in investment clubs such as Ladies with Leverage or California Investors, could serve as a bonding mechanism in the absence of financial success.

If continuing to make significant financial contributions to a losing enterprise constitutes a form of ritual sacrifice, to what or whom are the sacrifices being made? To the group? To the market deities?[13] Durkheim argues that ritual sacrifice creates a sense of shared identity; this identity is modeled on or partakes of the group's totem. The closest thing to a totem or fetish object in an investment club is cash itself. This begs the question, to what identity or totem do the sacrificial rites and other ceremonies in investment clubs refer? Chapter 3 reviews data suggesting that investor behavior is predicated on a set of identity claims: with every stock purchase, individuals stake a claim to being investors. As the social psychology literature indicates, such identity claims must be ratified in a social setting, a purpose for which investment clubs prove very useful.

But if claiming the social identity "investor" is the primary function—albeit a latent one—of investment clubs, it remains to be explained why the majority of investment club members join same-sex rather than mixed clubs. Most American adults have access to both male and female acquaintances through their personal and professional networks. While claiming the investor identity may be more problematic for women than for men, as outlined in chapter 2, it does not follow that same-sex groups would be the solution. Moreover, whatever advantage women may find in same-sex investment clubs would be more difficult to generalize to all-male clubs: for men, being an investor poses no identity problem.

So why *do* men choose to belong to same-sex clubs? It is not because they cannot find any women to join them. Further, my findings on the performance advantages of mixed over same-sex groups are not widely known in the investment club community, and in any case none of the individuals I interviewed mentioned performance as a factor in their decision to join a particular investment club. Yet there *was* a distinct preference expressed by many of the men I interviewed for investing in an all-male setting. For example, the men of Portfolio Associates—which briefly included one woman member after it was founded—passed a bylaw shortly after her departure from the club in the early 1960s stating that no women would be admitted in future. Among the men of the mixed club Bulls & Bears, there were many wistful references to the all-male group of founders—an era that Paul and Greg described with nostalgic warmth as a "men's club" or a "fraternity." And before the mixed group ESAP split up, one of the men left to join an all-male investment club. Shelley, the former president of ESAP, explained the decision as follows: "after Bert retired from the business world, he wanted to be with other men."

This rationale resonates powerfully with the accounts given by members of California Investors and Portfolio Associates about the benefits they experienced not only from investing together but also from gathering in an all-male setting. Such groups partake of a long tradition of fraternal organizations in American history,[14] and the persistent association between men and the world of finance. Finally, a single-sex group lends itself to the ritual functions of clubs like California Associates. In Durkheim's study and others, ceremonial groups have necessarily drawn rigid boundaries around gender and other characteristics of membership in order to advance the group's bonding and identity-formation functions. These activities take place in a wide variety of single-sex settings outside a religious context, including street gangs and work organizations.[15]

In fact, Brad of California Investors explained that the significance of the club for him—and he believed, for the other men—lay in the members' shared work history:

> Part of it is staying together with other [name of insurance company] veterans. Half of the club are ex-[name of insurance company], and there's a bonding that's almost irrational, like being in the marines. Those who came from outside [name of insurance company] were big-time movers and shakers, and often clients of ours on the benefits side of the business. It's a very clubby thing. The way we hired people at [name of insurance company] is the way we run things in the investment club: it was so informal, you wouldn't believe it. We interviewed candidates just about sports and business and everything but the firm and its financials. People who couldn't be flexible and converse with us didn't make the cut.

Thus, California Investors provided an environment in which a group of retired executives could reenact what Goffman calls the "call and response ritual" of (re)claiming their identity as businessmen.[16] This is important for men, because not only do they derive their identity from work to a greater extent than do women, but research on organizational attachment shows that men experience greater commitment to and satisfaction with work groups *to the extent that the groups are homogenous in terms of gender.*[17]

Other members of California Investors echoed this view of the club as a place for bonding in a particularly masculine register that drew its power from reference to the business world. At the February 2004 meeting I attended, Ken—the club president—remarked: "It's a very supportive network of men. We ask how each other is. There's interpersonal bonding, but it's very subtle, and they don't want to hear your whole story. We've had people die, people get sick. There's a genuine trust in each other—we'll buy five hundred shares on a member's recommendation, without knowing whether he did any research or not."

This framing of the group dynamic is reminiscent of the trust-building exercises sometimes used in corporate retreats, in which one member of a work group stands in the center of a circle of his coworkers and falls backward with eyes closed, allowing his coworkers to catch him. It is a gesture that simultaneously demonstrates bravery, trust, and commitment to the group.

In fact, I witnessed just such an exchange at the July 1998 meeting of California Investors, when Ted urged the other members of the club to buy more shares of Robert Half Corporation by asking, "who's got balls here?" (See chapter 3.) Such exaggerated masculine role-playing was expressed in a number of other ways within the group: members often referred to themselves and the other members in terms of classic male archetypes such as the soldier, the cowboy, the gambler, or the corporate mover and shaker. The importance of bluffing and role-playing in the group was institutionalized in the printed agendas distributed at the outset of every meeting, which always set aside time for an activity described as "Member Comments, Stock Tips and Lies." As Brad put it, "We got together in business, and now we get together to blow smoke at each other."

At the same time, the group provided a safe haven for the men to express support for one another and experience emotional vulnerability in ways that were not possible during their years together in the corporate world. The members described the club as a space where the affection and attachment that had evolved between them, but could not be expressed at work, at last found an acceptable outlet. As Terry, the club's former president and elder statesman, put it, "We were used to that business world where people were always looking to burn your tail feathers, and you had to keep your armor on. But we morphed from competitors to allies. We came to be friends, and it's a great relief to have the club setting where we can relax around one another." When asked why they chose this specific format—an investment club—to provide this space for male bonding, the men responded that it was the only set of interests they held in common *and* the only activity that their wives would not be interested in sharing. "We're paying money to get out of the house . . . but nobody says that to their wives," said Brad.

In a sense then, the men of California Investors invested together in order to experience themselves *as men*. Some of the historically and culturally specific reasons that they chose to conduct this gender performance through investing have been reviewed here, as well as in chapters 3 and 4. But it is also worth noting that in this regard, California Investors partook of a long-standing practice of enacting identity through exchange. As economic anthropologist Roy Dilley has noted, "representations of exchange are predicated on the recognition of *particular forms of personhood* and types of social agency."[18] The data from this study suggest that gender is among the most significant forms of personhood that figure into actors' understanding of their involvement in stock exchanges. This may be particularly salient for men, because the competitive market framework—and the rewards accorded within it to bravery and risk—coincide neatly with the demands of masculine performance. The linkage is deepened by accounts of other kinds of markets, such as the Chicago Board of Trade, which has been described as a "speculative tournament" built on "a mythology of circulation"—language that invokes the imagery of heroic epic.[19] Thus, to be an investor—at least in a highly ceremonial investment club like California Investors—is to enact masculinity in the most ideal-typical sense: bold, aggressive, and engaged in tests of wit and mettle.

But what of all-female investment clubs? As NAIC's enrollment figures show, women *are* interested in investing, in overwhelming numbers. Yet for the most part, these women are involved in single-sex groups. When I asked the women of Asset Accumulators and Ladies with Leverage why they chose to invest through an all-women's group, one woman—Liza of Asset Accumulators—mentioned the intrinsic value of social contact with other women. For the others, however, my question elicited a discussion of the gender politics of household finances. Among the women of Asset Accumulators, for example, learning to invest was part of their traditional gender role as homemakers; even though they were employed as full-time schoolteachers, they still had primary responsibility for maintaining the infrastructure of home and family. This is consistent with the general experience of American women, who work outside their homes for part of the day and return to perform a "second shift" by managing their households.[20] So while Mary worked full-time as a teacher, she also "did everything for the household, including the finances." Renee, another member of Asset Accumulators, said that her husband's demanding career as a surgeon meant that "he was saving lives at the hospital and was never at home, so I *had* to do the finances."

Similarly, for the members of Ladies with Leverage, learning to invest was understood as an extension of their household management responsibilities—an unintended reminder of the roots of the word "economy" in the Greek *oikos*, or household.[21] For these women—the majority of whom had not worked outside their homes for many years, if ever—learning about investments also provided a benefit to their family lives by giving them a topic and a vocabulary for connecting with their husbands and sons. As with California Investors, this investment club provided an opportunity to bond with men—but, in this case, the men were the participants' family members. Thus, my question about the women's membership in a single-sex club elicited the following discussion:

> *Georgia*: I joined the investment club because it was an opportunity to finally get on with it and learn about money . . . I got caught up in raising kids, and there wasn't a lot of communication between me and my husband at a professional level.
> *Teresa*: My sons are getting MBAs and now I can talk with them about money and investing.
> *Connie*: Since I joined the club, my husband and I watch the stock and business news as a couple. It stimulates conversation.
> *Georgia*: It opens up new channels of communication between us.

This discussion, along with the comments by the women of Asset Accumulators, suggests that while finance is still associated with men, investor perceptions of gender roles in the market are more nuanced than past analyses suggested. The data presented here suggest that just as some stocks are associated more with women than men (see chapter 3), some kinds of investing can be framed as "women's work" through extension of the notion of "managing the household." So while women's investment activity serves as a way of connecting with men and the masculinized realm of the stock market, it does so not at the expense of traditional gender roles but in a way that appears to reinforce them—bonding wives to husbands, and mothers to sons.

Summary

In returning to interview and observe the original group of seven clubs on which my study was based, I found data that confirmed the conclusions I had drawn about them earlier; but while the participants were still recognizable in their habits and perspectives, the intervening years and the end of the bull market had changed them in ways that were in some respects very surprising. Among the unexpected data from the follow-up study were these four findings:

- First, I expected that clubs would disband because of the market downturn, and while three of them did, I was surprised to find the majority remained intact—and that, whether intact or disbanded, every participant insisted that the finances of the club had nothing to do with its fate.

- Second, I expected to find that many groups had lost significant amounts of money after April 2000—and they had. But I did not expect that *all* the participants would continue to invest in stocks; I thought surely some would flee the markets as investors did after previous crashes, never to return. Yet while some of the participants in my study sat on the sidelines of the market for a year or two, they all came back.

- Third, I expected a sense of bewilderment or betrayal among these investors following the ongoing revelations of corporate accounting scandals, mutual fund fraud, and other events that might provoke a loss of faith in the U.S. financial system. But while I found some bewilderment, most of participants chose to blame themselves rather than see the financial scandals as evidence of betrayal. There was a kind of withdrawal of generalized trust from the market, as I expected, but that was accompanied by a motif of "I should have known better" and a passive resignation to corruption in the stock market.

- Fourth, given that three clubs had disbanded and the surviving four had incurred large losses in their portfolios, I was surprised by the goodwill and affection that all the participants expressed about their experience as investment club members. After spending a year with these investors, and listening to their many complaints about NAIC and its investing methods, I am confident that they did not view me as an agent of the investment club association or try to "spin" their remarks in a positive direction. Since NAIC had no control over the clubs, there would have been no motive to curry favor with the national organization in the first place.

Perhaps the most satisfying result of the follow-up study was finding answers to some of the questions that had been nagging me since I had last observed these clubs in the late 1990s. The unresolved issues included, why are there so many more single-sex investment clubs than mixed ones? and, why do members keep contributing significant sums each month to investment clubs that have consistently lost money over many years?

In seeking answers to the first question, I found confirmation of the earlier study I had conducted on disbanded clubs, which indicated that the origins of many mixed groups in work-related networks caused them to break up at a higher rate than their same-sex counterparts. But I also developed a more nuanced view of the situation, having spent a year observing two mixed clubs that subsequently disbanded: ESAP and Bulls & Bears. In essence, the data from the follow-up study suggested that the greatest strength and the greatest weakness of mixed clubs may derive from the same source. That is, diversity may be inextricably and reciprocally linked to instability.

On the one hand, the structural forces—such as work and school—that bring together diverse groups of men and women also create the outward pressures that drive these networks apart. Transfers, promotions, and other work-related moves, along with graduations from school, create a built-in vulnerability in mixed networks that does not appear to affect same-sex groups as powerfully. On the other hand, instability may be necessary to preserve diversity, since long-standing relationships tend to become more homogenous over time in terms of ideas and decision-making processes.[22] Instability in membership can thus mean renewal of crucial knowledge resources for groups that remain intact.

In contrast, I was struck by the resilience of the same-sex groups, and the significant role they played in defining the gender boundaries in members' lives. If there is a common thread among all the single-sex clubs in my study, it is the sense that investing creates social bonds—and not just with other members of the group. While the club members do forge a bond and a shared identity through their shared finances, investing also connects them to a world outside the group: the world of men and business. For the men of California Investors, that meant connection with their preretirement identities as corporate movers and shakers. For the women of Asset Accumulators and Ladies with Leverage, however, investing together meant creating a bond with their husbands and sons. So another surprise in the follow-up study was that the bonding that occurred in same-sex groups had a distinct gender valence, in that it drew both men and women toward closer relationships with men.

In pursuing questions about the gender mix and resilience of investment clubs, the data also brought me back to themes outlined in chapters 2 and 3—what I called *identity investing*. The mapping of masculine and feminine gender identities onto investment decisions continued to mark the behavior of the intact clubs I observed in 2004. But the new perspective of the follow-up study helped me develop a broader picture of the identity formation process: one framed by the notion of tribe or clan. In this, I found the anthropological literature especially helpful, because it refers explicitly to societies and economic practices in which finance and money are not separated from their social and cultural contexts.

Part of the valued added by looking at investment clubs through a lens that has most often been turned toward "primitive" peoples and underdeveloped societies is a better understanding of "irrational" behavior in our own midst. A group of men in California "throwing money down a rat hole" for years on end while claiming to be investors has some important features in common with a group of men in Australia jumping around while claiming to be kangaroos. Both are creating a sense of communal identity in their culturally and historically specific modes.

At the same time, the "investing ritual" in which these clubs engage has implications beyond the creation of identities for particular groups of people. As Durkheim observed of the totemic cults he studied, the most important function of their rituals was to produce an experience of and connection to society writ large. To worship a kangaroo or a wallaby was ultimately incidental, he argued; the celebrants were actually worshipping the idea of society itself. While this might seem to attribute too much symbolic weight to the actions of small groups, Durkheim and subsequent researchers have noted that awareness is not a prerequisite for ritual function. The key is to look at the outcome of the ritual, because ritual "works" whenever a repeated behavior delivers the required emotional significance.[23] As organizational sociologist Gideon Kunda has written in a study of ceremonial behavior in a large high-tech firm, "Outcomes of ritual performances . . . are a more complex matter than those who stage them might claim."[24]

APPENDIX ◆
Exit Interview for a Researcher

In the final part of my follow-up study, I posed a methodological question to all the research participants: did they believe that my presence had affected their group dynamics during my original 1997–98 observations, and if so, how? This is of course a classic problem in observational research.[25]

While it cannot be avoided, it must be taken into account as explicitly as possible; sometimes it can even elicit useful data. The key is to observe and record one's influence rather than to pretend it does not exist.[26] My field notes from the 1997–98 study are replete with reflections on how my presence might have been influencing the behavior I was observing; in the follow-up study, I wanted to go further by querying the participants directly about this issue. So before telling them what I thought was significant about my presence as an observer, I asked them for their recollections.

I found that the degree of influence participants ascribed to my presence increased in direct proportion to the percentage of men in the club. Both of the all-women's groups said they felt my presence had done little to perturb their decision-making and other interpersonal dynamics within the club. What little they could formulate on the subject came across in phrases such as "you became one of the family" (Karen of Ladies with Leverage) or "we hardly noticed you" (Berry of Asset Accumulators).

In the mixed clubs, the initial reaction to my question was that I had "absolutely not" affected the group dynamic (Greg of Bulls & Bears), and that my "presence didn't change anything" (Carla of Asset Accumulators). Yet after a moment or two, some members (such as Janet of ESAP) added that they might have worked harder to look like serious investors while I was present. Paul of Bulls & Bears offered his thought that "if anything, it [a researcher's presence] affected us positively; some of the sleepy minds woke up and participated—it was almost as if their supervisor was watching." This suggested that a version of the "Hawthorne Effect" might have been in operation, biasing my data toward observation of a greater rigor or industriousness than would normally have characterized the group.[27] However, it is difficult to gauge how widespread this influence might have been, since other members of the same clubs later reiterated their position that my presence had no effect on their groups.

With the all-male clubs, however, it was a different story. All the members recalled being acutely aware of my presence throughout the year of observation, and—among the straight men—their remarks about my influence on the group had distinct sexual overtones. For example, when I arrived at the February 2004 meeting of Portfolio Associates, the security guard in the building—whom I had never seen before—said "you must be Brooke." When I nodded yes and expressed surprise that he knew my name, he said, "The investment club guys told me to look out for a good-looking woman coming in after hours." This was consistent with the club's view of me during the original year of observation, in which they referred to me as "our little filly" or "a pretty critter" (this from the cattle rancher); they also made frequent "jokes" about my being their "date" for the evening, and compared my presence in the group to Snow White among the Seven Dwarfs (apparently a reference to the fact that many of the men were noticeably shorter than I).

Goffman once observed that you know you have become fully incorporated into a research environment "when the members of the opposite sex . . . become attractive to you."[28] The corollary for many female ethnographers has been that integration is signaled by participants' expression of attraction to *you*. This can be a problem for female ethnographers, limiting their legitimacy in the field as well as their access to data.[29] On the other hand, rebuffing such comments can have equally limiting effects. It was a line I recognized and walked carefully. Mostly I smiled and laughed, but did not respond verbally.

During the meeting of Portfolio Associates I attended in 2004, the pattern of sexualized banter reemerged during a discussion of the group's portfolio: the treasurer noted that their Pfizer stock was down and that they all needed to start taking *more* Viagra. Before I had a chance to pose the question about whether I had influenced the group's behavior, the members broached the subject themselves. As they prepared to vote on a major purchase of SunCor stock, the following exchange occurred:

> *Andy*: It's not often that we spend $7,000 on stocks.
> *Dave*: We have to impress Brooke while she's here.
> *Ralph*: She's good luck for us.

After the meeting, when I was able to question the members more directly about how they thought I had influenced their behavior, Skip said, "everybody was at least subconsciously trying to impress you; there was less of a ribald atmosphere." This was consistent with an observation Dave had made back in September 1997, after I had attended two meetings of the club; he said at that time that he noticed the club was "having better discussions" and was "more serious about discussing stocks" when I was around.

The men of Valley Gay Men's Investment Club shared a similar desire to look serious and smart, albeit without the sexual overtones. Frank, the treasurer, said, "I felt like I was onstage; I was more careful about what I said, more careful to mind my p's and q's to not sound stupid." They also said that I and my study had become part of the club's "creation myth." As Jeremy, who did not become a member until 2002, noted, "when I joined the club, you were part of the group's history, so I've heard about you for years without meeting you." On my return to observe the group in 2004, I did notice that they seemed more serious and skillful as investors than they had in 1998. This may have been the result of my presence— which, in the words of another new member, "gave us a sense of legitimacy"—or it may simply have been a case of "practice makes perfect." Most people get better at things if they keep practicing for five years, and given the effort that the members of Valley Gay Men's Investment Club had put into learning the ropes of investing, it would be presumptuous for me to claim any credit for their development.

The men of California Investors did not claim that my presence had made them more serious or hardworking about their investing, but I did notice that they had switched from a show-of-hands voting method to a secret ballot—a method I had told them about back in 1998 when they pressed me for details on the most financially successful clubs in my study (further evidence of their curious commitment to the *idea* of making profits in investing, if not always the practice). They also noted that although I was not present at the inception of their group, as I was with Valley Gay Men's Investment Club, I had nonetheless become a "character" in their history. As Josh put it, "we have referred to you on numerous occasions by saying 'that was back when Brooke was studying us.' "

Among the uncertainties about the perturbations I may have created in all seven clubs as an observer, one of the few things about which I feel truly confident is that my presence in California Investors worked in large part because I facilitated their "performance" of masculinity. That was readily apparent in their behavior back in 1997–98, but was reinforced repeatedly during my return visit. Even before I set foot in the meeting room in February 2004, I overhead Brad telling the other members that a surprise guest from the club's past would be arriving any minute—an announcement that was greeted with the exclamation, "Oh yes, lovely what's-her-name!" When I asked them directly about my impact on their behavior, they told me that from the very beginning, my request to observe their meetings had heightened their awareness of gender in a negative way. They were skeptical of my motives, and worried that I might attack them for being in an all-male group: an article critical of all-male investment clubs had appeared in the local newspaper shortly before I arrived to make my request. And, after all, they were based in the Berkeley Hills, where exclusion based on gender did not generally meet with anyone's approval. "But after you showed up," Brad said, "we saw how pretty you were and just melted." And like the other all-male groups I studied, they found a way to live with my presence through "role encapsulation": labeling me in terms of categories familiar to them, and then interacting with me on the basis of the label.[30] In a version of the "drag queen" episode in VGMIC, my presence was explained to an incoming member of California Investors in terms that were culturally relevant to former businessmen: "she's the new secretary."

To me, the evidence suggests that my presence generally had the effect of accentuating characteristics that were already present in each group, rather than modifying the groups' behavior in a significantly different direction. In groups where my gender was not salient, members claimed that I had no effect on their behavior, and I noticed none. In mixed groups struggling to "get serious" about learning to invest, members said that my presence perturbed the group dynamic just enough to nudge them to put forth greater effort. While this variation of the "Hawthorne Effect" was definitely real, it is important to note that performance and decision-making style did not change significantly during the yearlong period of my observation. While my presence may have evoked more serious participation on the part of some club members, it did not appear to make a big enough difference to substantially change the performance or interpersonal dynamics of the group; even the members of mixed clubs who *could* identify some way in which my presence might have influenced them were tentative in their suggestions, and could offer only a couple of words to describe their impressions.

The most pronounced effect of my presence as an observer appeared to be among the all-male clubs, but they denied that it influenced the stocks that they bought. Because of the salience of gender—both mine and theirs—they may have been moved to behave more aggressively than they otherwise would have. But the evidence supports only the notion that they spent more extravagantly and bought larger amounts of stocks than they would have purchased even if I had not been present.

The most barbarous and the most fantastic rites and the strangest
myths translate some human need, some aspect of life, either indi-
vidual or social. The reasons with which the faithful justify them
may be, and generally are, erroneous; but the true reasons do not
cease to exist, and it is the duty of science to discover them.
—EMILE DURKHEIM[1]

Theories and schools, like microbes and globules, devour each
other and, through their struggle, ensure the continuity of life.
—MARCEL PROUST[2]

Implications and Conclusions   ◆ 6

Investment Clubs as Microfinance for the First World

What do you call a voluntary association whose members make monthly
contributions to a collective enterprise designed to build their financial
independence? The World Bank calls it "microfinance"—a grassroots form
of economic development commonly employed in countries whose infrastructure of financial and social institutions is not sufficient to meet the
needs of the population. Across Southeast Asia and Africa, one of the most
popular forms of microcredit is rotating credit associations, whose members typically contribute a small sum of cash every month to a "purse,"
which one member receives in full at each meeting in order to finance a
business or some other project. Such organizations are popular among the
poor, people of color, and women, for whom do-it-yourself financing is
often the only way they can gain access to capital.[3] These organizations
have a significant economic impact in developing countries; for instance,
a number of microfinance associations have gone well beyond lending
money, extending into investment in commodities such as steel roofing
material or even currency equivalents. Some rotating credit associations in
Cameroon are reported to hold assets in excess of U.S. $1 million, and
many have developed written rules and procedures for governance.[4]

    To find essentially the same techniques in use by middle-class citizens
of one of the world's most economically developed nations is a startling
irony produced by a generation-long unraveling of institutions designed

to provide collective economic goods. Like microfinance organizations in developing countries, investment clubs in the United States address needs that are not met by the existing socioeconomic infrastructure. But while microcredit associations primarily serve the poor, the techniques of "frontier capitalism" are being used by Americans who are far better off economically, but have real concerns about sinking into poverty through holes in the social safety net. The popularity of investment clubs can be read as one indication of the growing gap in the United States between the very rich and everyone else, a phenomenon that social scientists have noted for the past two decades.[5]

Investment clubs have another important feature in common with rotating credit associations and other microcredit organizations: the use of social networks to achieve and enforce instrumental goals. In many investment clubs, as in rotating credit associations, economic activities are conducted in explicitly social settings. In rotating credit associations, not only money but also hosting duties cycle through the group's membership; sometimes the group meets at restaurants or bars, with one member footing the bill for the group. One World Bank economist recently argued that the sharing of food and drink in many rotating credit associations creates the social context and the rewards needed to ensure compliance with group rules:

> This transaction cost [providing refreshments at meetings] helps maintain group cohesiveness through eating or drinking together, and impresses on members the importance of continued loyalty to one another. Members can observe each others' health and moods, and gain impressions of each others' current financial status. While many transaction costs are an annoyance to those who pay them, the obligation to provide hospitality to one's friends at RoSCA meetings is usually regarded as an honor or as an opportunity for fun, something to be enjoyed.[6]

While investment clubs are subject to more stringent legal constraints than most microcredit organizations, they are similar to rotating credit associations in their reliance on group decision-making, as well as informal social means to monitor, sanction, and reward member behavior. Like rotating credit associations, investment clubs have no legal means of enforcing day-to-day member behavior.[7] If an individual refuses to do stock research or otherwise share the workload of the club, there is very little the club can do about it in a legal sense. Instead, the clubs must rely on the power of social bonds to influence member behavior, with ostracism as the ultimate sanction. The need to maintain the value of social connection—and to emphasize the cost of noncompliance with group rules—is one reason that some of the investment clubs I studied met just as rotating credit associations do: over food and drink, in restaurants or members' homes.

For the same reason, investment clubs, like microcredit associations, recruit and select members from preexisting social networks, based on friendship or family relationships, or work and school ties. Since, like rotating credit associations, investment clubs make decisions collectively (either through majority rule or consensus), financial success often hinges on the quality of relationships among members. As chapter 4 shows, these ties can be double-edged, invoking a host of interpersonal dynamics that run counter to the group's financial interests.

Despite the pitfalls of embedding economic activity in tightly knit social networks, this strategy allows investment clubs and microfinance associations to pool risk with reliable partners. In both kinds of organizations, individuals band together to compensate for the absence of social and political institutions for collectivizing risk. In underdeveloped countries, this takes the form of banks and other institutions refusing credit to the poor; in the United States, the problem is corporations (and increasingly the government) "outsourcing" the risks of retirement planning for workers to the employees themselves.

People who join microlending groups like rotating credit associations are pooling their risk of default—using their community network to assume a risk that financial institutions are usually unwilling to bear. While the poor may not have much to offer a bank loan officer in the way of collateral or credit history, microlending allows them to literally bank on their own reputations within their communities; those who are known to be trustworthy and industrious are most readily able to join grassroots financial organizations such as rotating credit associations.[8]

Investment club members are responding to a different kind of risk: the liability of supporting themselves in retirement. The decline of the "defined benefit" pension plan—in which employers were responsible for providing workers with a fixed pension—has created an institutional and economic vacuum. What was once a collective undertaking has devolved almost entirely upon the individual. Like microlending ventures, investment clubs address these risks by cashing in on the value of interpersonal networks.

One additional similarity is worth noting between the worlds of microfinance in the developing world and investment clubs in the United States: the prevalence of women participants. For example, the Grameen Bank of Bangladesh makes the majority of its development loans to small groups of women. This is in part an institutional decision—women have higher rates of loan repayment than men[9]—but the phenomenon is also driven by demand: though Grameen's clientele initially consisted primarily of men, women now apply for the majority of loans. Development economists speculate that this is because, unlike men, the women do not regard the group meetings as a transaction cost but rather as a benefit: an opportunity to socialize, learn, and reap other noninstrumental benefits from the loan process. By the same token, while investment clubs in the United States were initially a male-dominated activity, in recent years women have comprised just over 60 percent of investment club members. The group setting seems to make the difference: other investment education organizations that cater to individual investors rather than groups report that 95 percent of members are male.[10]

In keeping with the gendered character of microfinance organizations and investment clubs, both have been touted as vehicles for women's empowerment. Recipients of loans from the Grameen Bank must adhere to sixteen principles to improve their lives, including the use of family planning techniques and the refusal to pay or accept dowries.[11] Similarly, the Beardstown Ladies investment club grew out of an early 1980s initiative by the national Business and Professional Women's Association to develop financial literacy and independence among women. The idea was to promote investment clubs as financial self-help to cope with the economic vulnerabilities that women faced because of divorce, widowhood, and caregiving responsibilities.[12]

Table 6.1 summarizes the similarities and differences between microfinance organizations in the developing world and investment clubs in

Table 6.1
Investment Clubs versus Microfinance Organizations

	Investment Clubs	Microfinance Organizations
Similarities	Transactions in small amounts, compared with formal sector	
	Recruitment and selection via preexisting social networks	
	Use of face-to-face interaction and group decision processes	
	Importance of informal social mechanisms to monitor and sanction member behavior	
Differences	More stringent reporting requirements (IRS, etc.)	Formal reporting requirements minimal to nonexistent
	Partial visibility to institutions and researchers	Mostly invisible to institutions and researchers
	Significant barriers to exit, including legal and tax consequences, along with social sanctions	Minimal barriers to exit—social sanctions only

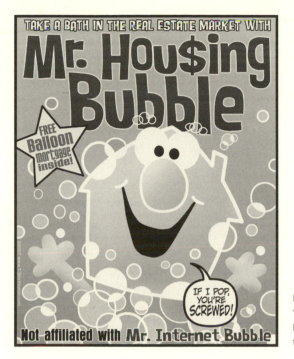

Figure 6.1
"Mr. Housing
Bubble" T-shirt (courtesy of
t-shirthumor.com ©2007)

the United States. Economists posit that microfinance organizations represent a step forward for developing countries, helping to evolve the kinds of formal financial institutions found in the United States and Europe.[13] Given that formal finance has made much greater inroads into American society than in almost any other place in the world, does the popularity and robustness of the investment club phenomenon therefore represent a step backward for economic development in the U.S.?

Recent data suggest that the withdrawal of socioeconomic "safety net" institutions that motivated the rise in investment club participation has also destabilized Americans' personal finances to an alarming degree. Increasing credit card debt (averaging $9,000 per household) and the lowest savings rate since the Great Depression (−1 percent annually) have given rise to a new set of grassroots financial associations to help individuals get out of debt.[14] Those who hoped to build a more secure future by investing in real estate seem to have gotten caught in a speculative bubble not unlike the internet stock boom of the 1990s. A small company in Austin, Texas, parodied the predicament in which many Americans found themselves by transitioning from stocks to real estate (see figure 6.1). Apparently the humor hit a nerve: not only did the image become a bestseller on T-shirts and other items; it made national news, leading to headlines such as "'Mr. Housing Bubble' Tries to Wash Away the Worries" in *USA Today*.[15]

The Policy Problem: Risk and Retirement Insurance

While Americans' scramble to make a profit, whether in stocks or real estate, can be attributed to greed and consumerism, there is also a pervasive fear that old age will bring poverty. For example, a 2001 *New York Times* poll—conducted more than a year after the stock market bubble had burst—showed that the majority of Americans expected to rely exclusively on their own savings, as opposed to private pension plans or Social Security, in retirement. Only 15 percent believed that Social Security would be a primary source of their retirement income—a belief driven by widely publicized (though controversial) predictions that the program would run out of money within the next thirty-five to forty-five years.[16] Even if the program remains solvent, many policy makers have argued that Social Security will not provide adequate benefits to retirees. As President Bush put it, "It's your money. It's part of your retirement benefits . . . I want to get a better rate of return for your own money than the paltry two percent that the current Social Security trust gets today."[17]

While historically Social Security has served multiple purposes—providing savings, insurance, and income redistribution in a single program—policy debates have shifted the terms of public discourse almost entirely toward individual assets. This is part of the larger trend toward distrust of government: twenty-five years of retreat from faith in public-sector institutions also appears to have brought detachment from the provision of collective goods. As one participant in the *New York Times* poll put it, "These decades to come are going to be more about what you do for yourself, as opposed to what you allow other people to do for you. It's not pro-government, not anti-government, just me, myself, and I."[18]

Building on this public willingness to treat retirement insurance as an individual responsibility, rather than as a collective undertaking, the Bush administration repeatedly advanced proposals to "privatize" Social Security, which would have allowed individuals to invest a portion of their contributions to the trust fund in the stock market. Privatization proponents (which include many conservative policy analysts and think tanks) rest their case on three claims: Social Security funds are comparable to private investments, like IRAs; since most Americans manage their own IRAs and employer-based retirement funds, there is no reason they should not manage their public pensions as well; and given the average returns on American stocks, we would all have much more money at retirement if we could take some of our Social Security funds out of government bonds and put them into the stock market. During the century just ended, the returns on the special-issue U.S. Treasury bonds in which Social Security funds are invested has been approximately 5 percent annually, average yearly return from U.S. stocks compared to the 11 percent. In this light, the policy choice seems obvious: pick the higher return.[19]

But the ability of Social Security participants to come out ahead financially in a privatized system would depend on their knowledge of and competence in managing their investments. Thus, while the Advisory Council on Social Security offered support for privatization during its 1999 meeting—an unprecedented move after more than sixty years of continuous, unanimous support for public management of the fund—members of the council also expressed considerable reservations as to the ability of ordinary Americans to manage investment decisions.[20] For example, the council's report acknowledges that "many workers do not have enough knowledge of investments to make sound choices."[21] In large part, the council's support for privatization was tempered by its uncertainty about the level of investment skills and knowledge that Americans possess. As one council member wrote: "We do not seem to know much about how individuals really make their portfolio decisions . . . Given our state of knowledge, we do not really know whether the proposed government transfers together with private investment decisions [in a privatized Social Security system] will be optimal."[22]

In this regard, the data from investment clubs are particularly valuable, because they offer insight into what has previously been a "black box" of investor behavior. Unfortunately, the evidence offers little reason to be encouraged about the prospects for enhanced financial returns under a privatized Social Security system. On the contrary, the findings of this study suggest that even individuals who are making a concerted effort to educate themselves about investing have a limited ability to navigate the overwhelming range of choices they face in the market. Through biases and heuristics of which many participants were only partially aware—including the purchase of stocks based on gender identity, or the use of stop-loss orders to avoid difficult sell decisions—the investment clubs in this study underperformed the market index by an average of 20.8 percent annually. The data support the views expressed by noted economist Robert Shiller on the privatization debate: "the notion that people will manage risks optimally may be excessively academic . . . *The public seems often to use naive rules of thumb for portfolio allocation* . . . and this behavior is a problem for models that presume proper public risk management."[23]

The Americans who consistently support privatization proposals tend to be young, wealthy, male, and well educated.[24] This is the same demographic group most interested in dropping out of Social Security altogether.[25] In other words, privatization appeals to those who believe they will be least dependent on Social Security benefits. But what of the huge number of people whose livelihoods will depend almost exclusively on Social Security? Currently, this group includes fifteen million people—one-third of all retirees.[26] Their numbers are likely to grow even further, as recent data indicate that more than half of Americans have virtually no personal assets as they approach retirement.[27]

As the Social Security trustees warned in their 1999 report, a system of privatized accounts would require measures to close the wide gap in investment knowledge between rich and poor, men and women, and whites and people of color. Otherwise, a privatized system would likely undercut the redistributive intent of the program and potentially leave vulnerable demographic groups worse off than they were under the previous policy. But if the federal government were to undertake such a massive investor education program to bring less-experienced investors up to speed, the costs would likely outweigh any of the financial benefits of privatization.[28]

Thus, imperfect as they are, investment clubs may represent one of the few affordable, available mechanisms to fill this educational need. Having already burgeoned in popularity by helping Americans meet the challenges presented by defined-contribution pension plans, investment clubs have a track record and an infrastructure for providing investor education en masse. In addition, investment clubs embody the kind of grassroots, voluntary organization—privately funded, with minimal government oversight—envisioned in the policy agendas of President George W. Bush as well as those of his father, who promoted such initiatives in his "one thousand points of light" campaign. But it is not clear whether participation in voluntary associations like investment clubs represents a renewal of participation in public life or a withdrawal from civic engagement.

Social Capital and Civil Society

This question speaks to a larger debate within sociology about the impact of social capital on civil society. As a voluntary, communal undertaking, investment clubs are a significant part of the associational life of the United States. But one of the dangers Robert Putnam warns about in his picture of declining civic life in America is a kind of isolation in which individuals retreat into settings where they interact exclusively with others who share their ideas and demographic traits. This is certainly the case in many voluntary associations, including investment clubs: the homogeneity of friendship and other socioemotional ties leads to self-selection into groups that have little variation on race, gender, age, and other characteristics.

On the other hand, by rewarding demographically diverse groups with higher returns on their investments—the "diversity premium" phenomenon—investment clubs may act as a positive force. Civic life thrives by bridging demographic and other boundaries, and investment clubs certainly provide the resources that Putnam argues define civic engagement: "trust, norms and networks that can improve the efficiency of society by facilitating coordinated action."[29] For example, recall the moment in Bulls & Bears when, following another frustrating exchange with Jeff over the Cisco decision, Greg turned to club president Paul and said by way of consolation, "you know that in real life, you would never associate with him [Jeff]." Even though all three men were employed by the same large firm, the barriers of functional specialty (engineering versus marketing), as well as race, would likely have kept them from crossing paths, professionally or personally. But the investment club brought them together under conditions that forced them to cooperate. In this sense, investment clubs help build the skills and competencies necessary to participate in the public sphere. The clubs create not only investors but citizens.

This is reminiscent of Habermas's theory of "communicative action," in which he foregrounds the role of small groups in building social capital and civic resources. Such groups, Habermas argues, help participants become "more competent members of modern societies" by teaching them to engage in constructive argumentation. Characteristics of such groups include:

- decision processes in which conflicts are resolved solely by the "force of the better argument";
- cooperation in defining and achieving shared goals;
- an equal voice in the process for all group members, including the ability to introduce proposals or call others' proposals into question;
- the absence of threats to free and equal expression of ideas.[30]

The case of investment clubs very closely approximates Habermas's vision of an "ideal speech situation." Learning to be an investor *through the vehicle of investment clubs*, as opposed to outside a group context, has the secondary consequence of teaching the "communicative ethics" and discursive rules on which, Habermas argues, civil societies are built.

Of course, there are also threats to the ideal-typical speech situation instantiated in investment clubs. In particular, as the evidence reviewed in this study shows, problems of power and ideology manifested themselves repeatedly in the form of club members who rubber-stamped each others' investment proposals (voting for ideas "just to fly the flag" of group cohesion, as Brad of California Investors put it) or who withheld valuable information from the group to avoid disrupting socioemotional relationships. But to the extent that the groups in this study *did* approach the high standards for candor stipulated in Habermas's vision, they were positively reinforced for it by improved profits. That is, investment clubs contribute to civil society by providing financial incentives to reward the development of argumentation skills such as candor, full engagement in the decision process, and respectful disagreement.

Finally, investment clubs contribute to civil society by creating an opportunity structure in which individuals have more to gain, or less to lose, by cooperating with others than by acting as free agents. The microlevel interaction context—including opportunity structures, such as economies of scale in investment, as well as monitoring and sanctioning—constitutes a unique contribution of small, face-to-face groups like investment clubs to civil society. Macrolevel entities such as states, complex organizations, or large associations (like bowling leagues) cannot reproduce these structures and capabilities effectively. When they attempt to do so, the costs are often prohibitive and the results often unsatisfactory in local contexts.[31] As one legal theorist put it, small groups excel at providing "order without law," which might serve equally well as a working definition of civil society itself.[32] Indeed, involvement in associations like investment clubs postulates a relationship to the larger civic arena—the state, the market, corporations, and other groups.[33] How a group positions itself with relation to these other actors can set the stage for a deeper engagement with civic life, as in phenomena like shareholder activism and socially responsible investing.

Implications for Publicly Traded Firms

With investor behavior increasingly linked to notions of citizenship, publicly traded firms may need to rethink *their* self-presentation strategies. While most such firms have a great deal of experience in shaping their corporate image for an audience of professional analysts and institutional investors,[34] strategies for presenting firms to a broader audience have lagged the growth of the amateur investor movement. Well-publicized instances of individual investors being rebuffed or ignored at shareholder meetings have contributed to the perception that many American firms are arrogant or out of touch when it comes to the groundswell of public involvement in the market. This is an issue not only of corporate governance but also of crafting a corporate identity to present to a new constituency—one that comes to investing from a decision model that assigns value to the identity implications of a stock purchase as well as to its prospects for financial gain.

Finance industry professionals are already issuing warnings about the likely changes to the traditional policy of benign neglect toward individual investors. Driven in part by regulatory changes such as the Sarbanes-Oxley legislation, and new disclosure rules issued by the New York Stock Exchange, the general trend will be toward much greater accountability, responsiveness, and personal interaction between executives and boards of directors, on the one hand, and individual investors on the other. As one former NYSE official wrote in 2004:

> The rules of the road for those who manage and steward large public companies *really are* different now . . . Many observers see 2004 as a template for what could follow in 2005 and future years. Shareholder activists are hailing some of the changes, believing now that after several decades of increasing activism, and the mounting challenges to nonresponsive companies, the scales are tipping in their favor (issuer ability to ignore or reject shareholder proposals is diminishing, they argue). *The players to watch from the boardroom and corporate suite especially include . . . individual and faith-based coalitions.*[35]

This trend toward greater activism and influence by individual investors has been facilitated by the Internet. As SEC commissioner Laura Unger noted, "companies may not be able to ignore individual investors in the future. Individual investors own close to half of the shares in U.S. companies. Internet-savvy individual investors are becoming increasingly interested in corporate governance issues." For example, she noted, a group of individual shareholders in Cincinnati created a website to mobilize other small stakeholders in a proxy battle against the management of Professional Bancorp; though the individual investors owned only 13 percent of the company in total, they ultimately won over 70 percent of the approximately one million votes cast by shareholders. Such activism by individual shareholders—alone or in groups—has had a significant impact on firms' finances, in some cases causing single-day swings of 20 to 30 percent in share price.[36] On the positive side, stocks of firms rated highest in terms of responsiveness to individual shareholders (i.e., investors that are not institutions, corporations, or finance professionals) outperformed the S&P 500 index by an *average* of 11.13 percent for the fiscal year March 1, 2004, through February 28, 2005.[37]

Such evidence suggests that just as firms are sensitive to the image they present to professional analysts, they will need to take great care in how they are perceived by the millions of individual investors who make up the "ownership society." Firms that have been willing to leave the NASDAQ for the NYSE, simply to project a more established image or to inspire greater confidence among analysts, may need to make similar accommodations to the perceptions of their individual shareholders. Clearly, in order for firms to build a relationship with these investors, they will need to understand who these investors are, as well as their concerns.

The present study of investment clubs is well positioned to shed light on such issues. Among other things, the data reviewed in this research suggest that corporate governance issues may be only the tip of the iceberg when it comes to changes firms will have to make in order to respond to this new group of investors. While media coverage has highlighted the changes in rules, regulations, and technology that will give small shareholders much greater authority in the management of firms in which they invest—particularly when it comes to hot-button issues such as executive compensation and board independence—the evidence from investment clubs suggests a set of issues that have not yet appeared on the radar screens of the professionals: issues of corporate image and identity, and the ways in which those issues may reflect on individual investors.

The evidence from the present study suggests that the consumer marketing analogy is particularly appropriate for firms attempting to address this new community of investors, since the investors themselves approach the stock market with mental models and decision heuristics derived from their consumer experience. This is not just a matter of women investors showing a preference for stocks within the consumer sector of the economy; it is a general orientation in which men and women alike invest based on stocks' congruence with their self-image. Thus, the investment club study yielded data showing that investors conceptualize their decisions in terms of the "logic of gender appropriateness." Some investors segment the market (to borrow a term from brand marketing) into "boy stocks" and "girl stocks"; others screen stocks by asking a related question: is this stock congruent with my identity as a man/woman?

Data such as these suggest that firms adapting to the new exigencies of mass involvement by individual investors in the stock market must attend to the ways in which purchasing a stock affects the way investors see themselves. The issue of congruence with notions of self is woven throughout the data showing how investors make decisions among stocks: as illustrated in previous chapters, there were repeated instances in which investors rejected stocks because they "couldn't identify" with them (as in the decision by Ladies with Leverage to eliminate Consolidated Stores from consideration) or thought that the stocks would reflect negatively on them as moral people (as when Asset Accumulators rejected a proposal to invest in Harley-Davidson, despite the firm's promising financial outlook).

Such decisions highlight the second major theme in this new regime of "identity investing": the need for individual investors to maintain their self-concept as "good people" when making investment choices. The tension that individuals experience around this issue is suggested by the investment club naming conventions discussed in chapter 2: names like "Investors for Christ," "L'Chaim Investors," or "Episcobucks" indicate that the age-old conflict between ethics and virtue on the one hand, and money and profit on the other, is still highly salient to contemporary investors.

This suggests an increasing need for firms to be sensitive to their image, not only in terms of corporate governance, but in terms of corporate citizenship. The "new investor class" wants to know not only whether a company is well run, with appropriate oversight and compensation policies, but whether a company makes a positive contribution to society. Thus, grassroots organizations have successfully lobbied large multinational firms—largely through activism at shareholder meetings—to support environmental and economic justice movements. The corporate social responsibility movement[38] has already gained enough clout to induce British Petroleum to spend two years and $200 million to "re-brand" itself worldwide as an environmentally progressive firm, starting with its name change to "BP: Beyond Petroleum."[39] Similarly, shareholder activists concerned about labor practices and economic development in the Third World persuaded Starbucks to sell and serve so-called "Fair Trade" coffee, purchased directly from small producers at per-pound rates three to four times what they would normally receive from coffee brokers.[40]

Such changes, driven in large part by the kinds of investors represented in this study, ultimately provoke larger questions about the meaning and purpose of commerce. Notions such as "shareholder value," so central to the operation of financial markets, can no longer be defined simply in terms of earnings per share. The investment club data suggest that values, ethics, and identity will continue to grow in importance as elements in investor decision-making. Such social constructs define some of the new boundaries of the expanding community of amateur investors whose power to influence corporate behavior is on the rise.

Implications for Economic Sociology

Explaining how investors understand and estimate value is a matter of interest not only to leaders of publicly traded firms but to economic sociologists as well. Theory in economic sociology has evolved in part through debates about what value means, who gets to assign value, and how notions of value are socially constructed. This study supports a multidimensional conceptualization of value by illustrating the ways in which investors interact, negotiate, and contest with one another over which of many available metrics they should employ to assess the value of a stock. In addition, because financial metrics are rarely sufficient to narrow investment decisions to a single, obvious choice, narratives become a deciding factor in constructing assessments of economic value. The decision space that investors face and co-create can be described as a "marketplace of stories," in which they—along with finance professionals and executives of publicly traded firms—vie to construct persuasive narratives about the current or future value of stocks.

Thus, a unique contribution of this study is to push economic sociology toward a clearer understanding of the mechanisms at work in complex systems. Complex adaptive systems like financial markets involve learning and experimentation by participants *in interaction with one another.*[41] Observing how investment clubs assess the value of individual stocks provides unique insight into these interaction processes. The social interactions involved in investing suggest that complexity in financial markets is created in part by fad and fashion; Robert Shiller acknowledges this in his observation that "investment in speculative assets is a social activity."[42] The role of fashion in valuing stocks—from the "conglomerate craze" of the 1950s, through the dot.com bubble of the 1990s—has been documented elsewhere.[43] The present study contributes to social scientific understanding of financial markets by showing how the rise of investment clubs has brought not only a new set of participants, but also a new set of motives and behaviors, to an already complex system.

Historically, many of the models used to conceptualize and analyze economic behavior have been derived from the physical sciences. This is a matter of pride to many economists and finance scholars, and their strategies have brought enormous progress in our understanding of investor behavior. That is, economics and finance have advanced knowledge by treating phenomena like investment activity as a problem of "disorganized complexity," much like the behavior of particles. Within systems of "disorganized complexity"—a term coined by the biologist Warren Weaver in his seminal 1958 report to the Rockefeller Foundation—entities move autonomously and randomly, but in ways that can be predicted through probability calculations and statistical analysis, then aggregated into averages.

Weaver credited this method with some of the most important scientific discoveries in history. But he also warned against what he saw as the widespread *misapplication* of this model—particularly to complex problems in which entities (be they particles or people) are *interconnected* or *organized*. In such cases of "organized complexity," the connections among entities could be so subtle as to be overlooked, causing problems to be misclassified and subject to the misapplication of techniques designed to analyze "disorganized complexity." As a result, the "disorganized complexity" model began to act as an impediment to the development of knowledge, forcing data to conform to deductive randomness models and subsuming vital evidence of the nonrandom connections among variables into the error term—treating what was often valuable data as, in Weaver's words, "in some dark, foreboding way, irrational."[44]

This is where economics and behavioral finance have left off in examining the behavior of retail investors. Despite their many contributions to knowledge, research in these fields has not brought us much closer to answering the "why" questions evoked by so-called "irrational" behavior on the part of investors, such as, why do so many individual investors prefer cash dividends to stock dividends? Or, why do individuals so often buy the same stocks as their neighbors? Disciplines that look to the physical sciences for their models appear stuck at this juncture in explaining economic behavior.

This is where sociology shows the most promise for advancing the social scientific project of understanding the workings of the stock market. As a discipline that allows for rationality to be locally defined and variable, and which permits researchers to build theory inductively, sociology is well suited to solve what Weaver called problems of "organized complexity." Jane Jacobs—who defined cities and other mass social behaviors as cases of "organized complexity"—advanced Weaver's conceptual framework by specifying the kind of approach needed to grapple with such problems. In her approach, statistical or probabilistic methods may be used, but only as supplements to inductively grounded data-gathering and analysis.

Jacobs's description closely approximates the analytic techniques that define "sociological miniaturism"[45] and "grounded theory" development.[46] That is, sociology as a discipline has the tools ready at hand to address problems of "organized complexity" in an effective and insightful way. So while sociologists can use statistical and probabilistic methods, and reason from deduction and averages, they are not obliged to discount what Jacobs terms "the unaverage" because it is statistically inconsequential. In fact, as the present study demonstrates, sociology can gain a great deal of insight from engaging with "unaverage" data rather than relegating it to the error term or the "black box" of irrationality. Sometimes, as Jacobs points out, the "unaverage" is a vital clue in comprehending complex relationships. Thus, the sociological approach to understanding investor behavior proceeds from the notion that "the variables are many, but they are not helter-skelter ... although the interactions of their many factors are complex, there is nothing accidental or irrational about the ways in which those factors affect each other."[47]

The present study is intended to contribute to sociology's already considerable resources in addressing problems of organized complexity by identifying some of the microlevel social mechanisms that underlie economic behavior. As in Jacobs's approach to the problem of cities, this study focuses on processes—specifically, the processes involved in making investments in the stock market. I argue that this seemingly straightforward activity, in which millions of Americans routinely engage, is actually a set of tightly connected microroutines, including: creating a social identity; constructing lines of action within a bewildering array of choices; and developing the stories, collective representations, and "social poetics"[48] of the stock market through which investors give meaning to their actions.

Perhaps most importantly, what we gain from treating the "mass culture of investing" as a problem of organized complexity is the ability to understand the ways in which the millions of individuals involved in this phenomenon *interact with, interpret, and respond to one another.* This is the fundamental contribution of sociology to theories of complexity involving social agents. As sociologist Herbert Blumer wrote, "human beings interpret or 'define' each others' actions instead of merely reacting to each others' actions. Their 'response' is not made directly to the actions of another but instead is based on the meaning which they attach to such actions. Thus, *human interaction is mediated by the use of symbols, by interpretation, or by ascertaining the meaning of one anothers' actions.*"[49]

As the evidence reviewed in this study shows, investors' goals and decisions are emergent, evolving through interaction; further, investors develop lines of action not only through identifying their own preferences but also in response to the imagined motives of other agents within the system. In other words, investors do not choose stocks simply in response to their own ideas, or even to those of their investment club cohort; rather, participants in this study continually evolved their investment strategies based on their "theories of mind" about other investors.[50] Just as firms imaginatively construct their target audiences of investors or consumers, amateur investors develop mental models about other actors within the stock market. The models consist of beliefs about those actors' motives and likely behavior, and combine with individuals' own preferences to create lines of action.

This phenomenon was evident in Jeff's pitch to Bulls & Bears, detailed in chapter 3. His primary rationale for buying shares of Cisco Systems was the "buzz" the firm had generated, and what that was likely to mean for the stock's future price. "The whole Valley is talking about Cisco," he said. While his approach was not immediately persuasive to his fellow club members—because it had to be squared with the group's other metric of value, instantiated in financial calculations—Jeff was by no means the only member to invoke these "theories of mind" as valid means of assessing share value. Even the more quantitatively oriented members of the group who voted down Jeff's initial presentation agreed with his assessment of the stock's popularity and the likelihood that that would lead to an increase in its price. Greg, a self-described "conservative engineer" who was Jeff's most vocal opponent, acknowledged that Cisco was a "hot stock"; Cate, one of the most experienced and respected members of the group, described Cisco as "hot, hot, hot . . . the Microsoft of its market." The major difference between Jeff and the other members of Bulls & Bears was his willingness to treat this "theory of mind" about other investors' responses to Cisco stock as a *sufficient* condition for making the purchase; for the other members, it was necessary to have two metrics of value—the theorized attitudes of other investors as well as the financial calculations—in order to be comfortable making the purchase.

For other clubs, a persuasive "theory of mind" about other investors was reason enough to buy stock, even when the financial calculations suggested otherwise. For example, Ladies with Leverage decided to buy shares of Charles Schwab despite the poor financial prospects, purely on the basis of their "theory of mind" about Schwab's clientele—that is, other investors. As Lydia put it, "This company is going to be hot: it's a great industry, and *baby boomers will want to keep investing regardless of the economic outlook*."[51]

Thus, unlike behavioral economics, sociology does not stop at acknowledging the ways in which context complicates financial decisions. Rather, it specifies *what kinds* of context matter (the color of one's house probably does not, but one's neighbors do), *why* they matter (for reasons of identity, status, or network content), and *how* they affect our decisions (we talk with our neighbors, observe their choices, and—most critically—interpret what those choices mean). The ability to incorporate "theories of mind," and other ways in which social actors' behavior is modified in response to other actors, is a distinctive contribution of the sociological approach to understanding complex systems like financial markets.

A Theory of Competing Rationalities

To observe the kind of intellectual purchase this approach can provide, consider the term "rationality." From the point of view of neoclassical economic theory (or of rational choice theory within sociology),[52] rationality involves autonomous agents like *homo economicus* making choices under the following conditions:

- there are a given, fixed set of alternatives,
- with (subjectively) known probability distributions of outcomes for each alternative,
- and the objective is to maximize the expected value of a given utility function.[53]

This version of rationality requires a logical connection between means and ends; that is, rational actors make fully informed calculations to minimize costs while maximizing profits, rents, or utility. Most economists acknowledge that such assumptions are unrealistic[54] but maintain that the stylizations represented by the *homo economicus* model remain useful in terms of predictive power. Others—notably behavioral finance scholars—have made numerous critiques of the model. Behavioral finance shares with sociology a rejection of the normative approach to rationality. To make this approach possible, both disciplines privilege empirical evidence over theory, and concrete behavior over abstraction. For example, behavioral finance scholars, like sociologists, acknowledge that economic decisions are not made autonomously, in a cultural and historical vacuum, but in a context of interaction with others and the desire to maintain congruence with prevailing norms and one's own past behavior. Thus, behavioral finance shares many of the objectives of economic sociology, including "taking stock price values as the dependent variable . . . we recognize human investor behavior, rather than some abstract, external force, as the independent causative variable."[55]

But while behavioral finance does an admirable job of critiquing the neoclassical model of rationality, the critique falls short in two respects. First, while it acknowledges the role of interaction in shaping economic decisions, behavioral finance is fundamentally bound to the individual level of analysis. On the positive side, this has enabled decades' worth of fruitful collaboration with psychologists (such as that between

Daniel Kahneman and Amos Tversky) who also work at the individual level. But on the negative side, behavioral finance lacks the theoretical tools to cope with interaction processes.

A second limitation, corollary to the first, is that behavioral finance does not have the conceptual resources to address issues such as culture or meaning. While many fascinating works of behavioral finance document the importance of these issues (e.g., a 1997 study showing systematic differences in attitudes toward financial risk held by Jews, Buddhists, Catholics, and Protestants, among others[56]) behavioral finance can only gesture in the direction of culture, meaning, and interaction. Though it represents a vital critique of rationality from within the disciplines of finance and economics, it lacks the means to construct a more satisfactory alternative.

This is where sociology picks up the baton and advances understanding of economic behavior. To grasp the contribution of the sociological approach, consider the case of socially responsible investing addressed in chapter 2. Given that "socially screened" investments are the most rapidly growing segment of the stock market, this is an area of intense interest to economist as well as sociologists. By investing in a socially responsible fashion, the investment clubs I studied did not always make an economic sacrifice. Rather, they tried to invest profitably while *at the same time* remaining congruent with their self-image (and public image) as good or virtuous people. However, when faced with investments that would be economically profitable, but socially questionable, most chose to forgo the potential gains and preserve their image.

Behavioral economists might observe that while socially responsible investing represents a departure from profit-oriented, neoclassical rationality, it could nonetheless be subsumed under the commonplace economic concept of utility. In fact, many of the major contributions to knowledge made by behavioral finance scholars have been of this form: modifications to the utility function. Some of these important modifications include expanding the notion of utility to account for effects such as "loss aversion" or "hyperbolic discounting," which acknowledge that individuals assign variable utilities to the same entity depending on whether it represents a loss or a gain, and on whether it is available immediately versus at some time in the future.[57] These insights have advanced economics tremendously by bringing in greater empirical realism and acknowledgment of the contextual embeddedness of investment decisions.

But ameliorating the limitations of the neoclassical economic paradigm is not the aim of economic sociology. Rather, as the case of socially responsible investing shows, sociology requires us to examine economic behavior in situ, on its own terms, with the object of discovering the meaning and implications of the behavior for the participants. Thus, faced with evidence of economic activity that is not oriented *exclusively* to profit maximization, economic sociologists would have an entirely different response than economists of either the behavioral or neoclassical variety. While the neoclassicists might be inclined to place socially responsible investing inside the black box of irrationality, and behaviorists might see the phenomenon as requiring an expansion of the notion of utility, sociologists would accept neither conceptual strategy as satisfactory. Rather, sociologists would argue that, prima facie, the value accorded to culturally and historically specific modes of behavior cannot plausibly be reduced to either irrationality or utility.[58] What these aspects of behavior represent are in fact outside the conceptual realm of economics, and cannot be forced into either classical or behavioral models without doing violence to the data.

Competing Models of Exchange

Ultimately, the data from this study suggest a need to expand our definitions of economic rationality beyond the profit motive. This is not a new idea, but one whose time has come to be revived. Max Weber, a founding father of sociology, spoke to this issue nearly a century ago, in his distinction between "substantive" and "formal" rationality, also known as means/ends or process/product rationality. The former is instantiated in value perspectives such as compassion or honor, while the latter is embodied in the modern socioeconomic order. Weber describes the clash between the two systems of rationality as "one of the most important sources of all 'social' problems."[59]

This is not to deny the importance of "formal," profit-oriented rationality as understood by economists. Rather, this study takes the position that multiple forms of rationality coexist, sometimes unobtrusively and sometimes in open competition with one another. In this sense, the study also proposes an alternative to Kahneman's "two-system" view by arguing that individuals are not only capable of being rational and irrational at the same time, but in fact operate *at all times* within multiple, intersecting spheres of rationality.

This simultaneity is often obscured by value judgments that attempt to privilege some forms of rationality over others. Historically, economics has claimed precedence in imposing its version of rationality on social science; thus, Nobel Prize winner Paul Samuelson defined the division of labor between economics and sociology as the study of the rational and the nonrational, respectively.[60] To which sociologists might respond, by quoting from Hegel: "The real is the rational and the rational is the real."[61]

In this competition for primacy in defining rationality, the actual complexity of the data can sometimes be obscured, to the detriment of social scientific knowledge across disciplines. Often, this takes place through a crude sorting process that implicitly acknowledges multiple modes of experiencing and engaging with reality, but conceals their coexistence or simultaneity by differentiating them along lines such as "public/private" or "modern/primitive." These distinctions are not value-free; instead, "different ways of organizing and relating to experience . . . tend to be historically and culturally embedded in distinct social groups and even classes."[62] As those social groups and classes are valued, so are the modes of rationality associated with them. In neoclassical economics, and even behavioral economics, this typically results in the devaluation of modes of rationality associated with women, non-Western peoples, and those outside the realm of professional finance.[63]

The following table summarizes the characteristics of these "competing rationalities of exchange" as instantiated in the realm of economic transactions. Borrowing from the works of Marx and Granovetter, I have dubbed the two modalities "alienated" and "embedded." The "alienated" mode of exchange derives from what is currently the hegemonic conception of economic rationality: abstracted from social relations, cultural context, or the personal characteristics of the agents. Investors making decisions in this mode would be expected to buy or sell stocks based purely on the expectation of maximizing profits or minimizing costs or losses. The identity of the investor, and the context in which he or she makes decisions, are of little consequence. In contrast, the "embedded" mode of transaction derives from embodied experience and takes place in a context where identity, historical context, and future social consequences of decisions all matter a great deal. Table 6.2 summarizes these characteristics as defined—implicitly or explicitly—by the literatures in economics and finance on the one hand, and sociology, anthropology, and some branches of psychology on the other.

The data from investment clubs suggest the presence of both alienated and embedded forms of economic rationality in a contemporary, developed nation, involving ongoing interactions between men and women. It is unlikely that the simultaneous operation of these modes of rationality and exchange is unique to investment clubs. Indeed, similar observations have been made about the coexistence of the formal and informal economies within the United States.[64]

Table 6.2
Alienated Versus Embedded Modes of Exchange

Alienated		Embedded
Abstract	*Source of knowledge*	Embodied
Male/"genderless universal"	*Ideal-typical actor*	Female/"other"
Public sphere	*Location in social space*	Private sphere
Developed countries	*Global/political position*	Underdeveloped countries
Modern/contemporary	*Temporal location*	Primitive/historical
Transient interactions	*Relationship among actors*	Ongoing interactions

But the evidence reviewed in the present study sheds light on a phenomenon that is fully part of the formal economy (in the sense of being subject to government protection, oversight, and accountability) yet still invokes multiple modes of rationality and exchange. For example, as the interview excerpts in chapter 5 indicate, investment club members are very sensitive to social context in their decision making, including the impact of their investment choices on their self-image and public image, as well as to group dynamics produced by network content and demographic composition.

At the same time, it is important to recall the data that show these individuals behaving from time to time like hard-nosed profit seekers. Investment clubs, like many other financial decision-making bodies, show elements of *both* modes of economic rationality. Sociological studies of mortgage brokers, investment banks, and pension funds show a similar pattern of parallel, competing rationalities—although the alienated form has a far greater presence in the professional settings. As historian Barbara Rosenwein notes of two competing models of economy (gift and commerce) in early modern Europe, the "new" systems never fully supersede the "old," but rather "they can function together, and economic activity of every sort is produced by their mix in greater, lesser or equal degrees."[65]

The point is that neither investment clubs nor professional financiers are *globally* rational or irrational in the way that neoclassical economics defines the terms. Rather, sociological research—including this study—indicates that investment in stocks and other economic activities are subject to *multiple* forms of rationality, often simultaneously. Further, the relationships of individuals and groups to these modes of understanding are not binary (as in "rational" or "irrational") but variable along a continuum. Attempts to balance these competing rationalities, and their often-divergent claims, are among the processes that make the stock market a system of organized complexity for both participants and observers.

Amidst the variety of motives that influence investors' decisions, and the myriad of ways in which individuals are influenced by one another, it is easy to see how the stock market could be mistaken for a system of "disorganized complexity." But by providing analytical tools—such as those found within the symbolic interactionist tradition and social psychology—that can reveal the organized social processes underlying the complexity, sociology contributes in two ways to the project of making sense of financial markets.

First, in keeping with Jacobs's strategy, sociology provides methods for inductive analysis of "nonaverage" cases. This allows researchers to address a much broader scope of empirical phenomena than is possible within purely deductive frameworks. Thus, this study can treat investment clubs as "markets in microcosm," by reasoning from the specific (small voluntary groups making decisions within the stock market) to the general (such as professional groups that make decisions within the stock market, like corporate investment committees or the Federal Reserve Board). While the analogy has its limitations, the shared interaction processes—such as the construction of value, meaning, and identity—transcend the boundaries of specific empirical settings and offer insight into other small-group and financial phenomena.

Second, the notion of multiple rationalities provides historical coherence to interpretations of events such as the dramatic increase in the popularity of investment clubs during the 1990s. This is not just a matter of linking the recent stock market bubble to the Dutch tulip bulb craze or the South Sea Company stock issues, though these are in some ways useful comparisons. Rather, the sociological approach allows us to develop connections and insights that are both broader (such as linking investment clubs to the microcredit associations used in developing countries) and deeper (illustrating the similarities between investment clubs and aboriginal totem cults) than are possible in disciplines that draw a hard line between rational and irrational, or modern and "primitive" behaviors. These connections are particularly exciting given that the phenomenon under investigation is occurring in a wealthy nation where online trading—unmediated by any human interaction—is readily available. Yet the behavior of these clubs is informed by a mode of rationality that at times sacrifices profits in the name of preserving or enhancing social networks and social identities. This form of rationality links investment clubs with the socially embedded mode of exchange that has characterized human societies throughout history, and which continues to flourish worldwide in the shadow of modern modes of economic development.[66] So investment clubs are not only similar in specific ways to groups associated with archaic or underdeveloped societies; they partake in a general way of much older traditions of rationality and exchange that have been overshadowed— though never entirely superseded—by free market capitalism and formal, alienated modes of rationality.

This is among the greatest rewards that investment clubs offer to the social scientific enterprise of understanding financial markets. Investment clubs represent an inflection point at which complex systems—such as the "new" economy and the "old"—meet and interpenetrate, allowing us to observe the collision between the systems and their competing modes of rationality, as well as the terms of their coexistence. What anthropologist Ellen Hertz writes of the emergence of the Shanghai stock exchange is equally apt as a description of investment clubs and the insights they offer to social scientists: "It provides us with a means of bridging the great divide between modern and non-modern economic institutions, while neither ignoring the differences which mark them nor exaggerating the force of those differences."[67]

Put another way, this study provides a snapshot of what Marcel Mauss once dubbed the "very long transitional phase" between the "old" economy (the world of embedded transactions, as instantiated in the gift) and the "new" (the world of alienated, spot-market exchange).[68] Mauss made this pronouncement in 1923; now, more than eighty years later as this book is being written, the evidence from investment clubs suggests that the transition is far from complete. While some scholars—notably Levi-Strauss[69]—have argued for the inevitable dominance of the alienated, impersonal mode of economic rationality, many others have been struck by the resilience of the particularistic, embedded modes of economic rationality, noting "the extent to which commercial markets and gifts continue to exist side by side and interact."[70]

Ultimately, this study suggests that a complete transition may never be effected, and that multiple modes of exchange and rationality may continue to coexist—though not necessarily in harmony. Nor is such harmony or completion necessarily desirable. There are advantages to dynamic tension among models of interaction. For example, the embedded model of exchange provides an alternative to the "frictionless" but sterile mode of impersonal markets. Such markets have their uses, to be sure, but there is a great deal to be said for the long-standing role of particularistic economic relations (whether in the form of gift exchange or investment groups) in advancing civic engagement—what Albert Hirschman has called the "civilizing" aspects of capitalism, or "doux commerce."[71]

Notes ◆

Acknowledgments

1. Marcel Proust 1981, *Remembrance of Things Past* (New York: Random House), p. 1089.

Section One
Investment Clubs and the "Ownership Society"

1. Hertz 1998, p. 19.
2. U.S. Congress 2000, p. 1.
3. Weisberg 1998, p. 30.
4. Robert Samuelson 1999.
5. Buenza and Stark, 2004, p. 370.
6. National Association of Securities Dealers 1997.
7. Based on the nonincarcerated adult population at the beginning of 1997: 190,072,921 people. For sources, see the *Statistical Abstract of the United States*, http://www.census.gov/prod/99pubs/99statab/sec05.pdf, specifically, section 1, 1998, table 14, and section 9, 1999, table 380.
8. NAIC Factbook, 12/31/02, http://www.better-investing.org/about/fact.html. This organization—the National Association of Investors Corporation, usually known as NAIC—does not represent all investment clubs; no organization does, and so with the exception of the 1997 NASD survey the total number of investment clubs in the United States cannot be known with any certainty. But NAIC is the only organization that represents investment clubs nationally.

The organization recently changed its name to Better Investing, but it has retained the investment education strategies and tools used by the participants in this study.

9. Rao, Davis, and Ward 2000.
10. DeLong, Shleifer, and Waldmann 1993.
11. Hirsch, Michaels, and Friedman 1990; Adler and Adler 1984; Samuelson Paul 1983; Boulding 1966.
12. Thaler 1992.
13. CalPERS data as of September 30, 2001; NAIC data as of October 31, 2001. As of January 2001, total NAIC club investments actually exceeded those of CalPERS.
14. O'Barr and Conley 1992, p. 229.
15. Friedman 1993.
16. Stolte, Fine, and Cook 2001.
17. Hart 1990.
18. Thaler 1992.
19. E.g., Baker 1990; see also Uzzi 1999; Galaskiewicz 1985.

Chapter One
Stock Market Populism—Investment Clubs and Economic History

1. Weber 1946, p. 314.
2. Geist 1999.
3. National Association of Securities Dealers 1997.
4. Both quotations from Weisberg 1998, p. 30.
5. Markoff 1998.
6. With the exception of some highly visible women, such as Carly Fiorina of Hewlett-Packard, the high-technology industry was dominated by young men.
7. Back cover text of Kevin Kelly's *New Rules for the New Economy* (1998); text is from 1999 paperback edition.
8. Krugman 1998.
9. McGough 1997.
10. National Association of Securities Dealers 1997.
11. National Association of Investors Corporation 1999.
12. O'Hara and Janke 1998.
13. Ragsdale 1997. Note the similar language used to encourage people to invest in American stocks following the terrorist attacks of September 11, next note.
14. For example, I received the following e-mail on Friday, September 14, 2001, as part of a mass mailing sent to my great-aunt, who forwarded it to me:

> In the last two days, people have been asking themselves what they can do in the wake of Tuesday's terrible disaster. Here is a simple answer BUY STOCK ON MONDAY MORNING as an act of defiance against hatred and terrorism. 1 Share. 10 Shares. 100 Shares. It doesn't matter. Just buy something and send a message to the perpetrators of this awful crime that our nation will not be

cowed. If you own mutual funds or work with an investment firm call them and tell them you want your money in U.S. stocks because you believe in the strongest economy the world has ever known. Imagine how powerful it would be if together we could to send the stock market racing up, not down. Together we can make this happen. Together, as a nation, we can create a groundswell. Defy hatred by sending this e-mail to everyone you know and another e-mail to the news services below. Let's create a news story, so that in turn, we can create the greatest rally the stock market has ever known. And be sure to follow up on that message by not letting this terrible tragedy change the way you live. Go to a store and buy clothes for your kids. Go on vacation just like you planned. Replace that old car. If the economy falters, the terrorists win. We can't let that happen. We can do this. Send it on. Here is your chance to be part of the most powerful act of social and economic defiance in the history of man.

Best regards,
Joe Forte & Friends
GROUNDSWELL FOR AMERICA
—Copy the lines below and send it out today!
TO nightly@NBC.com, evening@cbsnews.com, netaudr@abc.com, community@cnn.com, inquiries@wsj.dowjones.com, foxnewsonline@foxnews.com
SUBJECT I'M BUYING STOCK IN AMERICA
BODY OF E-MAIL I'm buying stock on Monday as an act of patriotism."

15. Chancellor 1999, p. 29.
16. Thaler and deBondt 1992.
17. There are a variety of definitions of growth stocks. NAIC uses two benchmarks: the first is a 15 percent annual growth rate in five value of the stock, which will double the original investment in five years; in addition, the earnings growth rate of the firm issuing the stock must be greater than the growth rate of the gross domestic product.
18. Malkiel 1990.
19. Barsky, Juster, Kimball, and Shapiro 1997.
20. In constant 1982 dollars, hourly wages declined from $7.78 to $7.40 between 1985 and 1995, and weekly wages declined from $275 to $255; from 1996 *Statistical Abstracts*, census charts 868, 589, and 587.
21. According to the Pension and Welfare Benefits Administration, cited in *Fortune*, 18 August 1997, p. 114.
22. General Accounting Office 1996.
23. Harrington 2001.
24. Ibbotson Associates 2001, pp. 112–113; Bogle 1997.
25. Barboza and Oppel 2002.
26. Weisberg 1998.
27. Reskin and Roos 1990.
28. DiMaggio 1992.
29. Meir Statman 1997, quoted in *Wall Street Journal*, 15 July, p. C1.

30. Marsden, Cook, and Knoke 1994.
31. Scott 1992.
32. 15 July 1997, p. C1.
33. John Kenneth Galbraith 1990, p. 52.
34. Chancellor 1999.
35. Schumpeter 1939, p. 250.
36. Lynch 1989, p. 32.
37. Steiner 1996.
38. Cited in Chancellor 1999, p. 81. No further information on the Swift quotation is provided.
39. U.S. Securities and Exchange Commission 1998.
40. Chancellor 1999.
41. Ingrassia 1995.
42. Chancellor, 1999, p. 166.
43. Beardstown Ladies 1994, p. 10.
44. Chancellor 1999, p. 20.
45. Chancellor 1999, p. 28. During Lay's February 12, 2002, testimony before Congress, Senator Peter Fitzgerald (R-IL) played the avenging role, saying: "Mr. Lay, I've concluded that you're perhaps the most accomplished confidence man since Charles Ponzi. I'd say you're a carnival barker, except that wouldn't be fair to carnival barkers. A carnie will at least tell you up front that he's running a shell game."
46. Found at http://politicalhumor.about.com/library/images/blpic-marthastewart living.htm; no other citation information was given at this site.
47. Ingrassia 1995.
48. Ben-Yehuda 1980.
49. The overstatement was explained by Beardstown treasurer Betty Sinnock as an accident occasioned by misunderstanding of the club's accounting software, but was generally interpreted as an attempt to perpetrate fraud on the American public. See articles cited below.
50. *Seattle Times*, 21 March 1998, p. A11.
51. *The Guardian* (London), 23 March 1998, p. 3.
52. Kroll 1998.
53. Rick Horowitz 1998.
54. Buenza and Stark 2004, p. 381. See also Castells 1996.
55. Hertz 1998, p. 4.

Chapter Two
Investment Clubs as Markets in Microcosm

1. Marcuse 1964, p. 9.
2. Turner and Killian 1972, p. 129.

3. Kahneman 2003, p. 470.

4. Deleuze and Guattari 1995.

5. Hegel 1975, p. 137.

6. Simon 1982.

7. Simon 1982.

8. On professional investors, see Malkiel 1990; on individual investors, see Barber and Odean 1999.

9. Iyengar and Lepper 2000.

10. Thaler and Benartzi 2002.

11. Tversky and Kahneman 1971. See also Kahneman's 2002 Nobel Prize address for a review of some of these heuristics.

12. Indeed, many taxonomies for parsing the stock market into manageable chunks are reminiscent of Jorge Luis Borges' account of "a certain Chinese encyclopedia" that classified the animal kingdom into the following categories: "a) belonging to the Emperor; b) embalmed; c) tame; d) suckling pigs; e) sirens; f) fabulous; g) stray dogs; h) included in the present classification; i) that shake like a fool; j) innumerable; k) drawn with a very fine camel-hair brush; l) etcetera; m) having just broken the water pitcher; n) that, if seen from a distance, look like flies." See Borges 1999. Many stock classification systems are equally arbitrary, but not nearly as humorous.

13. Zelizer 1996; Thaler 1992.

14. Rogus 2001.

15. Catalyst 2004, p. 7.

16. Nicholas Barbon 1696, *A Discourse Concerning the Coining of Money Lighter,* cited in Chancellor 1999, p. 45.

17. Katona 1975.

18. Cialdini 1984.

19. Asch 1955.

20. Freud 1959; Barsade and Gibson 1998.

21. Klausner 1984, p. 61.

22. Snow and Parker 1984.

23. Pugh 2001; Hatfield, Caccioppo, and Rapson 1994.

24. Abrams, Wetherell, Cochrane, Hogg, and Turner 1990, emphasis added.

25. Cooley 1902; see also Mead 1934.

26. Cooley, 1902.

27. Goffman, 1956.

28. Hall 1992, pp. 275–276.

29. Abrams, Hinkle, Otten, and Hogg 2001.

30. Manis and Meltzer 1978.

31. Harrington 2004.

32. Rao, Davis, and Ward 2000.

33. Staw, McKechnie, and Puffer 1983.

34. Zuckerman 2000.

35. Deaux 1984.

36. Adam Smith 1969, p. 5.
37. Habermas 1985.
38. Debord 1983.
39. Debord 1983.
40. Ingrassia, 1995.
41. According to the World Federation of Exchanges—the trade organization for stock exchanges around the world—there were 9,003 stocks available on American exchanges and 26,508 stocks available through the rest of the world's exchanges as of the beginning of 1998. While these numbers change frequently as new stocks are listed and old ones delisted, the early 1998 figure was chosen because this was the time period during which data were being gathered for the present study; thus, the investment clubs discussed in this book were looking at a total decision universe of about 9,000 domestic and 26,000 international stocks. This is useful to keep in mind when considering the multitude of ways that clubs (and individual investors) seek to reduce this information overload through the use of shortcuts and other accommodations to "bounded rationality" (see March and Simon 1958). The numbers from the World Federation of Exchanges are available in their monthly statistical reports; the 1998 report is available online at http://www.fibv.com/publications/Tm598.pdf. The figures include only individual stocks, not bonds or investment funds; firms that issue multiple classes of stock (such as preferred and common) are counted only once.
42. Beardstown Ladies 1994.
43. Catalyst 2004.
44. Goffman 1956.
45. From two interviews with NAIC regional officers for the San Francisco Bay Area, 7 March 1997.
46. Mead 1934; Cooley 1902.
47. Rao, Davis, and Ward 2000.
48. Boje 1991.
49. Beach 1997, p. 193.
50. Ingrassia 1995, p. 207.
51. Thaler and Ziemba 1992.
52. Weisberg 1998, p. 30.
53. Staw, McKechnie, and Puffer 1983.
54. Porac, Wade, and Pollock 1999.
55. Martin 1982, 287.
56. Gurley 1999.
57. Boje 1991.
58. With apologies to Mr. Lynch, who might find this comparison unflattering given his commitment to Catholicism and Catholic social organizations.
59. www.fool.com/Features/1997/sp971219BestAndWorstOf1997LoserTeal.htm.
60. The AAUW has played an important role in encouraging women to form investment clubs around the country.

61. Hagstrom 1997.
62. Macmurray 1995.
63. Bakhtin 1993.
64. Goffman 1956.
65. Servers are machines that serve as central repositories of information for a network of computer users. They are the linchpins of electronic communication systems, and thus essential to modern business.
66. Boje 1991, p. 124.
67. On a split-adjusted basis, Cisco's stock closed at $8.48 when Bulls & Bears began discussing the firm (9 July 1997); when the club finally made its purchase on 11 March 1998, the stock closed at $10.44. Figures obtained from the Cisco corporate website: http://investor.cisco.com/phoenix.zhtml?c=81192&p=irol -stockLookup&t=HistQuot&submit=Submit.
68. Investors may also be expected to be white, as suggested by the name of one group in the sample: "Independent Black Investors." Unfortunately, data on race/ethnicity are too sparse in this study to permit further speculation.
69. The gendered assumptions underlying the role of "investor" are reflected not only in the tiny percentage of women who make it into the executive ranks in financial firms—see Catalyst 2004—but also in the lexicon of the profession, in which terms such as "big swinging dick" designate those who have earned the highest status and esteem of their peers. See Lewis 1989.
70. Hakim 2001.
71. Geczy, Stambaugh, and Levin 2003.
72. Shiller, 1993, p. 167.
73. Morgenson 2003.
74. Catalyst 2004.
75. Hakim 2001, p. 26.
76. O'Barr and Conley 1992, p. 159.
77. Odean 1998.
78. Iyengar and Lepper, 2000.
79. Rao, Davis, and Ward 2000.

Section Two
Cash and Social Currency: Performance in Investment Clubs

1. Trump and Schwartz 1987, p. 2.
2. Barber and Terrance Odean 2000. In their study, the average club underperformed the market index by almost 4 percent. The average club earned an annualized geometric mean return of 14.1 percent, while the market index earned 17.9 percent.
3. The performance figures for my sample were calculated using the industry-standard internal rate of return, adjusted for differences in market conditions and amount invested by each club. See the appendix a to this section for further details.

4. These rates of return are relative to the S&P 500 index over the lifetime of the club, to make comparison possible between clubs of different ages with differing amounts of contributions; more details on these calculations are available in the appendix to this section.
5. Fama 1976.
6. O'Barr and Conley 1992, p. 64, emphasis added.
7. O'Barr and Conley 1992, p. 157.
8. O'Barr and Conley 1992, p. 150.
9. O'Barr and Conley 1992, p. 159.
10. Frank 1985.
11. Campbell 1987, p. 190.
12. Malkiel 1990.

Chapter Three
Group Composition and the Business Case for Diversity

1. Mill 2004, p. 594.
2. van Knippenberg, de Dreu, and Homan, forthcoming; see also Lau and Murnighan 2004; Phillips 2003; Phillips, Mannix, Neale, and Gruenfeld 2004.
3. Wiersema and Bird 1993; Tsui, Egan, and O'Reilly 1992.
4. See the following studies: Tajfel and Turner 1979; Brewer 1979; Kanter 1977; Pelled 1996a.
5. Ancona and Caldwell 1992b.
6. Jehn, Northcraft, and Neale 1999.
7. Nemeth and Kwan 1987; Beach 1997.
8. Nemeth 1986.
9. Phillips, Mannix, Neale, and Gruenfeld 2004, p. 508; see also Damon 1991; Jehn 1995; Levine, Resnick, and Higgins 1993; Nemeth 1986; Nemeth and Rogers 1986.
10. Cox, Lobel, McLeod 1991; Nkomo and Cox 1996.
11. Jehn, Northcraft, and Neale 1999, p. 745.
12. For a review, see Williams and O'Reilly 1998.
13. Eisenhart and Schoonhoven 1990.
14. Ancona and Caldwell 1992.
15. Katz 1982.
16. Jehn 1995, p. 260.
17. Malkiel 1990; Fama 1976.
18. Lawrence and Lorsch 1967, p. 36.
19. National Center on Women and Aging 1998.
20. Associated Press 2001.
21. Lewellen, Lease, and Schlarbaum 1977.
22. Estes and Hosseini 1988; Prince 1993.
23. Barsky, Juster, Kimball, and Shapiro 1997.
24. Jianakoplos and Bernasek 1998.

25. Bielby and Baron 1986.
26. Reskin and Roos 1990.
27. Reskin and Roos 1990.
28. U.S. Department of Labor, Women's Bureau, 1997.
29. England 1992.
30. Smith 1997.
31. Zelizer 1999; see also. Thaler 1992 on mental accounting.
32. Marx and Engels 1978, p. 30.
33. Tversky and Kahneman 1973.
34. Bushman and Wells 2001.
35. Barber and Odean 2003; while it might not seem an entirely irrational strategy to buy stocks based on the previous day's news reports, the study found that these stock purchases—like many impulse buys—usually prove to be disappointing in terms of profits.
36. Abrams, Thomas, and Hogg 1990.
37. E.g., Deaux 1984.
38. Malkiel 1990.
39. Veblen 1898.
40. Veblen 1994, chapter 4, p. 1.
41. Veblen 1994, chapter 4, p. 1.
42. From *Printer's Ink*, 7 November 1929, p. 133, cited in Marchand 1985, p. 66, emphasis in original.
43. Quinlan 2003.
44. Hochschild 1997.
45. Brines 1994.
46. U.S. Department of Labor, Women's Bureau, 1997.
47. See Golden-Biddle and Locke 1993.
48. Although SIC codes were collected for these data, they were not used in this analysis for two reasons. First, the SIC system contains thousands of categories and is difficult to aggregate into high-level economic sectors. Second, most small investors do not classify stocks by SIC codes, instead relying on more user-friendly and readily available taxonomies such as *Standard & Poors Outlook* and *Value Line*. Since this study aims to examine investors' decision-making processes, it made sense to use the same classification schemes employed by the overwhelming majority of participants in this study.
49. Thanks to Matthew Boomershine, Aaron Katz, Andrei Muresianu, and Kristen Peterson for their assistance in this project.
50. The number of clubs included in the analysis was limited by the availability of data to calculate values on the dependent variables. Although there is an aggregate N of 578, missing or incomplete data for certain clubs may have led to their omission from the models. For consumer-sector allocation and industry diversification, approximately 30 portfolios (5 percent of the sample) were missing industry classification data for at least one trade. Therefore, N was limited to 548 for the analysis. For market capitalization, approximately 134

clubs (23 percent of the sample) were missing market capitalization data on at least one trade; thus, the sample size for diversification by market capitalization was limited to 444 clubs.

51. Malkiel 1990.

52. For information on COMPUSTAT, see http://www.compustat.com/www/.

53. Thanks to Professor Terrance Odean of the Haas School of Business at University of California at Berkeley, and to Professor Campbell Harvey of Duke University, whose financial glossary provides references on market capitalization and all other financial terms used in this study: http://www.duke.edu/~charvey/Classes/wpg/glossary.htm.

54. Additional analyses were conducted by operationalizing group gender composition according the proportions of men and women in each group, divided into five categories—skewed male, tilted male, balanced, tilted female, and skewed female, in keeping with the method outlined in Kanter 1977. Results available from author.

55. Malkiel 1990.

56. I tested a total of four model specifications using OLS and stepwise regression analysis, with substantively similar results across implementations. Results available from author.

57. The results of this research are also subject to alternative explanations, some of which have been considered in this study and some of which provide a basis for future research. For example, the impact of men on portfolio diversification could be explained by the greater resources available to all-male clubs, which have a mean portfolio value 1.74 times greater than those of all-female groups. The higher mean portfolio value may provide a basis for greater diversification: the more money invested, the greater the variety in investments. However, the controls used in regression analysis make this alternative explanation unlikely. While the analysis did not control directly for clubs' portfolio value, owing to multicollinearity problems it did control for the two components of portfolio value: club age and (in a separate analysis not shown here) the average monthly financial contributions of members to the club. While club age did have a significant impact on the analyses, the monthly financial contributions did not, suggesting that experience matters in diversification but the actual amount of money invested does not.

58. Barsky, Juster, Kimball, and Shapiro 1997; Jianokoplos and Bernasek 1998.

59. E.g., Barsky, Juster, Kimball, and Shapiro 1997.

60. Data on race and ethnicity were not made available.

61. Nemeth 1986.

62. Shiller 1993.

63. Byrne 1971.

64. During the late 1990s, when I collected the original data for this study, annual club dues were $35 per year, plus $11 per year for each member; thus, a club of average size (fifteen members) would have paid a total of $200 per year for NAIC membership. As of 2004, annual club dues are $40 per year, plus $25

per member: a total of $415 per year for a fifteen-member club. See the NAIC website, http://store.yahoo.com/betterinvesting/clubmembership.html, for more information.

Chapter Four
Getting Ahead versus Getting Along—Decision Making in Investment Clubs

1. Drucker 1974, p. 29.
2. Beach 1997, p. 138.
3. Janis 1972, p. 2.
4. Roethlisberger and Dickson 1939.
5. Wolfe, Lennox, and Cutler 1986; see also Hogan and Holland 2003.
6. Pelled 1996b.
7. Blau 1977; Granovetter 1973.
8. Byrne 1971.
9. McPherson and Smith-Lovin 1987; Kanter 1977.
10. Stinchcombe 1965.
11. Boje 1991.
12. Baron, Hannan, and Burton 2001, italics in original.
13. Antonelli 1999.
14. Sydow et al. 2007, p. 6.
15. Granovetter 1992, p. 34.
16. Festinger 1957.
17. Hirschman 2006.
18. See, for example, Reskin 1976 and Useem 1978.
19. Hallett and Ventresca 2006; see also Burawoy 1998.
20. Hallett and Ventresca 2006.
21. Harrington and Fine 2000.
22. Podolny and Baron 1997.
23. McPherson and Smith-Lovin 1987; Blau 1977.
24. Granovetter 1973.
25. Nemeth 1986.
26. E.g., Butcher and Atkinson 2002.
27. Halpern 1996; Koehn 1998; Sommers 1997.
28. Uzzi 1997, p. 61.
29. Granovetter 1973.
30. See the following studies: Marsden and Hurlbert 1988; Granovetter 1985; Hurlbert, Haines, and Beggs 2000; Campbell, Marsden, and Hurlbert 1986; Lin, Woelfel, and Light 1985.
31. Butcher and Atkinson 2002.
32. Renzulli, Aldrich, and Moody 2000, p. 526.
33. Gomez-Mejia, Nunez-Nickel, and Gutierrez 2001, p. 82.
34. Mullen and Copper 1994.

35. Gomez-Mejia, Nunez-Nickel, and Guttierez 2001.
36. Gulati and Westphal 1999.
37. Udy 1962.
38. Boje 1991, p. 111, emphasis added.
39. Boje 1991, p. 111.
40. Portes and Sensenbrenner 1993.
41. O'Barr and Conley 1992, p. 89.
42. Thomas 2002.
43. Reported by the U.S. Congress, House Financial Services Committee, 2 October 2002: http://financialservices.house.gov/news.asp?FormMode=release&id=203&NewsType=1.
44. Ibarra 1992; see also Uzzi 1997.
45. These questions were validated through pretesting; details available from author.
46. Of the 11,138 individual responses received, 5,956 (53 percent) were coded as instrumental, 4,568 (41 percent) were coded as affective, and 614 (5 percent) were coded as mixed. It is noteworthy that there were so few mixed responses, supporting the findings of other studies that group participants often have a very clear sense of distinct types of content in their interpersonal networks. The eta squared for this calculation exceeded Georgopoulous's threshold, indicating that aggregation is acceptable. See Georgopoulos 1986.
47. Since the seventh club, Valley Gay Men's Investment Club, was newly formed when I began the study and took several months to make its first decision, the N was too small to draw quantitative conclusions about decision making.
48. Again, I was unable to include the seventh club—VGMIC—because of its newness and lack of investing decisions to measure.
49. Wolfe, Lennox, and Cutler 1986.
50. Shefrin and Statman 1993.
51. Berger and Zelditch 1985.
52. Megargee 1969.
53. Phillips and Loyd 2005, p. 5.
54. For a review of the case for reviving the small-group tradition in sociology, see Harrington and Fine 2000.
55. Gargiulo and Bernassi 1999.
56. Granovetter 1973.
57. See the following small-group studies: Bales 1953; Janis 1972; and Hackman 1990.

Section Three
Aftermath and Implications

1. Aron 1999, p. 207.
2. I am indebted to David Stark for his account of this history; see Stark 2000.

See also Camic 1987.

3. White 1976.
4. Boltanski and Thevenot 1991.
5. Stolte, Fine, and Cook 2001.
6. See Uzzi 1999; and Baker 1990.
7. Resnick, Zeckhauser, Swanson, and Lockwood 2002.
8. Cutler, Poterba, and Summers 1993.
9. Jacobs 1992, pp. 439–441.
10. Stevenson 2000.
11. Weisberg 1998.
12. Putnam 2000.

Chapter Five
Reflections on Investing in the 1990s

1. Hoffer 1951, p. 11.
2. For a review of numerous international case studies of common-pool resource management, see Ostrom 1991.
3. Ralph Katz 1982.
4. Merton 1957, pp. 60–69.
5. Durkheim 2001, p. 17, italics added.
6. Durkheim 2001, p. 250.
7. Durkheim 2001, pp. 388 and 423, emphasis added.
8. Emile Durkheim 1997 [1897], *Suicide* (New York: Free Press).
9. Hertz 1998, p. 18, n. 20.
10. Hart 1990.
11. Durkheim 2001, p. 385.
12. Hertz 1998, p. 22.
13. It is telling in this regard that many banks and trading institutions are modeled on the design of Greek temples (see Finlay 1973). A statue of Ceres, the Roman goddess of the harvest, presides over the commodities exchange from the rooftop of the Chicago Board of Trade.
14. See Kaufman 1999.
15. Horowitz 1986; Ouchi 1980.
16. Goffman 1956.
17. Tsui, Egan, and O'Reilly 1992.
18. Dilley 1992, pp. 1–34, emphasis added.
19. Appadurai 1986.
20. Hochschild 1989.
21. Finlay 1973.
22. Ralph Katz 1982.
23. Victor Turner 1974, p. 56.
24. Kunda 1991.

25. For accounts of this problem in observational research, see, for example, Ruth Horowitz 1986; Shaffir 1991; and Snow Benford, and Anderson 1986.
26. Harrington 2002.
27. Roethlisberger and Dickson 1939.
28. Goffman 1989, p. 129.
29. For a review, see Warren 1989.
30. Kanter 1977.

Chapter Six
Implications and Conclusions

1. Durkheim 1965, p. 15.
2. Proust 1982, p. 844.
3. Mansell-Carstens 1995; von Pischke 1991; von Pischke, Adams, and Donald 1983.
4. von Pischke, Adams, and Donald 1983, p. 212–213.
5. For a review, see Krugman 2003.
6. von Pischke 1991, p. 17.
7. However, unlike microfinance groups, other aspects of investment clubs' functioning *are* tightly regulated (e.g., annual tax reporting to state and federal agencies).
8. von Pischke 1991.
9. von Pischke 1991, p. 236; Anthony and Horne 2003.
10. American Association of Individual Investors 1996.
11. von Pischke 1991, pp. 240–241.
12. Beardstown Ladies 1994, p. 12.
13. von Pischke 1991, p. 173.
14. Leland 2007.
15. Reuters News Service, 2005, "'Mr. Housing Bubble' Tries to Wash Away the Worries," *USA Today*, 17 August, p. 1.
16. Estimates of the insolvency date range from 2052 (from the Congressional Budget Office) to 2041 (from the Cato Institute); see Associated Press, 2004, "Greenspan's Social Security Alarm," 27 August.
17. Presidential debate, 3 October 2000.
18. Stevenson 2000, p. A1.
19. Ibbotson Associates, 2001.
20. Blitzstein 1999.
21. Diamond 1999, p. 12.
22. Jermann 1999.
23. Shiller 1999, p. 191, emphasis added.
24. Employment Benefit Research Institute 1996.
25. Rother and Wright 1999.

26. Diamond 1999.
27. Shiller 2000.
28. Diamond 1999.
29. Putnam 1995.
30. Habermas 1983, p. 99.
31. Ostrom 1991.
32. Ellickson 1991.
33. Habermas 1985.
34. Rao, Davis, and Ward 2000.
35. Boerner 2004, emphasis added in last sentence only.
36. Unger 1999.
37. Morgenson 2005.
38. For a review, see the volume of essays edited by Prahalad and Porter (2003).
39. Though this effort has been met with some skepticism in the business press; see Murphy 2002.
40. For details on this campaign, see the Organic Consumer Association website, which includes links to recent shareholder activities as well as media coverage: http://www.organicconsumers.org/Starbucks/.
41. Gell-Mann 1995.
42. Shiller 1993.
43. Malkiel 1990.
44. Weaver 1958.
45. Stolte, Fine, and Cook 2001.
46. Strauss and Corbin 1998.
47. Jacobs 1992, p. 434.
48. Katz and Shotter 1996.
49. Blumer 1962, p. 180, emphasis added.
50. Blumer 1969.
51. Emphasis added.
52. E.g., Hechter 1987.
53. Savage 1954.
54. E.g., Katona 1975.
55. Adler and Adler 1984.
56. Barsky, Juster, Kimball, and Shapiro 1997.
57. Tversky and Kahneman 1991; see also Laibson 1997.
58. Willer 1992.
59. Weber 1978, p. 111.
60. Paul Samuelson 1983, pp. 90–92.
61. Hegel 1967, p. 2.
62. Harris 2004, p. 137.
63. Nelson 1992.
64. Portes 1994.
65. Rosenwein 1989, p. 130.

66. Polanyi 1944; von Pischke 1991.
67. Hertz 1998, p. 23.
68. Mauss 1990, p. 4.
69. Levi-Strauss 1969.
70. Davis 2000, p. 6.
71. Hirschman 1982.

References

◆

Abrams, Dominic, Steve Hinkle, Sabine Otten, and Michael Hogg. 2001. "The Social Identity Theory Perspective on Groups: The Interface of Social and Individual Processes." Paper presented at the Conference on Assessing Theory and Research on Groups, College Station, TX, October 21–23.

Abrams, Dominic, Joanne Thomas, and Michael Hogg. 1990. "Numerical Distinctiveness, Social Identity and Gender Salience." *British Journal of Sociology,* 29:87–92.

Abrams, Dominic, M. Wetherell, S. Cochrane, M. Hogg, and J. Turner. 1990. "Knowing What to Think by Knowing Who You Are: Self-categorization and the Nature of Norm Formation, Conformity and Group Polarization." *British Journal of Social Psychology,* 29:97–119.

Adler, Patricia, and Peter Adler. 1984. "The Market as Collective Behavior." In Adler and Adler (eds.), *The Social Dynamics of Financial Markets.* Greenwich, CT: JAI Press.

American Association of Individual Investors. 1996. Unpublished member survey. Chicago: AAII.

Ancona, Deborah, and David Caldwell. 1992a. "Bridging the Boundary: External Activity and Performance in Organizational Teams." *Administrative Science Quarterly,* 37:634–665.

———. 1992b. "Demography and Design: Predictors of New Product Team Performance." *Organization Science,* 3:321–341.

Anthony, Denise, and Christine Horne. 2003. "Gender and Cooperation: Explaining Loan Repayment in Micro-Credit Groups." *Social Psychology Quarterly,* 66:293–302.

Antonelli, Charles. 1999. *The Microdynamics of Technological Change.* London: Routledge.

Appadurai, Arjun. 1986. "Introduction: Commodities and the Politics of Value." In A. Appadurai (ed.), *The Social Life of Things: Commodities in Cultural Perspective.* Cambridge, UK: Cambridge University Press, pp. 3–63.

Aron, Raymond. 1999. *Main Currents in Sociological Thought: Durkheim, Pareto, Weber, Volume 2.* Somerset, NJ: Transaction Publishers.

Asch, Solomon. 1955. "Opinions and Social Pressure." *Scientific American,* 193: 31–35.

Associated Press. 2001. "Census: Women Made Gains in Business World." *San Jose Mercury News,* 3 April, p. 1.

Baker, Wayne. 1990. "Market Networks and Corporate Behavior." *American Journal of Sociology,* 96:589–625.

Bakhtin, Mikhail. 1993. *Toward a Philosophy of the Act.* Austin: University of Texas Press.

Bales, Robert. 1953. "The Equilibrium Problem in Small Groups." In T. Parsons, R. Bales, and E. Shils (eds.), *Working Papers in the Theory of Action.* Glencoe, IL: Free Press, pp. 111–161.

Barber, Brad, and Terrance Odean. 1999. "The Courage of Misguided Convictions: The Trading Behavior of Individual Investors," *Financial Analyst Journal,* November/December: 41–55.

———. 2000. "Too Many Cooks Spoil the Profits." *Financial Analyst.* January-February: 17–25.

———. 2001. "Boys Will Be Boys: Gender, Overconfidence, and Common Stock Investment." *Quarterly Journal of Economics,* 116:261–292.

———. 2003. "All That Glitters: The Effect of Attention and News on the Buying Behavior of Individual and Institutional Investors." Working paper, Haas School of Business, University of California, Berkeley.

Barboza, David, and Richard Oppel Jr. 2002. "Enron's Many Strands: The Employees—U.S. Moves to Ease Harm from Enron." *New York Times,* 4 April, p. C1.

Baron, James, Michael Hannan, and M. Diane Burton. 2001. "Labor Pains: Change in Organizational Models and Employee Turnover in Young, High-Tech Firms." *American Journal of Sociology,* 106:1009.

Barsade, Sigal, and Donald Gibson. 1998. "Group Emotion: A View from Top and Bottom." *Research on Managing Groups and Teams.* Greenwich, CT: JAI Press, pp. 81–102.

Barsky, Robert, Thomas Juster, Miles Kimball, and Matthew Shapiro. 1997. "Preference Parameters and Behavioral Heterogeneity: An Experimental Approach in the Health and Retirement Study." *Quarterly Journal of Economics,* 112: 537–579.

Beach, Leroy. 1997. *The Psychology of Decision Making in Organizations.* Thousand Oaks, CA: Sage Publications.

Beardstown Ladies. 1994. *The Beardstown Ladies' Common-Sense Investment Guide: How We Beat the Market—and How You Can Too.* New York: Hyperion.

Ben-Yehuda, Nachman. 1980. "The European Witch Craze of the 14th to 17th Centuries: A Sociologist's Perspective." *American Journal of Sociology*, 86:1–31.

Berger, Joseph, and Morris Zelditch. 1985. *Status Rewards and Influence*. San Francisco: Jossey-Bass.

Berger, Peter, and Thomas Luckmann. 1966. *The Social Construction of Reality: A Treatise on the Sociology of Knowledge*. Garden City, N.Y.: Anchor Books.

Bielby, William, and James Baron. 1986. "Men and Women at Work: Sex Segregation and Statistical Discrimination." *American Journal of Sociology*, 91: 759–799.

Blau, Peter. 1977. *Inequality and Heterogeneity*. New York: Free Press.

Blitzstein, Steven. 1999. "An Organized Labor Perspective on Social Security Reform." In Olivia Mitchell, Robert Myers, and Howard Young (eds.), *Prospects for Social Security Reform*. Philadelphia: University of Pennsylvania Press.

Blumer, Herbert. 1962. "Society as Symbolic Interaction." In A. M. Rose (ed.), *Human Behavior and Social Processes: An Interactionist Approach*. Boston: Houghton-Mifflin.

———. 1969. *Symbolic Interactionism: Perspective and Method*. Englewood Cliffs, NJ: Prentice-Hall.

Boerner, Hank. 2004. "2004 Proxy Season: A Test of New Rules and Attitudes." *Corporate Finance Review*, March/April: 38–42.

Bogle, John. 1997. "The Investment Outlook and Strategies in Our Global World." Presentation to the World Affairs Council of Philadelphia, 17 July. http://www.vanguard.com/bogle_site/lib/jcb718.html.

Boje, David. 1991. "Organizations as Storytelling Networks: A Study of Story Performance in an Office-Supply Firm." *Administrative Science Quarterly*, 36:106–126.

Boltanski, Luc, and Laurent Thevenot. 1991. *De La Justification: Les Economies de la Grandeur*. Paris: Gallimard.

Borges, Jorge Luis. 1999. "The Analytical Language of John Wilkins." In Eliot Weinberger (ed.), *Selected Non-fictions*. New York: Penguin, pp. 229–232.

Boulding, Kenneth. 1966 [1941]. *Economic Analysis*. New York: Harper and Row.

Bowles, Samuel, and Herbert Gintis. 2001. "Prosocial Emotions." Paper presented at the workshop Economy as a Complex Evolving System, III, Santa Fe Institute, November 16–18.

Brewer, Marilynn. 1979. "In-Group Bias in the Minimal Intergroup Situation: A Cognitive-Motivational Analysis." *Psychological Bulletin*, 86:307–324.

Brines, J. 1994. "Economic Dependency, Gender and the Division of Labor at Home." *American Journal of Sociology*, 100:652–88.

Brown, Roger. 1986. *Social Psychology: The Second Edition*. New York: Free Press.

Buenza, Daniel, and David Stark. 2004. "Tools of the Trade: The Socio-technology of Arbitrage in a Wall Street Trading Room." *Industrial and Corporate Change*, 13:370.

Burawoy, Michael. 1998. "The Extended Case Method." *Sociological Theory*, 16:4–33.

Bushman, Brad, and Gary Wells. 2001. "Narrative Impressions of Literature: The Availability Bias and the Corrective Properties of Meta-analytic Approaches." *Personality and Social Psychology Bulletin,* 27:1123–1130.

Butcher, David, and Sally Atkinson. 2002. "Interpersonal Relationships at the Top." Working paper, Cranfield University School of Management, Cranfield, UK.

Byrne, D. 1971. *The Attraction Paradigm.* New York: Academic Press.

Camic, Charles. 1987. "The Making of a Method: A Historical Reinterpretation of the Early Parsons." *American Sociological Review,* 52:421–39.

Campbell, Colin. 1987. *The Romantic Ethic and the Spirit of Modern Capitalism.* Oxford: Blackwell.

Campbell, Karen, Peter Marsden, and Jeanne Hurlbert. 1986. "Social Resources and Socioeconomic Status." *Social Networks,* 8:97–117.

Castells, Manuel. 1996. *The Rise of the Networked Society.* Cambridge, MA: Blackwell Publishers.

Catalyst. 2004. *The Bottom Line: Connecting Corporate Performance and Gender Diversity.* New York: Catalyst.

Chancellor, Edward. 1999. *Devil Take the Hindmost: A History of Financial Speculation.* New York: Farrar, Straus and Giroux.

Cialdini, Robert. 1984. Influence: *The New Psychology of Persuasion.* New York: Quill.

Cooley, Charles. 1902. *Human Nature and the Social Order.* New York: Scribner's.

Cox, Taylor, Sharon Lobel, and Poppy McLeod. 1991. "Effects of Ethnic Group Cultural Differences on Cooperative and Competitive Behavior in a Task Group." *Academy of Management Journal,* 34:827–847.

Cutler, David, James Poterba, and Lawrence Summers. 1993. "What Moves Stock Prices?" In Richard Thaler (ed.), *Advances in Behavioral Finance.* New York: Russell Sage Foundation, pp. 133–152.

Damon, W. 1991. "Problems of Direction in Socially Shared Cognition." In L. Resnick, J. Levine, and S. Teasley (eds.), *Perspectives on Socially Shared Cognition.* Washington, DC: American Psychological Association, pp. 384–397.

Davis, Natalie Zemon. 2000. *The Gift in Sixteenth Century France.* Madison: University of Wisconsin Press.

Deaux, Kay. 1984. "From Individual Differences to Social Categories: Analysis of a Decade's Research on Gender." *American Psychologist,* 39:105–116.

Deaux, Kay, and Brenda Major. 1987. "Putting Gender into Context: An Interactive Model of Gender-Related Behavior." *Psychological Review,* 94:369–389.

Debord, Guy. 1983 [1967]. *The Society of the Spectacle.* Fredy Perlman (trans.). Detroit: Black and Red.

Deleuze, Gilles, and Felix Guattari. 1995. "Capitalism: A Very Special Delirium." In Sylvere Lotringer (ed.), *Chaosophy.* Cambridge, MA: MIT Press/Semiotext(e).

DeLong, J. Bradford, Andrei Schleifer, Lawrence Summers, and Robert Waldmann. 1993. "Noise Trader Risk in Financial Markets." In Richard Thaler (ed.), *Advances in Behavioral Finance.* New York: Russell Sage Foundation, pp. 23–58.

Diamond, Peter. 1999. *Issues in Privatizing Social Security: Report of the National Academy of Social Insurance Panel on Privatizing Social Security.* Cambridge, MA: MIT Press.

Dilley, Roy. 1992. "Contesting Markets: A General Introduction to Market Ideology, Imagery and Discourse." In R. Dilley (ed.), *Contesting Markets: Analyses of Ideology, Discourse and Practice.* Edinburgh: Edinburgh University Press.

DiMaggio, P. 1992. "Nadel's Paradox Revisited: Relational and Cultural Aspects of Organizational Structure." In Nitin Nohria and Robert Eccles (eds.), *Networks and Organizations: Structure, Form and Action.* Boston: Harvard Business School Press, pp. 118–142.

Drucker, Peter. 1974. *Management: Tasks, Responsibilities, Practices.* New York: Harper & Row.

Durkheim, Emile. 1965 [1915]. *The Elementary Forms of the Religious Life.* New York: Free Press.

———. 1977 [1897]. *Suicide.* New York: Free Press.

Eisenhardt, Kathleen, and Claudia Bird Schoonhoven. 1990. "Organizational Growth: Linking Founding Team, Strategy, Environment and Growth among U.S. Semiconductor Ventures, 1978–1988." *Administrative Science Quarterly,* 35:504–529.

Ellickson, C. 1991. *Order Without Law: How Neighbors Settle Disputes.* Cambridge, MA: Harvard University Press.

Employment Benefit Research Institute [EBRI]. 1996. *Retirement Confidence Survey.* Washington, DC.

England, Paula. 1992. *Comparable Worth: Theories and Evidence.* New York: Aldine de Gruyter.

Estes, Ralph, and Jinoos Hosseini. 1988. "The Gender Gap on Wall Street: An Empirical Analysis of Confidence in Individual Decision Making." *Journal of Psychology,* 122:577–590.

Fama, Eugene. 1976. *Foundations of Finance.* New York: Basic Books.

Festinger, Leon. 1957. *A Theory of Cognitive Dissonance.* Evanston, IL: Row, Peterson & Co.

Fine, Gary, and Brooke Harrington. 2004. "Tiny Publics: Small Groups and Civil Society." *Sociological Theory,* 22:341–356.

Finlay, Moses. 1973. *The Ancient Economy.* Berkeley: University of California Press.

Frank, Robert. 1985. *Choosing the Right Pond: Human Behavior and the Quest for Status.* New York: Oxford University Press.

Freud, Sigmund. 1959 [1922]. *Group Psychology and the Analysis of the Ego.* James Strachey (trans.). New York: W. W. Norton.

Friedman, Benjamin. 1993. "Comments and Discussion." Response to Shiller's "Stock Prices and Social Dynamics." In Richard Thaler (ed.), *Advances in Behavioral Finance.* New York: Russell Sage Foundation, pp. 207–216.

Galaskiewicz, Joseph. 1985. *Social Organization of An Urban Grants Economy.* Orlando, FL: Academic Press.

Galbraith, Jay. 1973. *Designing Complex Organizations*. Reading, MA: Addison-Wesley.

Galbraith, John Kenneth. 1990. *A Short History of Financial Euphoria*. New York: Viking, p. 52.

Gargiulo, M., and M. Bernassi. 1999. "The Dark Side of Social Capital." In R.T.A.J. Leenders and S. Gabbay (eds.), *Corporate Social Capital and Liability*. Boston: Kluwer Academic Publishers, pp. 298–322.

Geczy, Christopher, Robert Stambaugh, and David Levin. 2003. "Investing in Socially Responsible Mutual Funds." Working paper, Wharton School of Business, University of Pennsylvania.

Geist, Charles. 1999. *One Hundred Years of Wall Street*. New York: McGraw-Hill.

Gell-Mann, Murray. 1995. *The Quark and the Jaguar: Adventures in the Simple and Complex*. New York: Henry Holt.

General Accounting Office. 1996. *Report to the Chairman, Subcommittee on Social Security, Committee on Ways and Means, House of Representatives: 401(k) Pension Plans—Many Take Advantage to Ensure Adequate Retirement Income*. August.

Georgopoulos, Basil. 1986. *Organizational Structure, Problem Solving and Effectiveness*. San Francisco: Jossey-Bass.

Goffman, Erving. 1956. "The Nature of Deference and Demeanor." *American Anthropologist*, 58: 47–85.

———. 1989. "On Fieldwork." *Journal of Contemporary Ethnography*, 18:123–132.

Golden-Biddle, Karen, and Karen Locke. 1993. "Appealing Work: An Investigation of How Ethnographic Texts Convince." *Organization Science*, 4:595–616.

Gomez-Mejia, Luis, Manuel Nunez-Nickel, and Isabel Gutierrez. 2001. "The Role of Family Ties in Agency Contracts." *Academy of Management Journal*, 44:81–95.

Granovetter, Mark. 1973. "The Strength of Weak Ties." *American Journal of Sociology*, 78:1360–1380.

———. 1985. "Economic Action and Social Structure: The Problem of Embeddedness." *American Journal of Sociology*, 91:481–510.

———. 1992. "Problems of Explanation in Economic Sociology." In Nitin Nohria and Robert Eccles (eds.), *Networks and Organizations*. Boston: Harvard University Press.

Gulati, Ranjay, and James Westphal. 1999. "Cooperative or Controlling? The Effects of CEO-Board Relations and the Content of Interlocks on the Formation of Joint Ventures." *Administrative Science Quarterly*, 44:473–506.

Gurley, William. 1999. "The Great Art of Storytelling." *Fortune*. 8 November, p. 300.

Habermas, Jürgen. 1983. *Moralbewusstsein un kommunikatives Handeln*. Frankfurt: Suhrkamp.

———. 1985. *The Theory of Communicative Action, Volume 2: Lifeworld and System: A Critique of Functionalist Reason*. Thomas McCarthy (trans). Boston: Beacon Press.

Hackman, J. R. 1990. "Creating More Effective Workgroups in Organizations." In J. R. Hackman (ed.), *Groups That Work*. San Francisco: Jossey-Bass, pp. 479–504.

Hagstrom, Robert. 1997. *The Warren Buffett Way: Investment Strategies of the World's Greatest Investor*. New York: John Wiley and Sons.

Hakim, Danny. 2001. "On Wall St., More Investors Push Social Goals." *New York Times*, 11 February, p. 26.

Hall, Stuart. 1992. "The Question of Cultural Identity." In S. Hall, D. Held, and T. McGrew (eds.), *Modernity and Its Futures*. Cambridge, MA: Polity Press.

Hallett, Timothy, and Marc Ventresca. 2006. "Looking Back to See Ahead: Institutions and Interactions in Goudlner's Patterns of Industrial Bureaucracy." *Theory and Society*, 35:213–236.

Halpern, J. 1996. "The Effect of Friendship on Decisions: Field Studies of Real Estate Transactions." *Human Relations*, 49:1519–1547.

Harrington, Brooke. 2001. "Investor Beware: Can Small Investors Survive Social Security Privatization?" *The American Prospect*, 10 September, pp. 20–22.

———. 2002. "Obtrusiveness as Strategy in Ethnographic Research." *Qualitative Sociology*, 25:49–61.

———. 2004. "The Social Psychology of Access in Ethnographic Research." *Journal of Contemporary Ethnography*, 32:592–625.

Harrington, Brooke, and Gary Fine. 2000. "Opening the 'Black Box:' Small Groups and Twenty-First-Century Sociology." *Social Psychology Quarterly*, 63:312–323.

Harris, Lee. 2004. *Civilization and Its Enemies: The Next Stage of History*. New York: Free Press.

Hart, Keith. 1990. "The Idea of Economy: Six Modern Dissenters." In R. Friedland and A. Robertson (eds.), *Beyond the Marketplace*. New York: Aldine de Gruyter, pp. 137–160.

Hatfield, E., J. T. Caccioppo, and R. I. Rapson. 1994. *Emotional Contagion*. Cambridge, UK: Cambridge University Press.

Hechter, Michael. 1987. *Principles of Group Solidarity*. Berkeley: University of California Press.

Hegel, Georg. 1967 [1821]. *Philosophy of Right*. New York: Oxford University Press.

———. 1975 [1817]. *Encyclopedia of Philosophical Sciences, Part I. Section 94 (First Subdivision: Being)*. New York: Oxford University Press.

Hertz, Ellen. 1998. *The Trading Crowd: An Ethnography of the Shanghai Stock Market*. New York: Cambridge University Press.

Hirsch, Paul, Stuart Michaels, and Ray Friedman. 1990. "Clean Models versus Dirty Hands: Why Economics Is Different from Sociology." In Sharon Zukin and Paul DiMaggio (eds.), *Structures of Capital: The Social Organization of the Economy*. Cambridge, UK: Cambridge University Press, pp. 39–56.

Hirschman, Albert. 1982. "Rival Interpretations of Market Society: Civilizing, Destructive, or Feeble?" *Journal of Economic Literature*, 20:1463–1484.

Hirschman, Albert. 2006. *Exit, Voice, and Loyalty: Responses to Decline in Firms, Organizations, and States*. Cambridge, MA: Harvard University Press.

Hochschild, Arlie Russell. 1989. *The Second Shift*. New York: Avon Books.

———. 1997. *The Time Bind*. New York: Avon.

Hoffer, Eric. 1951. *The True Believer: Thoughts on the Nature of Mass Movements*. New York: HarperCollins.

Hogan, Joyce, and Brent Holland. 2003. "Using Theory to Evaluate Personality and Job-Performance Relations: A Socioanalytic Perspective." *Journal of Applied Psychology*, 88:100–112.

Hogg, Michael, and Deborah Terry. 2000. "Social Identity and Self-Categorization Processes in Organizational Contexts." *Academy of Management Review*, 25:121–140.

Horowitz, Rick. 1998. "Beardstown Ladies Finally Sing." *Milwaukee Journal Sentinel*, 22 March, p. 3.

Horowitz, Ruth. 1986. "Remaining an Outsider: Membership as Threat to Research Rapport." *Urban Life*, 14:409–413.

Hurlbert, Jeanne, Valerie Haines, and John Beggs. 2000. "Core Networks and Tie Activation: What Kinds of Routine Networks Allocate Resources in Nonroutine Situations?" *American Sociological Review*, 65:598–618.

Ibarra, Herminia. 1992. "Homophily and Differential Returns: Sex Differences in Network Structure and Access in an Advertising Firm." *Administrative Science Quarterly*, 37:422–447.

Ibbotson Associates. 2001. *Stocks, Bonds, Bills, and Inflation 2001 Yearbook*. Chicago: Ibbotson.

Ingrassia, Catherine. 1995. "The Pleasure of Business and the Business of Pleasure: Gender, Credit and the South Sea Bubble." In Carla Hay and Syndy Conger (eds.), *Studies in Eighteenth-Century Culture, Volume 24*. Baltimore: Johns Hopkins University Press, pp. 191–210.

Iyengar, Sheila, and Mark Lepper. 2000. "When Choice Is Demotivating: Can One Desire Too Much of a Good Thing?" *Journal of Personality and Social Psychology*, 79:995–1006.

Jacobs, Jane. 1992. *The Death and Life of Great American Cities*. New York: Vintage.

Janis, I. 1972. *Victims of Groupthink*. Boston: Houghton-Mifflin.

Jehn, Karen. 1995. "A Multimethod Examination of the Benefits and Detriments of Intragroup Conflict." *Administrative Science Quarterly*, 40:256–282.

Jehn, Karen, Gregory Northcraft, and Margaret Neale. 1999. "Why Differences Make a Difference: A Field Study of Diversity, Conflict and Performance in Workgroups." *Administrative Science Quarterly*, 44:741–763.

Jermann, Urban. 1999. "Social Security and Institutions for Intergenerational, Intragenerational and International Risk-Sharing: A Comment." *Carnegie-Rochester Conference Series on Public Policy*, 50:209.

Jianakoplos, Nancy, and Alexandra Bernasek. 1998. "Are Women More Risk-Averse?" *Economic Inquiry*, 36:620–630.

Kahneman, Daniel. 2003."Maps of Bounded Rationality: A Perspective on Intuitive Judgement and Choice." In Tore Frangsmyr (ed.), *The Nobel Prizes 2002*. Stockholm: Nobel Foundation.

Kanter, Rosabeth Moss. 1977. *Men and Women of the Corporation*. New York: Basic Books.

Katona, George. 1975. *Psychological Economics*. New York: Elsevier.

Katz, Arlene, and John Shotter. 1996. "Hearing the Patient's 'Voice': Toward a Social Poetics in Diagnostic Interviews." *Social Science & Medicine*, 43:919–931.

Katz, Ralph. 1982. "The Effects of Group Longevity on Project Communication and Performance." *Administrative Science Quarterly*, 27:81–104.

Kaufman, Jason. 1999. "Three Views of Associationalism in Nineteenth Century America: An Empirical Examination." *American Sociological Review*, 104:1296–1345.

Kelly, Kevin. 1999. *New Rules for the New Economy: 10 Radical Strategies for a Connected World*. New York: Viking.

Keynes, John Maynard. 2000 [1923]. *A Tract on Monetary Reform*. New York: Prometheus.

Klausner, Michael. 1984. "Sociological Theory and the Behavior of Financial Markets." In Patricia Adler and Peter Adler (eds.), *The Social Dynamics of Financial Markets*. Greenwich, CT: JAI Press.

Koehn, D. 1998. "Can and Should Businesses Be Friends with One Another and with Their Stakeholders?" *Journal of Business Ethics*, 17:1755–1763.

Kroll, John. 1998. "Sing No Sad Songs for Unlucky Ladies." *Cleveland Plain Dealer*, 23 March, p. 1C.

Krugman, Paul. 1998. "The Capitalist: The Web Gets Ugly." *New York Times*, 6 December, section 6, p. 40.

———. 2003. *The Great Unravelling: Losing Our Way in the New Century*. New York: W. W. Norton.

Kunda, Gideon. 1991. *Engineering Culture: Control and Commitment in a High-Tech Corporation*. Philadelphia: Temple University Press.

Laibson, David. 1997. "Golden Eggs and Hyperbolic Discounting." *Quarterly Journal of Economics*, 112:443–477.

Lau, D., and K. Murnighan. 2004. "Interactions within Groups and Subgroups: The Effects of Demographic Faultlines." Working paper, Northwestern University.

Lawrence, Paul, and Jay Lorsch. 1967. *Organization and Environment: Managing Differentiation and Integration*. Boston: Graduate School of Business Administration, Harvard University.

Leland, John. 2007. "Debtors Search for Discipline Through Blogs." *New York Times*, 18 February, p. 1.

Levine, J., L. Resnick, and E. Higgins. 1993. "Social Foundations of Cognition." *Annual Review of Psychology*, 44:585–612.

Levi-Strauss, Claude. 1969. *The Elementary Structures of Kinship*. James Harle Bell, John Richard von Sturmer, and Rodney Needham (trans.). Boston: Beacon Press.

Lewellen, Wilber, Ronald Lease, and Gary Schlarbaum. 1977. "Patterns of Investment Strategy and Behavior among Individual Investors." *Journal of Business*, 50:296–333.

Lewis, Michael. 1989. *Liar's Poker: Rising through the Wreckage of Wall Street*. New York: Penguin.

Lin, Nan, Mary Woelfel, and Stephen Light. 1985. "Social Resources and Mobility Outcomes: A Replication and Extension." *Social Forces*, 66:1038–1059.

Lynch, Peter. 1989. *One Up on Wall Street*. New York: Simon and Schuster.

Macmurray, John. 1995. *The Self as Agent*. London: Faber.

Malkiel, Burton. 1990. *A Random Walk down Wall Street*. New York: Norton.

Manis, J., and B. Meltzer. 1978. *Symbolic Interaction*. Boston: Allyn and Bacon.

Mansell-Carstens, Catherine. 1995. *Popular Finance in Mexico*. Mexico City: Center for Latin American Financial Studies.

March, James, and Herbert Simon. 1958. *Organizations*. New York: John Wiley.

Marchand, Roland. 1985. *Advertising the American Dream*. Berkeley: University of California Press.

Marcuse, Herbert. 1964. *One Dimensional Man*. London: Routledge.

Markoff, John. 1998. "Internet Helps to Keep Silicon Valley in a Boom." *New York Times*, 12 January, section D, p. 4.

Marsden, Peter, Karen Cook, and David Knoke. 1994. "Measuring Organizational Structures and Environments." *American Behavioral Scientist*, 37:891–910.

Marsden, Peter, and Jeanne Hurlbert. 1988. "Social Resources and Mobility Outcomes: A Replication and Extension." *Social Forces*, 66:1038–1059.

Martin, Joanne. 1982. "Stories and Scripts in Organizational Settings." In A. Hastorf and A. Isen (eds.), *Cognitive Social Psychology*. New York: Elsevier-North Holland, pp. 225–305.

Marx, Karl, and Friedrich Engels. 1978 [1848]. "Communist Manifesto." In Robert Tucker (ed.), *The Marx-Engels Reader*. New York: W.W. Norton.

Mauss, Marcel. 1990 [1923]. *The Gift: The Form and Reason for Exchange in Archaic Societies*. W. D. Halls (trans.). New York: W.W. Norton.

McGough, Robert. 1997. "Bears Will Be Right on Stocks Someday, Just You Watch." *Wall Street Journal*, 17 July, p. A1.

McPherson, J. Miller, and Lynn Smith-Lovin. 1987. "Homophily in Voluntary Organizations: Status Distance and the Composition of Face-to-Face Groups." *American Sociological Review*, 52:370–379.

Mead, George. 1934. *Mind Self and Society from the Standpoint of a Social Behaviorist*. Charles W. Morris (ed.). Chicago: University of Chicago Press.

Megargee, Edwin, 1969. "Influence of Sex Roles on the Manisfestation of Leadership." *Journal of Applied Psychology*, 53:377–382.

Merton, Robert K. 1957. *Social Theory and Social Structure*. Glencoe, IL: Free Press.

Mill, John Stuart. 2004 [1848]. *Principles of Political Economy, Volume 3*. Amherst, NY: Prometheus Books.

Morgenson, Gretchen. 2003. "Shares of Corporate Nice Guys Can Finish First." *New York Times*, 27 April, section 3, p. 1.

—————. 2005. "Companies Behaving Badly." *New York Times*, 6 March, section 3, p. 1.

Mullen, Brian, and Carolyn Copper. 1994. "The Relation between Group Cohesiveness and Performance: An Integration." *Journal of Personality and Social Psychology*, 115:210–227.

Murphy, Cait. 2002. "Is BP Beyond Petroleum? Hardly." *Fortune*, 30 September.

National Association of Investors Corporation [NAIC]. 1999. "Updated NAIC Statistics." *Better Investing*, 72:2.

National Association of Securities Dealers [NASD]. 1997. *National Investor Survey*. Washington, DC: Peter D. Hart Research Associates.

National Center on Women and Aging. 1998. "Financial Challenges for Mature Women." Working paper, Brandeis University, Waltham, MA.

Nelson, Julie. 1992. "Gender, Metaphor and the Definition of Economics." *Economics and Philosophy*, 8:103–125.

Nemeth, Charlan. 1986. "Differential Contribution of Majority and Minority Influence." *Psychological Review*, 93:23–32.

Nemeth, C., and J. Kwan. 1987. "Minority Influence, Divergent Thinking, and Detection of Correct Solutions." *Journal of Applied Social Psychology*, 17:788–799.

Nemeth, C., and J. Rogers. 1986. "Dissent and the Search for Information." *British Journal of Social Psychology*, 35:67–76.

Nkomo, Stella, and Taylor Cox. 1996. "Diverse Identities in Organizations." In S. Clegg, C. Hardy, and W. Nord (eds.), *Handbook of Organization Studies*. Thousand Oaks, CA: Sage, pp. 338–356.

O'Barr, William, and John Conley. 1992. *Fortune and Folly: The Wealth and Power of Institutional Investing*. Homewood, IL: Business One Irwin.

O'Hara, Thomas, and Kenneth Janke. 1998. *Starting and Running a Profitable Investment Club*. New York: Random House.

Odean, Terry. 1998. "Are Investors Reluctant to Realize Their Losses?" *Journal of Finance*, 53:1775–1798.

—————. 1999. "The Courage of Misguided Convictions: The Trading Behavior of Individual Investors." *Financial Analyst Journal*, November/December: 41–55.

Odean, Terrance, and Brad Barber. 2000. "Trading Is Hazardous to Your Wealth: The Common Stock Investment Performance of Individual Investors." *Journal of Finance*, 55:773–806.

Ostrom, Elinor. 1991. *Governing the Commons: The Evolution of Institutions for Collective Action*. Cambridge, UK: Cambridge University Press.

Ouchi, William. 1980. "Markets, Bureaucracies and Clans." *Administrative Science Quarterly*, 25:129–140.

Pelled, Lisa. 1996a. "Demographic Diversity, Conflict and Work Group Outcomes: An Intervening Process Theory." *Organization Science*, 7:615–631.

—————. 1996b. "Relational Demography and Perceptions of Group Conflict and Performance: A Field Investigation." *International Journal of Conflict Resolution*, 7:230–246.

Phillips, Katherine, 2003. "The Effects of Categorically Based Expectations on Minority Influence: The Importance of Congruence." *Personality and Social Psychology Bulletin*, 22:14–23.

Phillips, Katherine, and Denise Loyd. 2005. "When Surface and Deep-Level Diversity Meet: The Effects on Dissenting Group Members." Working paper, Northwestern University.

Phillips, Katherine, Elisabeth Mannix, Margaret Neale, and Lisa Gruenfeld. 2004. "Diverse Groups and Information Sharing: The Effects of Congruent Ties." *Journal of Experimental Social Psychology*, 40:497–510.

Podolny, Joel, and James Baron. 1997. "Resources and Relationships: Social Networks and Mobility in the Workplace," *American Sociological Review*, 62:673–693.

Polyani, Karl. 1944. *The Great Transformation*. Boston: Beacon Press.

Porac, Jerry, James Wade, and Timothy Pollock. 1999. "Industry Categories and the Politics of the Comparable Firm in CEO Compensation," *Administrative Science Quarterly*, 44:112–144.

Portes, Alejandro. 1994. "The Informal Economy and Its Paradoxes." In Neil Smelser and Richard Swedberg (eds.), *The Handbook of Economic Sociology*. Princeton, NJ: Princeton University Press.

Portes, Alejandro, and Julia Sensenbrenner. 1993. "Embeddedness and Immigration: Notes on the Social Determinants of Economic Action." *American Journal of Sociology*, 98:1320–1350.

Prahalad, C. K., and Michael Porter. 2003. *The Harvard Business Review on Corporate Responsibility*. Boston: Harvard Business School Press.

Prince, Melvin. 1993. "Women, Men and Money Style," *Journal of Economic Psychology*, 14:175–182.

Proust, Marcel. 1982 [1922]. *The Cities of the Plain*, book four of *Remembrance of Things Past*. New York: Vintage.

Pugh, Douglas. 2001. "Service with a Smile: Emotional Contagion in the Service Encounter." *Academy of Management Journal*, 44:1018–1027.

Putnam, Robert. 1995. "Tuning In, Tuning Out: The Strange Disappearance of Social Capital in America." *PS: Political Science and Politics*, 28:664–683.

———. 2000. *Bowling Alone: The Collapse and Revival of American Community*. New York: Simon and Schuster.

Quinlan, Mary Lou. 2003. *Just Ask a Woman: Cracking the Code of What Women Want and How They Buy*. New York: Wiley.

Ragsdale, James. 1997. "The Evolution of the Shareholder's Voice in American Capitalism." In Judith Hoover (ed.), *Corporate Advocacy: Rhetoric in the Information Age*. Westport, CT: Quorum Books.

Rao, Hayagreeva, Gerald Davis, and Andrew Ward. 2000. "Embeddedness, Social Identity and Mobility: Why Firms Leave the NASDAQ and Join the New York Stock Exchange." *Administrative Science Quarterly*, 45:268–292.

Renzulli, Linda, Howard Aldrich, and James Moody. 2000. "Family Matters: Gender, Networks and Entrepreneurial Outcomes." *Social Forces*, 79:523–546; p. 526.

Reskin, Barbara. 1976. "Sex Differences in Status Attainment in Science: The Case of the Postdoctoral Fellowship." *American Sociological Review*, 41:597–612.

Reskin, Barbara, and Patricia Roos. 1990. *Job Queues, Gender Queues: Explaining Women's Inroads into Male Occupations*. Philadelphia: Temple University Press.

Resnick, Paul, Richard Zeckhauser, John Swanson, and Kate Lockwood. 2002. "The Value of Reputation on eBay: A Controlled Experiment." Working paper, Economics Society of America Conference, Boston. http://www.si.umich.edu/~presnick/papers/postcards/.

Roethlisberger, Fritz, and William Dickson. 1939. *Management and the Worker*. Cambridge, MA: Harvard University Press.

Rogus, Deborah. 2001."Individual Stocks Fuel a Passion for Profits." *Public Management*, 83:24.

Rosenwein, Barbara. 1989. *To Be the Neighbor of Saint Peter: The Social Meaning of Cluny's Property*. Ithaca, NY: Cornell University Press.

Rother, John, and William Wright. 1999. "Americans' Views of Social Security and Social Security Reforms." In Olivia Mitchell, Robert Myers, and Howard Young (eds.), *Prospects for Social Security Reform*. Philadelphia: University of Pennsylvania Press.

Samuelson, Paul. 1983. *Foundations of Economic Analysis*. Cambridge, MA: Harvard University Press.

Samuelson, Robert. 1999. "Stocks without Risks?" *Newsweek*. 11 November.

Savage, L. J. 1954. *The Foundations of Statistics*. New York: Wiley.

Schumpeter, Joseph. 1939. *Business Cycles I*. New York: McGraw-Hill.

Scott, W. Richard. 1992. *Complex Organizations: Rational, Natural and Open Systems*. Englewood Cliffs, NJ: Prentice-Hall.

Shaffir, William. 1991. "Managing a Convincing Self-Presentation: Some Personal Reflections on Entering the Field." In William Shaffir and Robert Stebbins (eds.), *Experiencing Fieldwork: An Inside View of Qualitative Research*. Newbury Park, CA: Sage, pp. 72–81.

Shefrin, Hersh, and Meir Statman. 1993. "The Disposition to Sell Winners Too Early and Ride Losers Too Long: Theory and Evidence." In Richard Thaler (ed.), *Advances in Behavioral Finance*. New York: Russell Sage Foundation.

———. 2002. "Behavioral Portfolio Theory." *Journal of Financial and Quantitative Analysis*, 35:127–151.

Shiller, Robert. 1993. "Stock Prices and Social Dynamics." In Richard Thaler (ed.), *Advances in Behavioral Finance*. New York: Russell Sage Foundation.

———. 1999. "Social Security and Institutions for Intergenerational, Intragenerational and International Risk-Sharing." *Carnegie-Rochester Conference Series on Public Policy*, 50:191.

———. 2000. *Irrational Exuberance*. Princeton, NJ: Princeton University Press.

Simon, Herbert. 1982. *Models of Bounded Rationality, Vol. 2*. Boston: MIT Press.

Smith, Adam. 1969. *The Money Game*. New York: Vintage.

Smith, Kelly. 1997. "New Survey: Blacks and Whites Differ as Investors—Sharply." *Money*, March, pp. 22–23.

Snow, David, Robert Benford, and Leon Anderson. 1986. "Fieldwork Roles and Informational Yield: A Comparison of Alternative Settings and Roles." *Urban Life*, 14: 377–408.

Snow, David, and Robert Parker. 1984. "The Media and the Market." In Patricia Adler and Peter Adler (eds.), *The Social Dynamics of Financial Markets*. Greenwich, CT: JAI Press.

Sommers, M. 1997. "Useful Friendships: A Foundation for Business Ethics." *Journal of Business Ethics*, 16:1453–1458.

Stark, David. 2000. "For a Sociology of Worth." Keynote address at the Meetings of the European Association of Evolutionary Political Economy, Berlin, November 2–4.

Staw, Barry, Pamela McKechnie, and Sheila Puffer. 1983. "The Justification of Organizational Performance." *Administrative Science Quarterly*, 28:582–600.

Steiner, Robert. 1996. "Were They in Japan, Beardstown Ladies Would Be Busted." *Wall Street Journal*, 13 February, p. A1.

Stevenson, Richard. 2000. "Bush to Advocate Private Accounts in Social Security." *New York Times*, 1 May, p. A1.

Stinchcombe, Arthur. 1965. "Social Structure and Organizations." In J. March (ed.), *Handbook of Organizations*. Chicago: Rand-McNally.

Stolte, John, Gary Alan Fine, and Karen Cook. 2001. "Sociological Miniaturism: Seeing the Big through the Small in Social Psychology." *Annual Review of Sociology*, 27:387–413.

Strauss, Anselm, and Juliet Corbin. 1998. *Basics of Qualitative Research, 2nd Edition*. Thousand Oaks, CA: Sage.

Sydow, Jörg, Arnold Windeler, and Guido Möllering. 2007. "Path-Creating Networks in the Field of Next Generation Lithography: Outline of a Research Project." Technology Studies Working Paper. Berlin: University of Technology.

Tajfel, Henri, and John Turner. 1979. "An Integrative Theory of Intergroup Conflict." In Stephen Worchel and William Austin (eds.), *The Social Psychology of Intergroup Relations*. Monterey, CA: Brooks-Cole.

Thaler, Richard. 1992. "Savings, Fungibility, and Mental Accounts." In Richard Thaler (ed.), *The Winner's Curse: Paradoxes and Anomalies of Economic Life*. Princeton, NJ: Princeton University Press, pp. 107–121.

Thaler, Richard, and Shlomo Benartzi. 2002. "How Much Is Investor Autonomy Worth?" *Journal of Finance*, 57:1593–1616.

Thaler, Richard, and Werner deBondt. 1992. "A Mean Reverting Walk down Wall Street." In Richard Thaler (ed.), *The Winner's Curse: Paradoxes and Anomalies of Economic Life*. Princeton, N.J.: Princeton University Press, pp. 151–167.

Thaler, Richard, and William Ziemba. 1992. "Pari-Mutuel Betting Markets." In Richard Thaler (ed.), *The Winner's Curse: Paradoxes and Anomalies of Economic Life*. Princeton, NJ: Princeton University Press, pp. 122–138.

Thomas, Landon. 2002. "Ford and Goldman: So Cozy at the Top." *New York Times*, 8 December, p. C1.

Trump, Donald J., and Tony Schwartz. 1987. *The Art of the Deal.* New York: Random House.

Tsui, Anne, Terry Egan, and Charles O'Reilly. 1992. "Being Different: Relational Demography and Organizational Attachment." *Administrative Science Quarterly,* 37:549–579.

Turner, Ralph. 1990. "Role Taking: Process versus Conformity." In Dennis Brissett and Charles Edgley (eds.), *Life as Theater: A Dramaturgical Sourcebook.* New York: Aldine de Gruyter, pp. 85–100.

Turner, Ralph, and Lewis Killian. 1972. *Collective Behavior.* Englewood Cliffs, NJ: Prentice Hall.

Turner, Victor. 1974. *Dramas, Fields, and Metaphors: Symbolic Action in Human Society.* Ithaca, NY: Cornell University Press.

Tversky, Amos, and Daniel Kahneman. 1971. "Belief in the Law of Small Numbers." *Psychological Bulletin,* 76:105–110.

———. 1973. "Availability: A Heuristic for Judging Frequency and Probability." *Cognitive Psychology,* 5:207–302.

———. 1991. "Loss Aversion in Riskless Choice: A Reference Dependent Model." *Quarterly Journal of Economics,* 106:1039–1061.

Udy, Stanley. 1962. "Administrative Rationality, Social Setting, and Organizational Development." *American Journal of Sociology,* 68:299–308.

Unger, Laura. 1999. "Remarks at the American of Society of Corporate Secretaries." Greenbrier, WV, June 25. Transcript available at http://www.sec.gov/news/speech/speecharchive/1999/spch287.htm.

U.S. Congress. 2000. *Joint Economic Committee Study,* April, p. 1. http://www.house.gov/jec/tax/stock/stock.htm.

U.S. Department of Labor, Women's Bureau. 1997. *The Wage Gap between Men and Women.* January. www2.dol.gov/dol/wb/public/programs/1w&occ.htm.

U.S. Securities and Exchange Commission. 1998. *Trading Analysis of October 27 and 28, 1997: A Report by the Division of Market Regulation,* September. http://www.sec.gov/news/studies/traderep.htm.

Useem, Michael. 1978. "The Inner Group of the American Capitalist Class." *Social Problems,* 25:225–240.

Uzzi, Brian. 1997. "Social Structure and Competition in Interfirm Networks: The Paradox of Embeddedness." *Administrative Science Quarterly,* 42:35–67.

———. 1999. "Embeddedness in the Making of Financial Capital: How Social Relations and Networks Benefit Firms Seeking Finance." *American Sociological Review,* 64:481–505.

van Knippenberg, D., C.K.W. de Dreu, and A. C. Homan. Forthcoming. "Work Group Diversity and Group Performance: An Integrative Model and Research Agenda." *Journal of Applied Psychology.*

Veblen, Thorstein. 1898. "The Barbarian Status of Women." *American Journal of Sociology,* 4:503–514.

———. 1994 [1899]. *The Theory of the Leisure Class.* New York: Penguin.

von Pischke, J. D. 1991. *Finance at the Frontier: Debt Capacity and the Role of Credit in the Private Economy.* Washington, DC: World Bank.

von Pischke, J. D., Dale Adams, and Gordon Donald. 1983. *Rural Financial Markets in Developing Countries.* Baltimore: Economic Development Institute of the World Bank.

Warren, Carol. 1989. *Gender Issues in Field Research.* Thousand Oaks, CA: Sage Publications.

Weaver, Warren. 1958. "A Quarter Century in the Natural Sciences." In the *Annual Report* of the Rockefeller Foundation. New York: Rockefeller Foundation.

Weber, Max. 1946 [1904]. "The Protestant Sects and the Spirit of Capitalism." In H. H. Gerth and C. Wright Mills (eds.), *From Max Weber.* New York: Oxford University Press, pp. 302–322.

————. 1978 [1914]. *Economy and Society.* Guenther Roth and Claus Witich (eds.). Berkeley: University of California Press.

Weisberg, Jacob. 1998. "United Shareholders of America." *New York Times Magazine,* 25 January, p. 30.

White, Harrison. 1976. "Where Do Markets Come From?" *American Journal of Sociology,* 81:330–380.

Wiersema, M. F., and A. Bird. 1993. "Organizational Demography in Japanese Firms: Group Heterogeneity, Individual Dissimilarity, and Top Management Team Turnover." *Academy of Management Journal,* 36:996–1025.

Willer, D. 1992. "The Principle of Rational Choice and the Problem of a Satisfactory Theory." In J. Coleman and T. Fararo (eds.), *Rational Choice Theory.* Newbury Park, CA: Sage Publications, pp. 49–77.

Williams, Katherine, and Charles O'Reilly III. 1998. "Demography and Diversity in Organizations: A Review of 40 Years of Research." *Research in Organizational Behavior,* 20:77–140.

Wolfe, Raymond, Richard Lennox, and Brian Cutler. 1986. "Getting Along and Getting Ahead: Empirical Support for a Theory of Protective and Acquisitive Self-presentation." *Journal of Personality and Social Psychology,* 50:356–361.

Zelizer, Viviana. 1996. "Payments and Social Ties." *Sociological Forum,* 11:481–495.

————. 1997. *The Social Meaning of Money: Pin Money, Paychecks, Poor Relief, and Other Currencies.* Princeton, NJ: Princeton University Press.

Zuckerman, Ezra. 2000. "Focusing the Corporate Product: Securities Analysts and De-diversification." *Administrative Science Quarterly,* 45:591–619.

Index

26. *See also* South Sea Bubble (1720); stock market bubble of 1990s
Spitzer, Elliott, 151
spot markets, 144
SSG. *See* Stock Selection Guide (SSG)
Standard & Poor's classification system, 39, 97–98
Standard & Poor's 500 index, 66, 74, 80
Standard Industrial Classification (SIC) Codes, 39, 207n48
Starbucks, 187
status: commerce involves, 144; investing associated with, 46–47, 77–79; in sociological perspective, 8
Stewart, Martha, 27, *28*
Stinchcombe, Arthur, 116
"Stock-Jobbing Ladies, The" (song), 30
stock market: and American identity, 15–16; average annual gain since 1926, 20, 41; continuing faith in, 153–54; disenchantment after 1990s, 149–55; equity premium for stocks, 41; "girl stocks" and "boy stocks," 90–94; identity in behavior in, 43–47; mapping gender onto, 93–98; mental maps of, 39–71; microlevel behavior has aggregate effects on, 70, 71; NASDAQ, 17, 45, 186; neighborhood associated with stock purchases, 42; New York Stock Exchange, 45, 185, 186; number of stocks available on world's exchanges, 204n41; as organized complexity, 189–90, 196–97; percentage of adults invested in, 2; portfolio as social accessory, 48; rationality of, 37; risk-return relationship, 41–42; social relations ignored in study of, 4–5; Social Security privatization and, 147, 180–82; stories and stock purchases, 48; "telephone" game compared with, 51; as value neutral, 67; value of stock owned by investor clubs, 3, 5; volatility as permanent feature of, 145. *See also* brokers; Dow Jones Industrial Average; investing; stock market bubble of 1990s
stock market bubble of 1990s: average annual return during, 20; decline beginning April 2000, 146, 150; disenchantment after, 149–55; Dow increase during, 11–12; investment club increase during, 15;

investors take some responsibility for, 153–54, 167; as speculative mania, 23–25, 26, 29, 31; storytelling in, 49–51; technological innovation in, 23
stock options, 20
Stock Selection Guide (SSG), 51–52, *54–55*; for Callaway Golf, 56, 57; for Charles Schwab, 93; for Cisco Systems, 62, 63; as conceptual framework for stories, 52; investment clubs seek alternatives to, 53; "Mad Lib" compared with, 52; "new economy" rhetoric contrasted with, 52–53; as weeding mechanism, 52
stop-loss orders, 134–36, 149, 181
stories (narratives): competing logics of exchange conducted through, 145; in constructing assessments of value, 188; decision making influenced by, 48; "everybody's talking" narrative, 62, 191; happy versus unhappy endings in investing, 70; NAIC as storytelling community, 51–60; as organizing principle, 48; in sociological perspective, 8; in stock market bubble of 1990s, 49–51; for understanding group context of investment behavior, 70–71
STOXX system, 39
Swift, Jonathan, 25
symbolic interactionism, 44, 47–48, 64, 145, 197

task-related relationships. *See* instrumental (task-related) relationships
Teachman's entropy index, 100
Thaler, Richard, 40
theories of mind, 145, 190–92
Thornton, John L., 127
totems, 160, 161, 162, 169, 197
transaction costs: commissions, 18; lowering of, 17–18; in microcredit organizations, 176, 178; with stop-loss orders, 135, 136; subtracting in calculating performance, 80
TriTeal Corporation, 53
Trump, Donald J., 73, 77, 78
trust: civic engagement requires, 183; commerce involves, 144; Greenspan on, 152; in same-sex clubs, 164